The Unknown Coleridge

The Life and Times of Derwent Coleridge
1800–1883

D1800148

Derwent Coleridge
St Mark's College Chelsea.
Nov 15 1850—

The Unknown Coleridge

The Life and Times of Derwent Coleridge
1800–1883

RAYMONDE HAINTON and
GODFREY HAINTON

JANUS PUBLISHING COMPANY
London, England

First published in Great Britain 1996
by Janus Publishing Company
Edinburgh House, 19 Nassau Street
London W1N 7RE

British Library Cataloguing-in-Publication Data.
A catalogue record for this book is available from the British Library.

ISBN 1 85756 288 7

Cover design Harold King

Photosetting by Keyboard Services, Luton, Beds
Printed and bound in Great Britain by
Antony Rowe Ltd, Chippenham, Wiltshire

CONTENTS

ILLUSTRATIONS

PREFACE

My husband, Godfrey Hainton, intended to write this book. He was Head of the History Department at the College of St Mark and St John, which moved from Chelsea to Plymouth in 1973. St Mark's College, Chelsea, was combined in 1926 with St John's College, Battersea (founded by Kay-Shuttleworth in 1841).

Godfrey Hainton did extensive research on the life of Derwent Coleridge in England and in the Humanities Research Center in Texas, before his sudden death in 1976.

After doing further research on the ground and among books and archives, I eventually wrote the book over an extended period.

I wish to thank the late Mr A. H. B. Coleridge, his wife, Mrs Joan Coleridge and the Humanities Research Center, The University of Texas at Austin, for permission to use the manuscripts there, and also the Nash portrait of Derwent Coleridge. I thank Mrs Mary Coleridge and her son, Capt. Gerard Peter Derwent Coleridge, for permission to use documents and family portraits. I thank Mrs Alison Bidgood, Librarian at the College of St Mark and St John, for much help with the College archives and the illustrations.

I am grateful to our granddaughter, Harriet Bazley, for helping me to shorten the book and for typing the manuscript; to our daughter, Dr Julia Bush, for reading the manuscript and giving helpful advice; and to our daughter, Mrs Joanna Bazley, for checking the typescript.

Raymonde Hainton

Exminster,
March, 1996.

ix

PROLOGUE

On 19 December 1799 Samuel Taylor Coleridge, his wife Sara and their infant son Hartley moved into lodgings at 21 Buckingham Street, a dingy turning off the Strand between Hungerford Market and the elegance of the Adam brothers' Adelphi estate. For Samuel it was another attempt to revive a marriage that had long been wilting. He was now a staff writer for the *Morning Post*, with an opportunity to pay his debts and to achieve financial independence to enable him to resume his proper role as a freelance man of letters.

For Sara it was an even more deeply felt fresh start – Samuel had returned in July from a ten-month visit to Germany. In her lonely insecurity when she had suffered the agonising loss of their baby son Berkeley, his letters had breathed tenderness and love. They had holidayed together in Somerset and Devon on his return; but he had again left her at Nether Stowey in October, saying that he was going to seek out some missing luggage in Bristol. Then silence – until the summons, with borrowed fare money, to join him in London two months later. In fact he had been on a journey whose full significance was yet unknown to either of the Coleridges. He had gone north to County Durham to join William and Dorothy Wordsworth at the home of Mary Hutchinson, William's future wife, whose sister was another, more exciting Sara. From there Wordsworth had taken him for an ecstatic introduction into the romantic beauty of the Lake District. But now they were together again, and Sara Coleridge had escaped once more from humiliating dependence on the sympathy and support of her brother-in-law Southey and their friend Thomas Poole of Nether Stowey. Dare she now hope for the security and domestic stability the marriage had so far failed to provide?

Samuel felt better and worked harder than he had done for years. 'We newspaper [men] are true galley slaves,' he wrote to his patron Josiah Wedgwood.[1] He relished the political influence his role as leader writer for the *Morning Post* brought him at a crucial stage in the war against revolutionary France. He spent his evenings in the House of Commons or at the theatre. He enjoyed the company of William Godwin, though Godwin's atheistical socialism was losing its savour, of Mary, Mrs Robinson, former mistress of the Prince Regent and now a fellow poet and journalist, and of Charles and Mary Lamb. But he did not intend to stay in London. To the despair of his friends, especially of those to whom he owed money, he scorned all inducement from Daniel Stuart, the proprietor of the *Morning Post*, to stay with the paper and to make a career in London journalism. The lodgings in Buckingham Street were cramped and draughty. Young Hartley was noisy and boisterous, to the particular distress of William Godwin when he was whacked on the shin with a ninepin. Samuel yearned for the country and for the society of his literary intimates. But which ones? Robert Southey was planning to go overseas to recover his health, and Samuel would have dearly liked to go with him. That plan, however, was the first to be given up – in January 1800 he told Southey 'I must stay in England for I fear that a circumstance has taken place which will render a sea voyage utterly unfit for Sara'.[2] Their reconciliation had borne fruit. Sara was pregnant again.

But already Samuel was having guilty second thoughts about the expected child which could be confided to his friend Josiah Wedgwood only in Latin: 'There are those who complain because they remain childless' (a reference to Southey) ... 'sometimes I can't help giving a sigh – an anxious sigh, in case Juno and the Gods of Marriage favour me more than I desire ...'[3]

Samuel's search for a house was conducted with ambivalent earnestness. 'God knows where we can go; for that situation which suits my wife does not suit me, and what suits me does not suit my

[1] 4 February 1800. Collected Letters of Samuel Taylor Coleridge. Ed. E. L. Griggs. OUP. 1956–1972.
[2] 25 January 1800. Ibid.
[3] 4 February 1800. Ibid.

wife.'[1] His patrons were in Bristol, Somerset, to which Sara wanted to return. His family home was at Ottery St Mary in Devon, where he was expected to rejoin the clan. But, as he wrote to Southey, 'Elder Brothers, not senior in Intellect, and not sympathizing in main opinions, are subjects of occasional Visits, not temptations to a Co-township.'[2]

So Thomas Poole at Nether Stowey was instructed to comb the Quantocks for a cottage. But Coleridge's heart was with William Wordsworth, for whom he now had an ardent and self-abasing admiration – 'the Society of so great a Being is of priceless Value ... since Milton no man has manifested himself equal to him'.[3] He longed to recreate the communion of souls at Alfoxden which had before created the *Rime of the Ancient Mariner*, *Frost at Midnight*, *Christabel*, *Kublai Khan* and *Lyrical Ballads*. In March Hartley and Sara were packed off to stay with friends. In April he was at Dove Cottage, Grasmere, again, though still in debt, devoting his energies not to his own literary undertakings, for which he had given up his London career, but to Wordsworth's affairs and to the enjoyment of the company of Sara Hutchinson. It was then that he found the house he really wanted, large enough for a community of poets, and in a sublime setting of lakes, streams and mountains, at Greta Hall, by Derwent Water.

Meanwhile a withdrawal from the personal and financial entanglements of Somerset had to be undertaken. In May Samuel was back at Stowey, dutifully house-hunting in the country between the Quantocks and Minehead and dreaming of a Lakeland Parnassus. The breach with Stowey and Bristol was at last accomplished. To the chagrin of Coleridge's friends in the south-west, Wordsworth won the contest for his allegiance. In mid-June the family left Bristol by chaise for Cumberland. They broke the journey to stay with friends near Liverpool, and Samuel caught a severe cold which was still heavy upon him when they reached Grasmere on 29 June. Here Wordsworth insisted that he should sail upon Rydal Water in his own boat.

[1] Samuel Taylor Coleridge to Thomas Poole. January 1800. Ibid.
[2] Samuel Taylor Coleridge to Robert Southey. 12 February 1800. Ibid.
[3] Samuel Taylor Coleridge to Thomas Poole. 21 March 1800. Ibid.

Samuel's condition rapidly worsened, and for three weeks he was more severely ill than at any time since the acute rheumatic fever which had kept him in the sick bay at Christ's Hospital during his last year at school. But by 25 July he was able to move on from Grasmere and to install Sara and Hartley once more in a home of their own. Greta Hall was a large new Regency villa, with an Ionic portico. It had just been built by a retired carrier, William Jackson, a bachelor with literary tastes, who occupied part of the house with his housekeeper, Mrs Wilson, and who doted on children. He had been looking for a congenial family to occupy the rest of the house, the parlour of which contained the main part of his library of five hundred books. The arrival of a poet and writer with a young wife and child appeared so providential that he completed Samuel's happiness by refusing any rent for the first half-year and accepting only a nominal one thereafter.

The situation of Greta Hall was superb. It stood on a peninsular hillock with the river Greta 'roaring like an untamed Son of the Hills'[1] around its base. Its grounds were extensive but as they were under cultivation as nursery and orchard land they satisfied Samuel's longing for a private garden that required no work. Close at hand was the little town of Keswick. The house was large enough for him to escape from Sara and Hartley into a study with a view which gave him fresh delight every time he looked out of the windows. Soon after moving in, he discovered the perfect fine-weather eyrie on the roof, where he day-dreamed 'enjoying the Godlikeness of the Place ... with the voluptuous and joy-trembling Nerves of Convalescence'[2] and wrote ecstatic accounts of his new situation to his distant friends 'from the leads on the housetop of Greta Hall, Keswick, Cumberland, at the present time in the occupancy and usufruct-possession of Samuel Taylor Coleridge, Esq., Gentleman-poet and Philosopher in a mist'.[3] Through the mist he saw a splendid panorama of lakes, mountains, woods and valleys. To the north-west lay Bassenthwaite lake, seen beyond the woods and meadow-lands of the pastoral plain and encased in mountain ranges. Close by,

[1] Samuel Taylor Coleridge to Josiah Wedgwood. 1 November 1800. Ibid.
[2] Samuel Taylor Coleridge to S. Purkis. 29 July 1800. Ibid.
[3] Samuel Taylor Coleridge to J. W. Tobin. 25 July 1800. Ibid.

to the north, ever dominant, rose the mighty bulk of Skiddaw, its smooth flanks seamed with steep-sided ghylls. The westward prospect led the eye across the broad mouth of the Newlands valley to Coledale, running deep under Grisedale Pike into the mountains of Grasmoor – 'a great Camp of Mountain Giants seem to have pitched their Tents there ... and how the light streams from them – and the Shadows that travel upon them!'[1]

Most often, however, he looked south along the whole length of island-dotted Derwent Water to the narrow jaws of Borrowdale, beyond the guardian fang of Castle Crag and the white gleaming Lodore Waterfall, to the distant curtain wall of the central fells, Glaramara, Scafell and Great Gable. It was a view whose elements of water, land and air were differently compounded not only with the changing seasons but with the changing light and weather of a single day – 'endless combinations as if heaven and earth were for ever talking to each other'.[2] Above all he delighted in Derwent Water itself, of all lakes the most perfectly framed in mountains, the most capricious, responsive to sun and cloud, to wind and rain.

But Sara, expecting their child in a few weeks, in no mood to do all the work of moving in unaided while her husband admired the view, found his lofty hideout. 'My wife will not let me stay on the leads – I must go and unpack a trunk for her – she cannot *stoop* to it – thanks to my late Essay on Population!'[3]

While Sara prepared the new home and Hartley rejoiced in the freedom of the large garden, Samuel spent much time at Dove Cottage devoting himself to the interests of William Wordsworth, working on the second edition of *Lyrical Ballads,* and entirely neglecting his own literary and financial responsibilities. He agreed to the exclusion of his own major contributions to the book, the *Ancient Mariner* and *Christabel.* Eventually the difficulty of replacing the *Ancient Mariner* led to a compromise – a revision of the piece by Coleridge and an apologetic foreword by Wordsworth to explain that Coleridge himself had wanted to suppress it as a failure but had been prevailed upon by Wordsworth to allow it to appear again.

[1] Samuel Taylor Coleridge to Humphrey Davey. 25 July 1800. Ibid.
[2] Samuel Taylor Coleridge to Josiah Wedgwood. 1 November 1800. Ibid.
[3] Samuel Taylor Coleridge to S. Purkis. 29 July 1800. Ibid.

Between visits to the Wordsworths, Samuel walked the fells alone.

The long busily unproductive summer of Wordsworth-worship was drawing to an end. The real world was again obtruding itself: for a time at least, he had to confront it. It was as well that his landlord required no rent for Greta Hall, for Samuel had no money by mid-September. At that 'unseasonable time', as he ruefully described it, the consequences of that reunion at 21 Buckingham Street finally declared themselves. On the night of Sunday, 14 September 1800 Sara gave birth to a son.

PART I

The Lake District 1800–1820

Samuel Taylor Coleridge's second surviving son was to be identified from the beginning with the new world of romantic beauty that lay around Greta Hall. In naming his son Derwent he confessed to 'a sort of sneaking affection for the poetical and the novellish'.[1] Both the birth and name must soon have been known in nearby Keswick, for on the day after Sara's *accouchement* Cumbrian voices beneath her window called up congratulations to her and 'Good morning to li'le Darran'. In far away London Derwent's birth was celebrated with less promptitude but more sophistication by an 'Ode, inscribed to the Infant Son of Samuel Taylor Coleridge, Esq., Born September 14th at Keswick in Cumberland' which appeared in the *Morning Post*. The author was Samuel's fellow journalist-poet, Mary Robinson, whom he had met in London the year before. Mrs Robinson, known also as 'Perdita', had been one of the Prince Regent's mistresses twenty years earlier, subsequently descending the social scale in the Whig interest while cultivating a new career. The 'Ode' proclaimed that the genius of his father would ensure that Derwent would hear 'the soft voice of wood-wild harmony'. It was her last poem, for she was already ill, and died in December.

Meanwhile, Samuel's immediate financial embarrassment had been relieved by a loan, not this time from his Somerset friends the Wedgwoods and Thomas Poole, but from William Godwin, the atheist political philosopher, whom he had half-seriously invited to be Derwent's godfather. He discussed with Godwin his doubts about baptism. He was still poised uncertainly between the traditional Christianity of his upbringing and the determinism that

[1] Samuel Taylor Coleridge to Josiah Wedgwood. 1 November 1800. Ibid.

7

had led him to call his first son Hartley and his second son Berkeley, after the political philosophers who had shaped his thinking at Cambridge. At times when he saw 'the follies and superstitions' of man as 'ever-varying incarnations of the Eternal Life' he veered towards baptism for his boys. But when he watched Hartley as a creature of Nature – 'he looks at the clouds, the mountains, the living beings of the Earth, and jubilates!' – he wondered 'Shall I suffer him to see grave countenances and hear grave accents while his face is sprinkled and while the fat paw of a Parson crosses his Forehead?'

It was not until 2 November 1803 that Derwent was baptised at Crosthwaite, together with Hartley, then seven years old, and his baby sister, Sara, who was born on 23 December 1802. William and Dorothy Wordsworth were the godparents. Many years later Derwent recalled:

A Christian name my uncle Southey would never allow it to be. Accordingly he always called me John – John Derwent when he was serious. Christian indeed it was not until I had borne it some two years and when at last it was confirmed to me at the font I was graceless enough to resent the lustral effusion '*par voie de fait*' in my nurse's words by slapping the Parson in the face. As recorded elsewhere I was christened at the same time with my elder brother and younger sister, being at the unlucky age when I could neither share the reticence of the one nor the unconsciousness of the other.[1]

The mountains filled Samuel with ecstasy, but their damp climate had a devastating effect upon his rheumatism and gout, which confined him to bed for months during the winter of 1800 to 1801. The frequent doses of laudanum, which he took to combat the pain, increased his addiction to opium which had begun with large doses of laudanum administered for his rheumatic fever at Christ's Hospital. He was too ill to provide for his family by writing and they depended on an annuity from Josiah and Thomas

---

[1] Derwent Coleridge MSS. HRC, Texas. 'Recollections'.

Wedgwood and on what he could borrow from other friends. The temperamental incompatibility with his wife was aggravated by his constant illness and lack of a steady income, and, after that first winter at Greta Hall, by Samuel's growing attachment to Sara Hutchinson and by his constant wanderings.

In July 1801 Samuel stayed for a month with the Hutchinsons near Durham, and read Duns Scotus in the Cathedral Library. He was planning to go to St Nevis in the West Indies in search of health. In October he wrote to Southey, '... and Sara – alas! We are not suited to each other ... Carefully have I thought thro' the subject of marriage and deeply am I convinced of its indissolubleness. – If I separate I do it in the earnest desire to provide for her and them...'[1]

From November 1801 to March 1802 Samuel was in London and Nether Stowey. He stayed at Gallow Hill, Sara Hutchinson's home, from 2 to 13 March, before returning to Keswick. On 4 April 1802 he sent Sara Hutchinson the first draft of the Ode to Dejection, including the lines:

> My own peculiar Lot, my household Life
> It is, and will remain Indifference or Strife...
> My little Children are a Joy, a Love,
> A good Gift from above!
> But what is Bliss that still calls up a Woe,
> And makes it doubly keen
> Compelling me to *feel*, as well as KNOW,
> What a most blessed Lot mine might have been.
> Those little Angel Children (woe is me!)
> There have been hours, when feeling how they bind
> And pluck out the Wing-feathers of my Mind,
> Turning my Error to Necessity,
> I have half wish'd, they never had been born!

Nevertheless, by 7 May 1802, Samuel was writing to Thomas Poole 'Mrs Coleridge is indisposed and I have too much reason to

[1] 21 October 1801. Collected Letters of Samuel Taylor Coleridge. Ed. E. L. Griggs. OUP.

suspect that she is breeding again – an event which was to have been deprecated'.

After writing to Southey of a reconciliation with his wife in July 1802, in August he went on an eight-day solitary walking tour in the mountains, including risking his neck sliding down precipices on Scafell. In November he went to London and then to Bristol to join Thomas Wedgwood and accompany him to Wales. He returned to Keswick with Thomas Wedgwood on 24 December, the day after Sara Coleridge was born. At the end of January 1803 Samuel departed again with Thomas Wedgwood for two months in the south, after which he hoped to go with his patron to France, Italy and Sicily and to look for two houses in Italy or Sicily for the Wordsworths and for himself and family. His plans were frustrated by the renewed outbreak of war and he returned to Keswick in April 1803. In August he was off again to Scotland with the Wordsworths but he parted from them because of the constant rain and returned to Keswick on 15 September 1803. Robert Southey and his wife Edith had arrived at Greta Hall, seeking solace for the death of their little girl, their only child. They came from Bristol on a visit, but in fact never left, and Southey was to provide for Coleridge's children the stability that their own father was unable to create.

On 20 December 1803 Samuel and Derwent went to the Wordsworths at Dove Cottage, Grasmere. Samuel left Derwent there, on the understanding that he would be returned to Keswick shortly, and departed for London and Ottery, to try to arrange the means of going abroad. On 8 April 1804 Samuel sailed from Portsmouth for Malta, where he became Secretary to the governor. He arrived back in London in August 1806, but as Wordsworth wrote to Sir George Beaumont, 'In fact, he dare not go home, he recoils so much from the thought of domesticating with Mrs Coleridge...' When, after a delay of more than two months, he eventually arrived in the Lake District, he went first to Penrith to see Sara Hutchinson. She had left for Kendal to join the Wordsworths and Samuel followed her there and spent three days in Kendal before proceeding to Keswick. He arrived back at Greta Hall on 30 October 1806. Three weeks later Samuel wrote to the Wordsworths: 'We have *determined* to part absolutely and finally;

Hartley and Derwent to be with me but to visit their mother as they would do if at a publick school.'

In fact Coleridge took only Hartley with him in December 1806 to stay with the Wordsworths at Coleorton, Leicestershire, while Derwent stayed with his mother. In March 1807 Mrs Coleridge, Derwent and his little sister Sara went to stay with Mrs Coleridge's relations at Bristol. The plan was that Samuel and Hartley should join them at Bristol and proceed to the home of George, Samuel's elder brother at Ottery St Mary. Sara had been invited to visit Ottery and Samuel had been invited to help the Reverend George Coleridge with his school. But when Samuel wrote to George explaining the state of his marriage, George replied begging him not to come to Ottery – 'as you are going to Bristol and determine to separate from your wife (a step which in my opinion no argument in your situation can justify), make your arrangements there among her Friends ... It is necessary now for me to tell you that I have made my final arrangements for giving up the School ... so that I cannot offer you to take the children under my care...'

In September 1807 Mrs Coleridge returned to Keswick with the three children, escorted by De Quincey. In late November Coleridge went to London and lodged at the office of the *Courier* newspaper in the Strand. That winter, in the intervals between illness, he delivered a series of lectures at the Royal Institution on the Principles of Poetry, dealing with Shakespeare, Spenser, Chaucer, Milton, Dryden, Pope and Modern Poetry.

Despite his estrangement from his wife and his increasingly prolonged separation from his family, Samuel Taylor Coleridge had an undoubtedly deep affection for his children and exercised a powerful influence over their lives. 'If my wife loved me, and I my wife, half as well as we both love our children, I would be the happiest man alive.'[1]

He wrote to Southey: 'Derwent is the Boast of the County – the little River God is as beautiful as if he had been the Child of Venus Anaduomene previous to her Emersion.'[2] In a letter to Sara Hutchinson: he said:

[1] Samuel Taylor Coleridge to Southey. 9 November 1801. Ibid.
[2] 6 May 1801. Ibid.

There is something in children that makes love flow out upon them, distinct from beauty, and still more distinct from good behaviour. I cannot say, God Knows! that our children are even decently well-behaved – and Hartley is no beauty – and yet it has been the Lot of the two children to be beloved. They are the general Darlings of the whole Town: and wherever they go, Love is their natural Heritage.[1]

On 21 September 1802 he told Basil Montagu: 'Derwent 2 years last Tuesday – on which day he could tell all his letters and tell the names of upwards of 60 animals, on the picture Cards. He is as quick a Learner for his age as any child I know of – and there is not a child of his age in Christendom that I love so well.'[2]

Over a year later he remarked to Matthew Coates: 'Derwent is a large, fat, beautiful Child, quite the *Pride* of the Village, as Hartley is the Darling – Southey says that all Hartley's Guts are in his Brains, and all Derwent's Brains are in his Guts – Verily, the constitutional Differences in Children are great indeed ... Oh bless them! Next to the Bible, Shakespeare and Milton, they are the three books from which I have learnt the most – and the most important – and with the greatest Delight.' He wrote to his wife from Malta: 'O my children! my children! I cannot write their names. Even to speak of them thus is an effort of courage',[3] and 'How deeply I love – O God! It is agony at Morning and evening.'[4] Derwent later recalled his father's arrival back at Keswick in October 1806: 'I well remember his expected arrival. My Mother had taken my pillow for my father's bed, who required several. In her telling me of this, I exclaimed "Oh! by all means, I would lie on straw for my father", greatly to my mother 's delight and amusement. How well does this speak for my mother.'

As a small child Derwent, together with his brother and sister, had the freedom of the fields. His father wrote to William Sotheby on 27 September 1802: 'It is in very truth a sunny, misty, cloudy, dazzling, howling, omniform Day and I have been looking at as

[1] 10 August 1802. Ibid.
[2] Ibid.
[3] 12 December 1804. Ibid.
[4] 21 July 1805. Ibid.

pretty a sight as a Father's eyes could well see – Hartley and little Derwent running in the Green, where the Gusts blow most madly – both with their Hair floating and tossing, a miniature of the agitated Trees below which they were playing, inebriate both with the pleasure – Hartley whirling round for joy – Derwent eddying half willingly, half by the force of the Gust – driven backward, struggling forward, and shouting his little hymn of Joy.'

Mr Jackson's housekeeper, Mrs Wilson, soon became Nanny to the Coleridge children and later to Southey's children. They were all very fond of 'Wilsy'. In later years Derwent described her as 'a person of marvellous sweetness of temper and sterling good sense'.

In his sixth year Derwent went for a short time to a day school in Keswick kept by a Unitarian preacher called Grattan. 'Here I learned my *strokes* and well remember the feeble, tremulous sensation in my fingers with which these first efforts in calligraphy were accomplished.'[1]

Derwent evidently made rapid progress in his education. On 7 February 1807 Samuel Taylor Coleridge wrote to Derwent: 'It will be many times the number of years you have already lived before you can know and feel thoroughly, how very much your dear Father wishes and longs to have you on his knees, and in his arms ... So it must needs be a horribly wicked Thing, ever to forget, or wilfully to vex, a Father or a Mother: especially a Mother.' He goes on to urge Derwent 'always to tell the Truth'. Then I am greatly delighted, that you are so desirous to go on with your Greek; and shall finish this letter with a short Lesson of Greek.' On 3 March 1807 he wrote Derwent a letter about poetic metre concluding:

If Derwent be innocent, steady and wise,
And delight in the Things of Earth, Water and Skies;
Tender Warmth at his heart, with these metres to shew it,
With sound Sense in his Brains, may make Derwent a Poet!
May crown him with Fame, and *must* win him the love
Of his Father on earth, and his Father above,

---

[1] Puerilia et Juvenilia. Derwent Coleridge MSS. HRC, Texas.

My dear dear Child!
Could you stand upon Skiddaw, you would not from its whole
    Ridge
See a man who so loves you, as your fond S. T. Coleridge.

On 1 September 1808 Coleridge came to stay with the Wordsworths at their new home at Allan Bank, Grasmere. He spent two days at Greta Hall, with Wordsworth, and on 7 September they returned to Grasmere, taking little Sara with them. On 16 September Coleridge saw the Reverend John Dawes and arranged for him to take Hartley and Derwent into his small school at Ambleside.

This was the Kelsick Grammar School founded in 1723. From the low-lying land by Lake Windermere the boys would climb the steep Smithy Brow and take the road towards the Kirkstone Pass to the school, opposite St Anne's Church. It was quite a small building, about 44ft by 22ft.[1] Sara Hutchinson mentioned that she had heard from Mrs Coleridge that Dr Tillbrook and Bloomfield 'are both grieved that Hartley and Derwent are not at a better school where something might be made of their great Talents'.[2]

Derwent described the school in his Memoir of Hartley Coleridge (1851):

Elsewhere he might have had higher advantages in the way of scholarship; for his master, an excellent and in many respects a remarkable man, was a native of the place, and had been educated after the fashion of the North-Country, where little attention is paid to the niceties or graces of classical learning, and though possessed of a vigorous understanding, by no means disposed to repair his deficiencies by severe study in after years. He was a man of lofty stature and immense bodily strength, and though sufficiently exact in the discharge of his scholastic duties, yet he evidently attached quite as much importance to the healthful recreations and out of door life of

[1] Tithe Map – Ambleside above Stock. 7 December 1838. County Record Office, Kendal.
[2] Letters of Sara Hutchinson. Ed. K. Coburn, Routledge and Kegan Paul 1954. P.50 – letter to Mrs Hutchinson – 19 November 1812.

his scholars, as to their progress in Greek and Latin ... he carried in every word and gesture the evidence of a manly and cordial nature. No wonder that his scholars regarded him with more pleasant feelings than boys usually entertain towards their master...

In the overgrown disused churchyard of St Anne's there is a flat stone inscribed to John Dawes 'the incumbent Minister & Instructor of the Youth of Ambleside through a period of 35 years' who died in 1845 aged 79 years. It was erected by his pupils, 'who regarded him with love & esteem', including Derwent Coleridge and the sons of William Wordsworth.

Derwent and Hartley, like all the other pupils, were day-boys. They lodged with old Mrs Longmire and her son James, a maltster, at Clappersgate, a small hamlet a mile from Ambleside. Clappersgate consists of a row of cottages overlooking the Brathay River which runs into Lake Windermere. Todd Crag and Loughrigg Fell rise steeply behind the cottages and beyond the river are low meadows, in which lies Brathay Hall, then rented by the artist John Harden. In 1810 he painted a slate wharf at Clappersgate.

To the east, Wansfell descends to the shores of Lake Windermere. The River Brathay runs through shallows, past a small island where beech trees grow, before turning to rapids under the bridge. Sycamores and oaks, with ferns in the crooks of their branches, grow on river banks fringed with pussy willows, hazel, wild roses and arum lilies. In his Memoir of Hartley Derwent remembers 'Our freedom, out of school-hours, was unlimited; our play-place was the hillside, the river-bank, or the broad bosom of the lake, and our bounds the furthest point to which our inclinations led, or our strength could carry us.' He goes on to recall that they were joined by two companions, sons of a Liverpool merchant. After they went to bed Hartley would tell them a long continuous improvised story, which went on for years. 'It turned upon the injustice of society, and the insufficiency of conventional morals to determine the right or wrong of particular actions.'

At the beginning and end of term the boys walked the 17 miles between Keswick and Ambleside by way of Dunmail Raise and

Grasmere, stopping for lunch at the Nag's Head, Wythburn. But Ambleside was only four miles south of Grasmere. From September 1808 to May 1810 Samuel Taylor Coleridge was staying with the Wordsworths at Allan Bank, with its view of Grasmere and of Easedale and Helm Crag, and Derwent and Hartley would frequently walk over there for weekends. During this time Coleridge was writing *The Friend*, a weekly periodical concerned with establishing principles relating to religion, philosophy and politics. He had hoped to make a profit of £12 to £20 a week from this venture but it resulted in further debts to his friends of about £300. It was as well that the Reverend John Dawes in a letter of February 1810 waived the fees for Hartley's instruction 'while I have the honour of having Hartley under my care'. Later he remitted the fees for Derwent also.

On 29 April 1810 Coleridge wrote to his wife how pleased he was with the accuracy of Derwent's knowledge in Greek.

> Today, I pitched on a Chapter in St Paul (I.Corinth.XV) – and having satisfied myself that Derwent had not read this Epistle at School, I bade him read it to me – and to my surprise he read it as well as I could have done – and not at all in the words of the common translation ... I assure you, Derwent is a very clever boy – the rapidity, with which he reads and comprehends, is extraordinary. In the course of three days he read three Plays and half of a fourth, of Massinger – tho' he was with me only in the afternoon and evening – and he gave a very intelligent account of the story and characters of each. – May God turn it to good account![1]

Coleridge left Grasmere in May 1810 and until October he stayed at Greta Hall. He was deeply troubled by his addiction to opium and had decided to go to Edinburgh and place himself 'in the House, and under the constant eye, of some medical man.' However, the Basil Montagus, who were visiting the Wordsworths, persuaded Coleridge to accompany them to London and consult

[1] Collected Letters of Samuel Taylor Coleridge. Ed. E. L. Griggs. OUP.

their physician, Carlisle. Wordsworth tried to dissuade Montagu and spoke to him frankly about Coleridge's habits. Two days after their arrival in London, Montagu asked Coleridge to leave his house, telling him 'Wordsworth has commissioned me to tell you, first, that he has no Hope of you', that 'for years past you had been an ABSOLUTE NUISANCE in the Family', and that Wordsworth had spoken of him as a 'rotten drunkard' who was 'rotting out his entrails by intemperance'. Coleridge was heart-broken. He recorded in his notebook on 3 November 'Now for fourteen years of my life ... I am conscious to myself of having felt the most consummate friendship, in deed, word and thought inviolate, for a man whose welfare never ceased to be far dearer to me than my own...' Wordsworth offered no explanation and for eighteen months there was no communication between Coleridge and Wordsworth. Eventually, on 11 May 1812 Wordsworth sent to Coleridge 'an unequivocal denial of the Whole *in spirit* and of the most offensive passages in Letter as well as Spirit'. But the relationship between the two men was never the same. Coleridge wrote to Thomas Poole 'A Reconciliation has taken place, but the Feeling ... can never return.' The association with Sara Hutchinson was also at an end.

Derwent's earliest surviving letter is one he wrote on 15 January 1811 to Mary Lawrence at Gateacre, near Liverpool. He says it is four years since they were under the same roof and he hopes she has not forgotten him.

My brother and I continue at Mr Dawes' school at Ambleside. Hartley makes great progress except in Arithmetic, which he dislikes, but I am very [?fond] of and my father intends me to begin Geometry soon ... My father is at this time in Town. He left us in October to consult a physician and we all most ardently wish he will return home in perfect health ... My sister Sara is reading Metastasio's plays with my mother but they are at a sad loss for my father's assistance, who having been in Italy so long understands the Italian language thoroughly ... A lady near school gave us each a pair of Scates. I feel very happy on the ice – the winter before the last I slid over to the first Island and my mother and sister walked over

17

on a path strewn with ashes made for the accommodation of ladies but they never intend to venture again.

It is a very well-written letter for a boy of ten, but Sara Coleridge added the deprecatory comment: 'I am sometimes flattered by our partial friends concerning the abilities of my sons. I cannot say that I feel much pride or even satisfaction in either of them when they attempt a letter to a friend.'

In February 1812 Samuel Coleridge returned briefly to Keswick. He stopped at Ambleside to collect Hartley and Derwent, and passed through Grasmere but to the astonishment of the boys did not call on Wordsworth. He left Keswick for good on 26 March 1812 and returned to his friends the Morgans in London. He did not see Hartley again until 1815 and Derwent not until 1820.

Derwent and Hartley continued to visit the Wordsworths regularly while at school and used Wordsworth's library at Allan Bank, at the Parsonage from 1811 to 1813 and after 1813 at Rydal Mount. Derwent went for long walks with Wordsworth, discussing poetry and Nature; according to his daughter Christabel, Derwent said that Wordsworth had done more to form his mind than anyone else.[1]

The school holidays were spent at Greta Hall, where Robert Southey acted as father to his own seven children, to the three Coleridge children and to the orphan Robert Lovell, who lived there with his mother, widowed sister of Mrs Southey and Mrs Coleridge. As the three women were all aunts to the children not their own, Southey called the house the 'ant-hill'. After Mr Jackson's death in 1809, Southey took over the tenancy of the whole house. It was none too large, especially as a fourth sister, Eliza Fricker, arrived on a long visit in 1814, shortly before their brother George died of consumption there. The rooms were relatively small, considering that most of them were shared. The triangular wing bedroom shared by Hartley and Derwent measured 14 feet along two walls, but the third wall was a long curve, with a large window looking out on Lord's Seat.

---

[1] A memoir of Derwent Coleridge by Christabel Coleridge. Dated 26 October 1909. Derwent Coleridge MSS. HRC, Texas.

Southey was a steadily prolific writer, in strong contrast to the erratic genius of Coleridge. He produced a regular flow of works for publication: poetry, histories, biographies, travels, reviews, translations and articles for the *Quarterly Review*, with which he maintained this large household. In 1813 he was appointed Poet Laureate.

Yet Southey was by no means a recluse and always found time to play with the children, to teach them and to take them out for picnics, swimming, boating and climbing. He also enjoyed the large family of cats who lived in the house. He was a lifelong collector of books, which overflowed the whole house, and Derwent had the run of this vast library of 14,000 volumes. His sister, Sara, and her mother, were employed in cataloguing the books and covering many of them with scraps from their cotton dresses, which led Southey to christen that room the 'Cottonian Library'.

Mrs Coleridge wrote to Thomas Poole that they kept regular school in Greta Hall from 9.30 a.m. to 4.00 p.m., with Mrs Lovell teaching English and Latin in her small room, Mrs Coleridge teaching writing, figures, French and Italian in the dining-room with the assistance of Aunt Eliza, and Southey teaching his wife and daughters to read Spanish and his sons Greek.

Derwent's mother appears in the miniature painted by Matilda Betham in 1809 as quite a good-looking woman, with dark curls and blue eyes, a strong nose and a kind but firm mouth. Coleridge complained that she was ill-tempered, 'my friends received with freezing looks, the least contradiction occasioning screams of passion', that she was worldly-minded and concerned far too much about what other people would think. She was certainly lacking in imagination, writing to Poole in 1816, about her husband: 'he has been so unwise as to publish his fragments of "Christabel" and "Koula-Khan".'[1] Dorothy Wordsworth called Mrs Coleridge a 'sad fiddle-faddler' because of the time she took to get the children dressed in the morning, and 'the lightest, weakest, silliest woman',

[1] *Minnow among Tritons: Letters of Mrs Sara Coleridge to Thomas Poole*, ed. S. Potter, London, 1934. p. 48.

but it must be remembered that the two women disliked each other, Sara being jealous of her husband's intellectual friendship with William and Dorothy Wordsworth and of his love for Sara Hutchinson, and Dorothy feeling that Coleridge's unhappy marriage had been the ruin of his genius. Mrs Coleridge was a woman of practical intelligence who was sorely tried by her husband's unreliability and failure to provide for his family.

Her daughter Sara wrote to her husband Henry Nelson Coleridge in 1834 an interesting analysis of her mother's character:

> the sort of wife to have lived harmoniously with my father need not have possessed high intellect or a perfect temper – but greater enthusiasm of temperament than my mother possessed. She never admires anything she doesn't understand ... This faith, this docility, is quite alien to the Fricker temperament ... They are too literal and do not believe as I do that matters of imagination ... can work as many practical effects as what we see with our eyes and touch with our hands ... Neither had my mother that dexterity in managing the temper of others which is often a substitute for an even temper in the possessor. She has no power over her mind to keep the thought of petty cares and passing interests ... in abeyance ... though her talents are above mediocrity and her understanding clear and good – on its own range – she has no taste whatever for abstractions and formerly had less toleration for what she did not relish than now.[1]

Mrs Coleridge emerges from her long series of letters to Thomas Poole as a person for whom prudence and respectability were the most important qualities. She was, quite understandably, constantly worried about money. She lived for her extended family and wrote long accounts of their illnesses and achievements, but she believed any brilliance in her children to be confined to Hartley. She was very diffident about herself and her claims on Poole's time. Her great wish was that her children should be respectably

---

[1] Quoted by E. L. Griggs: Coleridge Fille pp. 105–6.

settled and financially secure and should not inherit their father's instability.

During the summer months there was a constant flow of visitors to Greta Hall. Among them were the Wordsworths, Hazlitt, De Quincey, Walter Scott, Shelley and his wife, Thomas Clarkson, Humphry Davy, William Wilberforce and Dr Bell. Although the combined dining-room and general sitting-room was downstairs, Southey's study on the first floor was used as a drawing-room for company. It was the biggest room in the house, with a large triple window with an arched central light looking out across the green to Derwent Water and the jaws of Borrowdale, and two smaller windows looking across the lake towards Newlands, Grasmoor and Grisedale Pike. The room was lined with books and here the visitors drank tea from blue and white willow-pattern gold-rimmed dishes with deep saucers while Derwent listened to their talk of philosophy, literature, politics and religion.

The fact that he could not be sent off for the conventional public schooling of the time greatly influenced Derwent's future attitudes to education. On 16 May 1862 he delivered a lecture in Chelsea on 'Poetry as a teacher'. He began 'The child is father of the man. To explain what I am I must tell you what I was. I was born in the loveliest of our English vales – but nature, as such, is not poetical. There must be an interpreter.'

Derwent went on to describe the three 'interpreters' who 'spoke to my childhood'. First, his father. 'One grey-haired man there was – a noticeable man, with large grey eyes, whose voice was as the sound of many waters, led by whom and holding by his hand, I have climbed the mountainside – and his speech has ever come back to me in soft mysterious echoes...'[1] Then, Southey – 'who living in a world of books looked out from them upon the world of nature – his vocation being to tell in varied numbers what he daily learned from both.' Finally, Wordsworth – 'it was my lot to listen, weekly to the deep bourdon of another voice, not less impressive. I lived much, as a child and growing boy, with him, who has been styled the Priest of Nature – rather let us say the Prophet ... The men of

---

[1] Derwent wrote this 28 years after his father's death. Coleridge had black hair which was grey by 1810, when he was 38.

whom I speak were Poets. Knowing them as I did, I grew up in the belief that this was a title of high and special privilege – almost divine...'

Great as his debt was to his unconventional upbringing, it deprived Derwent of that 'influence' which was an important contribution of a public school education to a successful public career, so that later in life he was to suffer constant rebuffs in his efforts to fulfil his talents and his vision.

There was no money for the university education of either Hartley or Derwent. In 1814 Coleridge's opium addiction was at its worst. He was living in Bath, earning nothing, and Josiah Wedgwood had been obliged by financial difficulties to withdraw his half of the annuity which he and his brother had settled on Coleridge. The income of Samuel Taylor Coleridge and family in 1814 was £76 10s. Wordsworth and Southey took it upon themselves to write to Coleridge's relations and friends to raise money for Hartley to go to university. An uncle managed to obtain a small scholarship for him and with this and subscriptions from his father's friends and relations Hartley went up to Merton College, Oxford, in 1815.

Derwent's letter to his mother on 20 October 1816 speaks for itself:

> I shall forthwith attend the epistolary committee to take into consideration the state of my wearing apparel. My strong shoes are completely worn out ... I have sent proposals to Mr Walton to fabricate a new pair. My ex-white trousers, now vice-breeches, are completely superannuated. My stockings, being composed on three generations, viz. the patriarchal grandfather at the top, yellow with age, ironing and bad washing, the son in the middle, a hue whiter (not snowy) and the hand-wrought grandson at the toes (of a dark brown tint) are completely shown off ... by the distressing lack of longitude. My sombre trousers (the seam at the knees now visible) are very shabby. My nankeens are blanching very fast... [1]

[1] Derwent Coleridge MSS. HRC, Texas.

In April 1816 Samuel Coleridge placed himself under the care of Dr Gillman in Highgate for a month, hoping that he could bring his opium addiction under control. In fact he remained with the Gillmans until his death in 1834 and his drug consumption was regulated. They took him into their family, looked after him and welcomed his children and his friends. During the next eight years he published *The Statesman's Manual*, revised *The Friend* and wrote *Aids to Reflection* (1825) and *The Constitution of Church and State* (1830). With his improved health came a renewed sense of responsibility for his sons.

At the end of August 1817 Coleridge wrote to his wife 'I wish to know about my dear Derwent and whether you can afford to send him up to me by the first week of November ... If you will order him the proper fit out that he may want, I will try to defray great part of it within the six months. I should, if it be thought proper, wish him to be at Highgate by the last week of October.'

But Derwent did not go to join his father.

On 29 October 1817 Southey wrote to his old friend Grosvenor Charles Bedford:

> Today however his wife has received a letter from Mrs Gillman saying that Mr Coleridge is not well enough to receive his son; that his illness is chiefly occasioned by his having engaged to write the introduction to the New Cyclopædia, which he now repents of having undertaken, finding it cannot be done in time etc. etc...
>
> Without affecting any love for Derwent, I feel much compassion for him: it is a truly pitiable situation; for his father not only does nothing for him, but stands in the way of having any thing done, because there is not that claim on his relations to bestir themselves, which there would be if he were an orphan. I can contribute nothing toward placing him in College, if such a scheme were set on foot, because there are much nearer claims which take from me all I can spare, which are likely to grow heavier, and which will continue as long as I live.'[1]

[1] K. Curry. *New Letters of Robert Southey*. Vol. II p. 175–6.

Southey's views on Coleridge are confirmed in a letter to Joseph Cottle in February 1819: '... when I think of the manner in which he has left these boys to sink or swim, I cannot speak of him with patience.[1]

In the autumn of 1817, on the recommendation of his teacher Mr Dawes, Derwent became tutor to the two sons of the Hopwood family, at Summerhill, three and a half miles north-east of Ulverstone, Lancashire, a position which he held until December 1819. Here he was living in a wealthy environment for the first time. After the cottage at Clappersgate and the simple and economical housekeeping at Greta Hall, it was a new world of fine ladies and pretty girls, flattery and snubs. He met other young men with a different background and had a sense of his social deficiencies. Although by January 1819 his manners were 'much improved' in Mrs Hopwood's eyes, he records in his Commonplace Book his chagrin and mortification when he allowed a lady to fall when helping her to dismount.

His mother wrote to Thomas Poole in June 1818 .'... nothing on earth would induce him to pass a great many years of his life as a private Tutor; but he is determined to do his duty in it as long as he is in it; and the greatest difficulty he finds is, making the children tractable, which he says he could much easier do, if he was <u>older</u> and <u>Mama</u> were not so very indulgent ... you see, he is not overworked; but he says, if they were not uncommonly quick he could do but little for them in so short an allotment of time.' The Commonplace Book[2] which he began to keep in August 1818 records signs of homesickness as well as mathematical exercises, Greek and Latin verse, and a series of poems of unrequited love, of increasingly sophisticated vocabulary and sentiments.

When dejected at Summerhill Derwent would walk the mile and a half across to Pennybridge Hall to visit Mrs Anne Machell, a married lady of forty, with two boys younger than Derwent. He would read her his poetry and his father's; she praised his compositions and listened sympathetically to his doubts and fears

[1] Ibid. p. 196.
[2] Derwent Coleridge MSS. HRC, Texas.

for the future and to his religious questionings. 'Receive my heartfelt thanks,' she wrote, 'for the Treasures you have bestowed and <u>allow</u> me <u>once</u> to say that I believe my admiration of them to be as <u>just</u> as it is ardent ant sincere.' She advised him: 'Abstain at present from Metaphysic – Indulge your admiration of the Deity in the magnificence of eternal Nature, and suffer your wounded or doubting spirit to be healed and harmonized by the benignant touch of Love and Beauty.' In Derwent's Commonplace Book there is a poem addressed to her.

Derwent later called her 'my sainted Mrs Machell – the guiding light of my earliest youth'.[1] When Derwent left Summerhill he sent her in 1820 a copy of his father's *Christabel, Kubla Khan, The Pains of Sleep,* and *Zapolya,* the 1816 text of *Christabel* having many emendations in Derwent's writing. She continued to write to Derwent at intervals over the next twenty years, showing a warmly affectionate interest in his progress.

In addition to tutoring the Hopwood boys for entry to Eton, Derwent was trying to raise money for a University career by translating from the Latin at Southey's suggestion *An account of the Abipones, an Equestrian People of Paraguay* by Martin Dobrizhoffer. He began work on volume I late in 1818 and his sister Sara, wishing to assist him, started on volume III. Sara eventually completed the translation and had it published by Murray in 1822.

Sara had grown into a beautiful and intellectually gifted girl with a charming and modest personality. Mrs Coleridge wrote to Poole in September 1819: 'Derwent encourages and instructs her; they read Tacitus, Livy, Virgil and Cicero together; and when tired of these, she turns to Ariosto, Tasso, Chiabura and Dante.'[2] De Quincey wrote 'at seventeen, when I last saw her, she was the most perfect of all pensive, nun-like, intellectual beauties that I have seen in real breathing life'.[3] She set Derwent a high standard of girlhood.

Hartley told Thomas Poole in February 1819, 'Derwent is well satisfied with his situation, and what is perhaps still better, gives

---

[1] Derwent Coleridge to Mary Pridham. 9 November 1825. Derwent Coleridge MSS. HRC, Texas.

[2] ed. Samuel Potter. Minnow among Tritons.

[3] Ibid, p. XXXV.

Derwent Coleridge in 1819 or 1820, attributed to Edward Nash, sketched at Greta Hall. *(By permission of Mrs A. H. B. Coleridge and Humanities Research Center, The University of Texas at Austin, Texas)*

26

satisfaction in it.' Derwent got on well with the Hopwood family, choosing in 1818 to stay over Christmas at Summerhill – 'at that time so full of attractions, so many beautiful and accomplished young ladies, such good music and singing' – rather than with his family at the Wordsworths', at Rydal Mount. In 1819 the Hopwoods came to Keswick with him, and Mrs Coleridge wrote to Jane Coleridge (wife of Samuel's brother George) of 'the good fellowship that subsisted between them'.

In January 1819 Derwent wrote to his mother that Mrs Hopwood wished that he could remain with the family at least another year and a half. At the same time she was 'interesting herself for me more than I have given her credit for, or gratitude'. She was trying to obtain for him a scholarship at Oxford, which would suit him very well, since he could study the classics rather than mathematics, and 'in Oxford reside my relations, my friends and my interest'. Moreover he hoped that the surroundings at the University would be more conducive to work than the frivolous atmosphere at Summerhill where, he admitted, 'I am not at present, I confess, in <u>cue</u>'.

Mrs Hopwood's attempts to help Derwent to get to University did not bear fruit but eventually Samuel Coleridge's friends came to the rescue; J. H. Frere contributed £300 and Lady Beaumont also assisted. Coleridge wanted Derwent to join him immediately, but he could not leave his situation at such short notice. He left Summerhill in December 1819 and went to Highgate in April 1820 to study under his father. He was 19 years old and had not seen his father since he was 11. On 10 May he was entered at St John's College, Cambridge.

Hartley had been elected by examination to a probationary Fellowship at Oriel in Oxford in April the previous year, to his father's joy. But on 29 June 1820, Coleridge's nephew, John Taylor Coleridge, wrote to James Gillman asking him to convey to his Uncle the distressing news that the provost and fellows of Oriel had decided not to confirm Hartley's Fellowship on the expiration of his probationary year. 'The charges against him are very painful ones to repeat . . . they are "sottishness, a love of low Company, and general inattention to college rules".' Derwent records the effect of the news on his father. 'I was with him at the time, and have never seen any human being, before or since, so deeply afflicted: not, as he said, by the temporal consequences of his son's misfortune, heavy as these were, but for the moral offence which it involved.'[1]

The Fellows of Oriel were noted for their austerity, sobriety and decorum. Hartley's misdemeanours seem to have been his continued association with undergraduates, his irregular attendance at chapel and his occasional drunkenness.

Coleridge immediately sent Derwent to Oxford to enquire into Hartley's affairs. Derwent reported that Hartley had disappeared, probably to the north. His father wrote to Derwent in deep distress on 3 July 1820 'O surely if Hartley knew or believed that I love him and [hunger] after him as I do and ever have done, he would have come to me ... I wish that I dared believe that Hartley is bona fide on his road to Keswick – but the same dread struck at once on Mr G.'s mind and mine – that he is wandering on some wild scheme, in no dissimilar mood or chaos of feelings to that which possessed his unhappy father at an earlier age during the month that ended in the Army-freak, and that [he may] even be scheming to take passage from Liverpool to America...'[2] But Hartley returned to London and by September was staying with the Montagus in Bedford Square, whence he wrote to explain the facts of the affair to his father.

Samuel Taylor Coleridge spoke of Hartley's loss of the Oriel Fellowship as one of the four major sorrows of his life. Hartley had shown signs of genius as a boy and his brilliant mind had won him the probationary fellowship, but after his rejection by Oriel he went slowly downhill and eventually became increasingly addicted to drink.

The shock and humiliation of Hartley's failure made both parents apprehensive about Derwent's activities at university. Coleridge was haunted by the fear that his own instability and personality defects had somehow been transmitted to his children; and Derwent's career as a student was under close scrutiny from the beginning.

---

[1] *Poems by Hartley Coleridge with a Memoir of his life by his Brother*, 1851. Moxon.
[2] Collected Letters of Samuel Taylor Coleridge. Ed. E. L. Griggs. OUP.

PART II
Cambridge 1820–24

Derwent went up to St John's College on 7 October 1820. He was a pensioner, the status of the majority of undergraduates, and soon after his arrival he was elected to a Foundress Scholarship (the Foundress being Lady Margaret Beaufort, mother of Henry VII). At this time, the college consisted of the first three courts of mellow red brick, although the chapel was the original thirteenth-century one of the old Hospital of St John. Mrs Coleridge wrote to Thomas Poole in 1824 that Derwent never had rooms in college but resided always in lodgings. He did however have to dine in Hall every day and attend chapel. Since the days of Newton, mathematics were pre-eminent in studies at Cambridge, whereas classics were still the principal study at Oxford. Until 1822 it was not possible to take an Honours Degree in classics or theology at Cambridge, only in mathematics. In May 1822 the Cambridge Senate passed a proposal that an Honours Examination in classics should be held, but only those were admissible who had obtained Honours in the Senate House examination in mathematics first.

Until 1822 the Senate House examination for the BA Honours degree consisted entirely of mathematics and moral philosophy, but in May 1822 the Senate passed a proposal that candidates for a pass BA degree should be examined in the first two days in the elements of mathematics, on the third day in Locke's *Essay on Human Understanding*, Paley's *Moral Philosophy* and *Evidences of Christianity* and on the fourth day be required to translate passages from the first six books of the Iliad and Æneid. Professor J. H. Monk stated in 1822 that the majority of undergraduates did not qualify for honours.[1]

---

[1] Philograntus. A letter to the Rt. Rev. John, Lord Bishop of Bristol.

It is strange that Derwent was entered for Cambridge rather than Oxford. He wrote to his mother from Summerhill: 'my rage for mathematics has declined ... My hope of <u>first-rate</u> distinction in them vanished ... still however I could resume, and I have no doubt acquit myself creditably in them ... on the contrary my love and good opinion of classics has warmed and rooted itself in me.'[1] It is likely that Derwent would have gained a much higher class degree in classics at Oxford with incalculable effect on his future career. The choice of Cambridge must have been his father's, possibly because Samuel Taylor Coleridge wanted Derwent to succeed where he had failed, having left Cambridge without a degree at all.

In his first year Derwent applied himself to his official studies. Hartley wrote to Lady Beaumont in December 1820: 'Derwent is hard at it at Cambridge. Heaven grant he may be wise from my imprudence...' His father wrote to Derwent in May 1821 'We are quite satisfied that you both do and do without, to the utmost of your power – and God forbid that by hook or crook you shall be enabled to make both ends meet, without incurring any Cambridge Debt – the very thought of which agitates me...' He went on to say that a very high degree, leading to a Fellowship, may be bought too dear if 'with the ruin of your Health'. His hopes were that Derwent would leave the University 'with an honourable character, as a Man, with a respectable degree ... and with <u>all</u> the several faculties of your mind ... cultivated in symmetry... You may be a Tutor in a wealthy or noble family – you may (and I truly hope, will) be a Clergyman – a man of Letters – a Secretary to a public man ... In short do you mean to find your World in the University, or to make use of the University as a stepping stone to the World?' He finished with a postscript: 'I need not say, my dear Derwent! that if I had reason to suppose you inclined to scatter the stream of your Power and Time in a multiplicity of Channels, or to be dallying with the Desultories, which is the sad case with Hartley, my advice would be as different as the source of my anxiety.' In June 1821 Derwent was bracketed fourth in the first class at his College and in July his father wrote to

[1] Derwent Coleridge MSS. HRC, Texas.

his brother George that Derwent had come back from College with a good report from his Head Tutor.

But Derwent's enthusiasm for mathematics was short-lived. One of Hartley's first letters to him at Cambridge sounded a prophetic note: 'My dear Snifter-breeches – ...I hope your mind is thriving on its dry food of Squares and Triangles. Do you take an occasional draft of the waters of Helicon to wash it down?'

His cousin, Henry Nelson Coleridge (son of Colonel James Coleridge of Ottery St Mary) who was at King's College, introduced Derwent to Cambridge society, especially to his fellow-Etonians. One of the most brilliant of the group was Winthrop Mackworth Praed, who came up to Trinity from Eton in October 1821. In his last year at Eton Praed had edited *The Etonian*, a large part of which he wrote himself in prose and verse. It also contained contributions from Cambridge undergraduates who had recently left Eton, including Henry Nelson Coleridge and John Moultrie, who was to become Derwent's closest friend. *The Etonian* was published by Charles Knight.

When Praed came up to Cambridge, Derwent wrote in his Memoir: 'It was indeed soon apparent that neither his time nor his talents would be devoted exclusively or even mainly, to the pursuit of university distinction. His disposition was eminently social, his company gladly welcomed wherever he was pleased to bestow it, whether by his immediate contemporaries or by men of higher standing. In a word, his habits were by no means those of a severe or regular student, while ... it was not long before he found himself literary employment foreign to his academical pursuits, and sufficient of itself to occupy almost any pen but his own.'[1] Praed's father was Serjeant-at-Law and Chairman of the Audit Board. He had a London house in Bedford Row, near the Inns of Court, and a country seat at Bitton House, Teignmouth.

After the long struggle to get to university, Derwent responded with delight and a sense of liberation to the friendship of like minds in Praed and his associates. As Derwent wrote years later: 'To the circle in which he moved belonged many who became subsequently

[1] *The Poems of W. M. Praed with a Memoir by Derwent Coleridge*, 1864.

among the most distinguished men of their time, and who were certainly not less remarkable in the spring and promise of their powers, than in the maturity and fulfilment of after life. The discussions which occurred at the frequent meetings of these friends were conducted with a force of argument, a readiness of illustration, and a command of language on the part of more than one of the disputants, which the compiler of this memoir has seldom heard equalled . . . It may readily be supposed that the war of words was not exclusively aroused by matters of taste or literary judgement; the graver questions of social, political and mental philosophy were debated with at least equal interest, and with scarcely less ability.'[1]

Praed's circle included Thomas Babington Macaulay and his cousin John Heyrick Macaulay, Charles Austin, John Moultrie, and Derwent's cousin Henry Nelson Coleridge. Praed wrote 'Davenant Cecil [Derwent's nom de plume] of whose character I can convey in the course of a few lines, no idea except what will naturally be associated with a highly flushed cheek, a magnificent forehead and thick black hair and eyes of unusual brilliancy, stept into this glistening circle with a temporary look of embarrassment, and folded his arms over his breast – "I", he said, "have looked into the lakes and fields for those enjoyments which our friend Marmaduke has found in Buhl ornaments and Turkey carpets. There are few who understand me, fewer who sympathise with me!"' According to Derwent's daughter, Christabel, he was chaffed because of his devotion to Wordsworth (not yet fashionable) and his love of pretty bound editions of the poets.

Derwent developed an intense friendship with John Moultrie, who remembered in his poem *The Dream of Life* how they would walk to Grantchester, the Gogs and surrounding villages, would come home with cowslips in their caps and, after a shared meal, would go on talking until midnight. Moultrie recalled how, after an eloquent debate in the Union, their circle would repair to an oyster supper in his neighbouring rooms. The Cambridge Union, started in 1815, met once a week in a room at the back of the Red Lion Hotel in Petty Cury. Thomas Macaulay, Austin and Praed were the leading orators.

[1] Ibid.

In his poem *The Dream of Life* Moultrie paints a picture of Derwent as a student:

> Himself a poet born, and, from a child,
> With all a poet's sensibilities,
> Even to excess endued: – for him, a boy,
> The boisterous sports of boyhood were too rough, –
> The sympathy of school fellows too coarse,
> Save of some few like-minded with himself,
> With whom he roam'd apart – to all the rest
> A by-word and a laughing-stock; – now climb'd
> Some favourite hill – now ranged the vernal woods
> In search of wild flowers. – With advancing youth
> Such weakness had worn off, and though he still
> Retain'd a woman's beauty, manly thought
> Was his, and manly feeling; – Still the paths
> Of quiet contemplation – the mild haunts
> Of phantasy – and the mysterious realms
> Of painting and of music were his choice, –
> The world in which his spirit loved to dwell;
> And, I believe, no truer eye than his,
> No finer ear for concord of sweet sounds,
> No spirit more susceptible of pain
> Or pleasure from the spells of either art,
> Or their diviner Sister Poesy,
> Was found that day among us.

Derwent's father was desperately anxious about his son's activities at Cambridge, fearing a repetition of his own and Hartley's failure. He wrote to Derwent on 11 January 1822:

You cannot do without intermissions of Study, without recreation and such as society only can afford you – ? – Be it so! But is dissipation of mind and spirit the fit recreation of a Student? Or not rather the fever fit, of which your Studies are likely to be the cold, feeble and languid Intermittents? ... But extra-academic Society, Concerts, Balls – Dressing, and an hour and a half or two Hours not seldom devoted to so respectable a purpose – O God! – even the disappointment as to your success in the University, mortifying as I feel it, arising from such causes and morally ominous as it becomes in your particular case and with the claims, that <u>you</u> must recognize on your exertions, is not the worst. This accursed Coxcombry . . . sends a ferment into the very Life-blood of a young man's Sense and Genius – and ends in a schirrus of the Heart.

He went on to paint a somewhat fanciful picture of his own student days at Jesus, describing how he read all day and every day and evening too.

Samuel Taylor Coleridge continued 'There was a passage in your letter to Mrs Chisholm which shocked and wounded me so much that I could not speak of it to you at the time.' In this passage Derwent had evidently spoken of himself as 'a mere poor child of charity, a dependent on the I know not what' and had contrasted his state with those who were maintained by their fathers. Samuel Taylor Coleridge pointed out that J. H. Frere had given him the money to send Derwent to College in recognition of his intellectual debt to Coleridge. 'Suppose that a Bookseller had given me 300£ for my lectures, instead of Mr Frere – would you think the sum more earned by me?' Coleridge's pride was bitterly hurt by Derwent's derogatory remark – 'how little you have been taught or are in the habit of attributing to or connecting with me, as the Source, I mourn to see, chiefly for your sake and because too many others see and notice it'.

This letter ends 'I am not angry, Derwent! – but it is calamitous that you do not know how anxiously and affectionately I am your Father – Samuel Taylor Coleridge.

'P.S. I hear that you are Premier or Secretary of a Literary Club – about old books. If such things did not dissipate your time and thoughts, they <u>dissipate</u> and perplex your <u>character</u> – They are well enough for BA.s and MA.s –'

Four days later on 15 January Samuel Taylor Coleridge wrote again to Derwent. 'Be a student, a recluse, an <u>Autocrat</u> for the next two years and a half, and what are green Gooseberries and dry Colic or wasting flux now will be a handsome <u>Desert</u> afterwards. – For

God's sake, my dear Boy! for mine, for your Mother's, for dear little Sara's, do throw off these flappets and tag-points and appendages – Your business at present is to <u>learn</u>, to acquire, to <u>habituize</u> – not to teach – to <u>be</u> but not not to <u>shew</u> or rather to <u>become</u> ... Do, do, give your poor Brother an example, instead of an excuse –'

In December 1821 Derwent was eighth in the first class in his examination. His father was upset that he did not write with the result of his examination and in a letter to Thomas Allsop (19 January 1822) he lamented Derwent's 'failure'. On 9 February 1822 in a letter to his wife Coleridge conceded 'I have had no proof of Derwent's <u>Extravagance</u> from his Bills: tho' of course we began to fear, lest it might be so –'

In July 1822 the Gillmans probably saved Derwent's life. He was critically ill in their house at Highgate for six weeks with typhus fever and received constant medical attention from Mr Gillman. His father wrote 'Nothing is wanting that Skill, Tenderness and unwearied Attention can supply – and what if he had been taken ill at Cambridge where a Typhus is raging! and no friend near him.'[1] Five young men died of typhus at St John's College in this epidemic. To add to Coleridge's anguish, Hartley disappeared from Highgate on the nineteenth day of Derwent's illness, being quite unable to face any kind of mental pain. Derwent's diary for 1822[2] records that he was taken ill on 25 June: 'I am now (July 30th) convalescent, but weak. Gratia Deo.' Another entry reads: '15th July – This week in great danger. Mr Gillman came 6 times one day and Mr Watson probably as often.' At this point he interposed a jingle:

I met a pretty maid,
She called herself Jeanette
But I'm more than half afraid
That I've put her in a fret.

By 31 July he was 'tired of my porridge, Tea, Boiled Milk, Bread pudding'. On 6 August: 'Mutton chop for dinner! Wrote to

---

[1] Samuel Taylor Coleridge to John Taylor Coleridge. 15 July 1822. Collected Letters of Samuel Taylor Coleridge. Ed. E. L. Griggs. OUP.
[2] Derwent Coleridge MSS. HRC, Texas.

mother', and on 7 August: 'Much stronger. Dressed myself and walked into the other room.'

On 1 August Derwent wrote 'It is strange that during my illness I never felt that I was in any danger. Yet the fever was dangerous; and might have been fatal to another, or to myself at another place, as at Cambridge ... Mr Gillman has no doubt my bill at Cambridge would have come to an £100. How fortunate I was ill at Highgate!' The cheerful extrovert character of these notes is an interesting contrast to the neurotic preoccupation with physical symptoms in the notebooks and letters of Samuel Taylor Coleridge.

On 29 July Praed wrote to Derwent from Teignmouth: 'How have you managed to lay yourself up in this style? You have, I strongly suspect, been sitting up too late on a Heath Knoll, or helping some Sentimental One over a stile, when the grass was damp with a shower.'[1] On 15 August he wrote again to say he was glad to hear Derwent was recovering. 'I beg that you will abstain for some time from Champagne, Love, Château Mergeau, Sentiment, tiger-like reading, Politics and all other poisons.'[2]

Derwent's diary for 1822 lends some substance to his father's fears of Dandyism. He records, with no date 'The supposed amount of my debts'. The total is £21.10s, of which £11.5s is for lodgings, £3.10s for books etc., £2.5s for hairdressing etc., and £2.10s for a waistcoat. In March he records:

I want from Simon –
Suit of Clothes, gaters	£8
Common trowsers	£2
Box coat	£7
Also gloves, silk stockings,	
cravats and white handkerchiefs	
Also a wig	£2.10s

In August while convalescing at Highgate he wrote down a review of his wardrobe, which was not excessive, but its listing indicates Derwent's natural desire to dress suitably for the circle in which he

[1] Ibid.
[2] Ibid.

moved. He was strikingly good-looking but conscious of being short. He wrote to his mother from Summerhill in 1819 'My appetite is very good and I rather think I am growing. Four inches is all I want.' He was determined to make the most of himself and not to appear outwardly as 'a mere poor child of charity'.

The diary also reflects Derwent's continued interest in literature and the arts, and growing aversion to mathematics. He made a chronological list of Eminent Persons in Letters, Philosophy and the Arts and a list of Eminent Living Artists, Musical Composers, Musical Performers and Teachers and a list of Booksellers. By July 1822 Derwent, Praed and Moultrie were engaged in getting some of their writings published in a new periodical, *Knight's Quarterly Magazine*, of which Knight was the Editor and Praed the directing spirit.

Praed wrote the leading article to the first number of *Knight's Quarterly Magazine*: 'We will go forth into the world in high spirits and handsome type, with verse and prose, criticism and witticism, fond love and loud laughter, everything that is light and warm, fantastic and beautiful – while we will leave the Nation to the care of the Parliament and the Church to the Bishop of Peterborough.' The contributors all had *noms de plume*:

Peregrine Courtenay	Winthrop Mackworth Praed
Vyvyan Joyeuse	
Gerard Montgomery	John Moultrie
Davenant Cecil	Derwent Coleridge
Tristram Merton	Thomas Babington Macaulay
Hamilton Murray	Henry Malden
Joseph Haller	Henry Nelson Coleridge

Derwent's major contribution to *Knight's Quarterly* was *Beauty; a Lyrical Poem*, written in 1821 and originally entitled *Dream Love*. It describes a vision of an impossible 'ideal of a poet's love', beginning:

Since yesternight I've dreamt a dream,
Delicate maid, of love and Thee;
I know that it can only *seem* –
But let it seem to be.

It is a vision sent to bless
The spirit of my youth awhile;
Oh! Let it still upon my spirit smile!
It is a vision in whose soft caress
Today – perhaps tomorrow,
I may forget my sorrow, –
The pains of an unquiet mind
That ever seeks what it can never find,
That undiscover'd loveliness
Which is to youth a hope – a dark belief –
A somewhat dimly promising relief
To that which nothing natural can heal;
The unseen wound which makes us poets when we feel.

This handsome young man who wrote poetry had already fluttered several female hearts but he was searching for an apparently unattainable ideal love. He later confessed that his amorous adventures began at the age of 12 with the saddle-maker's daughter at Ambleside. At Summerhill he inspired the affections of Mrs Hopwood's niece, Cecilia Byng. She was still writing to Derwent in 1824: 'What would I not give to know a woman whom you could love. How perfect she must be: I dare say you have found one in fancy and in fancy it will always be – as in reality the woman will never exist whom I should deem worthy of you ... I wonder if you give one thought to me for the thousands I waste upon you...' Cecilia also refers to 'the girl you were in love with when with us', whom she guesses to be Agnes.[1] At Cambridge Derwent was attracted to Aline Malden, sister of one of the contributors to *Knight's Quarterly* and later to Anne Longueville, whom he met while staying with his friend, John Moultrie, at Shrewsbury.

Derwent's closest friendship at Cambridge was with John Moultrie – a friendship which lasted until Moultrie's death in 1874, despite a bitter quarrel which contributed much to Derwent's depression and sadness during his last year at Cambridge. The two friends spent part of the 1821 vacation together at Moultrie's home in Shrewsbury, where his father was Rector. They were supposed to

[1] Ibid.

be studying mathematics, but in fact were writing poetry. In August 1822 John Moultrie wrote to Derwent at Highgate saying that from childhood his parents had expected him to be a lawyer but he had always loathed the idea. He had undergone many changes of opinion in the last two years and a half; 'suffice it to say I have been for many months a speculative, that is to say a sort of Paley's Evidence Christian, and am now becoming (I hope) essentially one. But it is only in the last few months that I have felt sufficient confidence in myself, or in my religion, to think of taking orders.' Writing to his father to tell him of his change of plan would cause friction. 'I wish therefore that, partly for my own satisfaction, but more for that of my father and family, you would write to me immediately and state distinctly to me your opinion on the subject and the reasons on which they are grounded.'[1] By January 1823 Moultrie was acting as Tutor at Eton to the son of the Earl of Craven.

The quarrel between them was over religious and philosophical beliefs. Derwent had gradually lost all religious faith at Cambridge. Moultrie had also been a freethinker but rapidly and easily recovered his faith and decided to go into the Church. The gap between them widened until by October 1823 the breach seemed to be final. Derwent's impassioned letters to Moultrie reveal much of his lack of religious faith and his depression in his last complete term at Cambridge.

'Pardon me if I say that I cannot allow you to hold that high tone of moral superiority which you at present assume over me, as if everything was to be forgiven on your part. "Why", you say, "force these recollections upon me?" Because I am not conscious of having erred in these respects, and because I will be justified in your eyes. Again I must be allowed to say that I think a man might be argued out of Christianity – I was myself argued out of it. Yet more, I do not look upon my own Faith (by which I mean Austinism)[2] as a thing to be ashamed of... If

[1] Ibid.
[2] Austin, a prominent member of the Union, who later became an advocate and parliamentary lawyer, was a friend of J. S. Mill and a Utilitarian.

39

you mean to distinguish between a conscientious Infidel and an Epicurean[1] I am the <u>latter</u>. I am not a Godwinite or Words-worthian or a Shelleian or any other kind of unChristian-religionism – for all these have a religion and a worse one than that of Christ – whom I <u>almost</u> worship ... As to opposing a practical to a theoretical Epicurean if anyone <u>believes</u> one thing and does another, he is a silly fool, and such in this respect am not I.'[2]

On 23 September 1823 Derwent wrote to Moultrie: 'I have been your devoted friend for three years. I cannot accuse myself of one thought or one action incompatible with the sincerest, nay, the most romantic friendship. I have bestowed on you the most unreserved confidence. I have managed your wayward feelings and preferred their gratification to that of my own. In return, I demand from you a friendship equally devoted, a confidence equally unreserved, a consideration for my feelings approaching to that which I give to yours. I cannot maintain habits of half friendship with <u>you</u>...'[3]

There follows an undated letter from Derwent:

'You will be troubled no longer with explanations or what you call "blarney". In one word I <u>cannot bear</u> the feelings you entertain towards me, or the language you couch them in. Farewell, you lose nothing in me but a few pleasant associations. I am, you know, "the foe to all your hopes in earth and heaven"!...

I am on the point of being arrested for £4 8s 6d – I am going to sell my books. Send those you have of mine; but keep the desk, as a memento of one formerly dear to you. Do not refuse me this favour, I am not too proud to ask one of you in return. Send £3 to Edward to discharge my debts in Shrewsbury...

... Had I not lost you and Anne Longueville it might have been different; but the temper of my soul has lost its spring by

---

[1] Epicurus, an Athenian philosopher of the fourth century B.C., was a materialist who taught that the highest pleasure is tranquillity, which is to be attained by a virtuous and simple life.
[2] Derwent Coleridge MSS. HRC, Texas.
[3] Ibid.

these events. Since my frame of mind and fortunes have so fallen – it would be cruel to wish to retain any influence over the heart or prospects of that dear girl ... Farewell, may you obtain present happiness and final peace in your own way.[1]

On 30 October 1823 Derwent wrote again to Moultrie: 'Your letter of Monday reached me yesterday morning. I am neither "too proud nor too offended" to apply the sum it encloses to the relief of my present necessities: but your delicacy will readily suggest to you that this must be the last pecuniary favour I can receive.' He goes on to say that when it is necessary to disclose their separation 'I shall give the real cause – to wit, my inability to hold your Friendship, without your esteem, which I have forfeited on the score of my principles.' Derwent continues at great length to explain that they can no longer converse on equal terms on ethics, philosophy and religion (all subjects of which Derwent was passionately desirous of 'sympathy and social commune') or on literature or even on their affections for the opposite sex. 'I do not part with you because I am offended with "my heart's best brother" but because we have for several months made each other mutually unhappy...

As for my way of life, I sometimes fancy I resemble the Moriscoe in *The Remorse* as he was passing out of the cheerful sunshine into the dark and damp cavern whose termination was an empty and unfathomable pit, first a horrible dream and then destruction![2]

This correspondence reveals Derwent as a proud man, anxious to keep his self-respect, but able to understand different opinions. He is intellectually honest, and a man of deep feelings who has to commit himself completely to this friendship or not at all. Moultrie, somewhat bewildered, wrote in reply to Derwent's farewell letter: 'I cannot even now comprehend the reasonableness of the quarrel into which I have been unwillingly forced.'[3]

[1] Ibid.
[2] Ibid.
[3] Ibid.

41

Derwent was also penniless and without prospects (which is partly why he renounced Anne Longueville) and was feeling exceedingly lonely and depressed. Thanks to his father's canvassing, he obtained from the Mercers' Company in November 1822 the Lady North Exhibition of £20 p.a. and in May 1823 from the Goldsmiths' Company another exhibition of £20 p.a. but the latter was only paid until he left Cambridge, and the former not until 1828/9.

On 24 June Hartley sent brotherly advice and sympathy: 'I am sorry that you have been not well or not happy ... That you feel at times a want of inward strength, of faith, of hope, and of fortitude, I rather lament than wonder.' He went on to say: 'You mention nothing with respect to your plans, either at College or afterwards, but I am informed that you have resigned the pursuit of Academic honours ... Let me, my dear Derwent, advise you to be very cautious in your conduct to Father and to the Gillmans. When in their company be as little of a dandy, or even of a Beau, as you can. Write to them frequently and affectionately, and never argue with Mr G.'[1]

Derwent in fact had given up the unequal struggle to gain honours in mathematics. In June 1822 he was '5th in first class', in December 1822 he was 'Inferior to those in the first class, but entitled to Prizes if in the 1st Class at the next examination'. He was 'not classed' in May 1823, being 'absent from part of the Examination with leave'. In June his disappointed father described him as 'in a very unsettled unhealthy [state] of mind – I should be at a loss to say, [what] one advantage he has acquired by his University Campaigns'.[2] On 24 January 1824 Derwent was admitted to a pass BA degree.

However, Cambridge had given Derwent some lifelong friendships and had done something to remedy the lack of 'influence' which resulted from his lack of a public school education. He had made close links with people like Praed and Thomas Babington Macaulay who were to become MPs and politically influential. He owed his first job to John Heyrick Macaulay, cousin of Thomas

[1] Letters of Hartley Coleridge. Ed. E. L. Griggs. OUP.
[2] Samuel Taylor Coleridge to John Taylor Coleridge. 10 June 1823. Collected Letters of Samuel Taylor Coleridge. Ed. E. L. Griggs. OUP.

Babington Macaulay, who was Master of the new Proprietary Classical and Mathematical School which opened in Plymouth in 1822. He offered Derwent the post of Third Assistant Master.

Derwent wrote to Moultrie from St John's on 11 January 1824,

... to inform you of the turn my unsteady fortunes are about to take. The situation of third master to the new Grammar School at Plymouth has been offered me: and if the delay occasioned by the necessity of my obtaining permission from my Father has not obliged the Governors to give the appointment to another, on the 29th of this month I shall commence my laborious duties. The value is £190 p.a. – which is also about the amount of my present debts. To liquidate these I am going, with Praed's advice and through his means, to borrow £200 at the usual interest, for the payment of which he and Ord bind themselves as sureties.

My mind has been in a very weak and miserable state ever since we parted. I have sought refuge from inward malady partly in dissipation, partly in the acquirement of knowledge, which I find an operation more mechanical, and standing less in need of the lively spirit of hope to quicken and impel it than original composition. In the low estate to which it has pleased the dispensing power to call me, I trust I shall derive from continued mental activity, and the steady contemplation of such objects of rational desire as are still within my reach, a new strength sufficient to prevent me from being thoroughly worthless and miserable. At present I am suffering very much in body and mind – far more than even you <u>can</u> take account of, but I feel that something of my old character is beginning to reappear in me, in another shape: and I am again endeavouring to fix my eyes upon that *grandeur d'âme*, to which with boyish, but not unamiable pride, I once believed myself capable of attaining. I fear it will soon be impossible to command your respect: but I trust you will not again have to lament any of those "low declensions and descents of mind" to which recent events (with some of an older date) have lately sunk me. I know not whether I am impertinent in addressing this to you: I think <u>not</u>. I could not have wound up my affairs here to my satisfaction without entreating your forgiveness, for all that I have said and done amiss, during our late differences and assuring you, notwithstanding appearance, that I still feel for you all the love that my nature is capable of feeling – far more, I grieve to say, than I have ever felt for woman ... You spoke of "receiving me with open arms" – believe me I am withheld by no false pride from flying to them: but we must not deceive ourselves: it is not for you to mingle in daily commune with one who not merely resolves good and evil into pleasure and pain without reference to futurity, but who also gives them a practical meaning so widely different. Farewell: pardon this long letter, which I fear will give you fresh pain: yet not more than if I had left you in ignorance of my destinies. If you have any books of mine which you do not want send them in by the coach or they will not be in time.

Derwent wrote across the seal of this letter '*L'herbe ne doit pas croître sur le chemin de l'amitié*'.[1]

Derwent passed through Highgate on his way to Plymouth, leaving his father in a state of despair at his rejection of academic ambitions and of orthodox Christianity. Coleridge wrote to C. A. Tulk on 26 January 1824; 'I am under great affliction of mind from the diseased state of mind in relation to his moral and religious System of Thinking (N.B. – not of Action, thank God!) in which I find my second Son – O what a place of poisons that University of Cambridge is – Atheism is quite the Ton among the Mathematical Geniuses, Root and Branch Infidelity!'[2]

Derwent's mother wrote to Thomas Poole in January 1824: '... there is little else but disappointment for poor Sara, and me, to say nothing of S.T.C. and Hartley, the poor father is very much wounded by all this, but I hope his next letter will be written in a calmer state of mind, for my poor Derwent has now done his best in accepting the situation of third Master of Plymouth School, from whence I have just received a good account of his health and determination to perform all the duties of the situation with the

[1] Derwent Coleridge MSS. HRC, Texas.
[2] Collected Letters of Samuel Taylor Coleridge. Ed. E. L. Griggs. OUP.

utmost regularity. He will, however, find it a very different sort of employment to the studies of a College; though he tells me he shall have leisure for his own improvement which he shall make a point of, and that having been previously acquainted with the other masters he feels himself already quite at home.'[1] Mrs Coleridge and Hartley proposed to pay Derwent's debts, with hopes of future recompense. Her letter concluded: 'Hartley says, his brother is a beautiful Classic, and might have got a Fellowship at Oxford.'

[1] Ed. S. Potter. *Minnow among Tritons.*

PART III
Plymouth 1824–26

When Derwent arrived in Plymouth in January 1824 the old original town was crowded round Sutton Harbour but a new elegant Regency quarter was growing up behind the Hoe. Plymouth had a growing number of artists, following in the tradition of Reynolds (who had been Mayor of Plympton and had as his patrons the Parkers of Saltram), and men with a cultured interest in literature and science. The Athenaeum, the meeting place of the Plymouth Institution, was the centre for the intellectual life of the town and picture shows were held in the Gallery in Frankfurt Place.

Derwent arrived in Plymouth with a pass degree, pursued by bills and love letters, a handsome young man of twenty-three with romantic ideals but uncertain of what he wanted to do with his life. He had literary aspirations but no prospects, and had become estranged from his family and his closest friend. He had lost the faith he had absorbed from Southey. He was deeply depressed, but nevertheless resolved to improve himself by the acquisition of knowledge in pursuit of that '*grandeur d'âme*' to which he had always aspired. Hartley, now teaching at Ambleside, wrote to his father about Derwent's state of mind: 'I fear that you imagine that Vanity rules his heart and soul, no less than his words, looks and gestures – I do [not] and cannot think this ... His misfortune is that his intellect has no patience. He substitutes positiveness for certainty and must always be positive of something ... But ... the good which I am sure is in him is very hard to quench.'

Derwent was still having money problems. His mother had received a legacy of £115, which she had entrusted to Praed so that

47

Derwent's Cambridge debts could be paid without borrowing at interest. However, Praed never made the slightest allusion to the subject after March 1824 and Derwent was concerned to discover that his debts still remained unpaid. More than a year later he learned that Praed had in fact invested the money at interest; the debts were not paid until December 1825, by which time 'a considerable surplus'[1] had accumulated, which was duly returned to him.

Mrs Coleridge had hoped her legacy would be repaid out of Derwent's Exhibitions from the Mercers' and Goldsmiths' Companies; but one Exhibition ceased on his leaving Cambridge, while the arrears on the other were not paid until 1828/9. After a good deal of pressure Derwent sent his mother £10 to help towards sending Sara to Highgate for treatment of her eyes, but there is no record of further remittances, and he did not manage to save, as she urged him to do.

Mrs Coleridge's letters are always anxious and repetitious and sometimes fretful. She complains that Derwent does not write often enough and then he writes a short letter with a promise of a long one which never comes. She does however show a real concern for Derwent's moral state, for his health, particularly his eyes, and for all those minutiae which were so important to her. Does he send his washing out and how much does it cost? Did he send to Plymouth the tablecloths and spoons he had at Cambridge?

There were letters from Praed.[2] On 16 March 1824, despondent at only having come second for the Pitt and Battie prizes, he wrote to Derwent, who was then lodging at 3 Union Street: 'I perhaps disgusted the examiners by my apparent coolness, for I came into the first day's examination ten minutes too late in a postchaise from a journey – went to the Huntingdon Ball in the middle of the contest, and got into a whimsical scrape with Crawley (one of the Examiners) the day after its conclusion.' He continues: 'Your debts are in a state of clearance. How am I to get at your London taylors' names and addresses?'

On 10 October Praed wrote from his family's home in Bitton, near Teignmouth, where he was staying for a week: 'I found

---

[1] Derwent Coleridge MSS. HRC, Texas.
[2] Ibid.

Cambridge a bore.' He would come to the ball at Plymouth on 13 October – 'a flying visit to Plymouth . . . I am not clear that I shall see even the Breakwater'. However, he added: 'be of good cheer! – you are of more value than many breakwaters'. On another occasion Praed wrote that he had won the English Poem and Epigram Prize. 'I have had a young lady, tolerably plain and foolish, making the most annoying love to me in consequence! . . . You are used to these things but it is so horribly out of my line! Do you contrive to get entangled at all at Plymouth?'

Derwent evidently still retained the affection of Cecilia Byng, niece of Mrs Hopwood at Summerhill, whose employ he had left four years earlier. During 1824 she wrote several long letters to him clandestinely, under the pseudonym of 'Sebe'.[1]

'You <u>are</u> altered in that sincere affection I once flattered myself you felt for me . . . ask yourself if a year ago, or three or four, you would have told me you had "three important letters on your hands" which made you hurry in writing to <u>me</u> – I feel almost sure I should have been the principal object at any of the periods I name.' She protests: '<u>Our</u> affection I call purely platonic' and 'I believe I do not mean to), marry at all. I have not partially but <u>wholly</u> overcome my liking to' but concludes, 'I never can change though you may make me feel it necessary for me to conceal the extent of my regard . . . Ever your affectionately attached Sebe.' They had evidently met last in the summer of 1823 and she tried hard to arrange another meeting, signing herself '<u>Devotedly</u> yours, Sebe.'

Mrs Coleridge urged Derwent to be diligent at the school: 'I wish you would not say in yours that you are <u>heartless</u> and <u>aimless</u> . . . you say you "lounge into school" – and you go down to school in the mornings "half alive".' The turning point in Derwent's life was his meeting with Mary Simpson Pridham, late in 1824. She was to give him a new sense of the beauty of the world and a new sense of purpose.

Mary Pridham was a beautiful dark-haired girl of seventeen, the oldest daughter of John Drake Pridham, director of the Naval Bank in Whimple Street. He was a Freeman and Common Council-

[1] Ibid.

man of the city, Treasurer to the newly appointed Improvement Commissioners and to the Royal Eye Infirmary, and, like all the cultured men of Plymouth, a member of the Athenaeum. His wife was an orphan with a small independent income, who had been brought up by her aunt and uncle, retired tradespeople in comfortable circumstances. She was beautiful – her height and presence compared with Mrs Siddons. She had a strong character and great self-confidence and aplomb. She was also clever and her four daughters were unusually educated. When Derwent met Mary she was studying art under Ball and Italian with Signor Bezzi (an Italian political exile); she was in touch with current poetry, and had copied into her album of 1824 some of Davenant Cecil's poems from No. III of *Knight's Quarterly*, published at the end of 1823.

According to Christabel Coleridge, Derwent first met Mary in a picture gallery, where she was standing before a portrait of a lady. Derwent turned to the dark haired girl, with curls all round her face and neck, and said 'I hope you don't wear ear-rings!' Mary was glad to say she did not.[1]

On Christmas Day 1824 Derwent wrote for Mary a poem, 'Mary's Cove. In imitation of Wordsworth'. He tells how he set forth on a bright December noon –

> Intent to watch the ripling tide flow in
> And let the sea-wind blow among my hair.
> It was my chance, ere I could reach the shore,
> Winning upon her footsteps, to o'ertake
> A gentle maid, with a 'heart-robbing eye',
> Who govern'd by a kindred impulse, bent
> On a like object, in her sweetness did admit me
> To a companionship of her wild way.
> And with her walked her little sister meek,
> Her sister well-beloved. So we were three.
>
> . . .
>
> Anon we lit upon a little Cove,
> A cleft in the rude Rock, a shut-in place
> Defended from the eyes of all the world.

[1] A memoir of Derwent Coleridge by Christabel Coleridge. Dated 26 October 1909. Derwent Coleridge MSS. HRC, Texas.

. . .
Beside old England's guardian main she sat
An English maid, rich in the thoughts that stir
An English spirit – sensible to joy,
And grateful for the pleasure it received,
I following the sweet leadings of her mind,
Nor I nor she could bear that Memory
Should have no name for that delightful spot;
And so we called it Mary's Cove, – a sound
Already grown familiar to my ears.[1]

Derwent's courtship did not run smooth. Back in his lodgings he recorded minutely the course of his changing fortunes in a little book entitled 'Mary – A Record of Feeling',[2] which he kept from Monday 17 January 1825 to 11 April 1825. 'In lack of a friend I commit my thoughts and feelings, when they would otherwise be intolerable, to this book, *quasi fido amicus.*' He starts off with a rhyme:

Still idle with a busy air
Deep trifles to contrive
The gayest valetudinaire
Most thinking rake alive,

Such at least I was at College, I am sadder if not wiser now.

He continues

Monday 17th January 1825. Mary with her father and mother. A. B. also there. No good understanding between self and A. B. . . . in bed – her face seemed engraven on the retina of my eyes – talking, smiling, animated, her eyes flashing, her cheek glowing – inextricably involved in a *tête-à-tête* with A. B. . . . the endless lights and flashes of her countenance playing on his black phiz like the sparkles of running water on a pebble –

[1] Derwent Coleridge MSS. HRC, Texas.
[2] Ibid.

Several times she appeared to me sitting at the instrument – swinging round from it with a twine in her form such as Caracci has often painted and a smile on her lips and in her eyes such as Caracci never painted, nor anyone else – a smile brimful of love and bewilderment – that makes the ground sink from under your feet – that almost makes you forget you are not in Paradise – but restricted by a thousand rules and reasons and proprieties, so forcibly are you impelled by all the instincts of Love and Admiration to fold the lovely object in your arms and vent the turbulence of your feelings in a long, long kiss. But A. B. was there – neat, shaven, trim ... assuming all the rights of long and confidential amity.

The entry for Thursday, 20 January reads 'dined with Henry Woolcombe' (the founder and President of the Athenaeum). 'Resolved to lecture at the Athenaeum on Wordsworth according to Mr Woolcombe's advice ...' Subsequent entries continue:

Saturday, 22nd January ... I do not now call 18.1t1 every day as I used to do, but every other day. Why do I make this change? Because I feel that my visits are less acceptable than formerly ... Ere long I will learn more, for my suspense at present is intolerable ...

Sunday, 23rd January. I saw her at Church. She did not look unkindly at me – but her Mother?

Monday, 24th January. It is – it must be as I feared. What have I done to merit, to occasion this sudden coolness of manner, 'How do you do, Sir! Thank you for this call' – gentle girl, <u>thou</u> didst not frown. I saw thee but for a moment – it must serve me for many days ...

25th January. From what a dream of fields and flowers have I awakened? We had agreed to spend the ensuing summer in each other's society. To arrange our plans so that we might see each other daily – early in the morning and late at night – walk together – be in the woods together – watch the sun rising and setting together. I thought to have done something under these influences, that might have made me a name ... not a durable one – I look not for immortality – but such a reputation as might have given me authority in my own circle – which might have supplied the want of rank and wealth. Where shall I go now? One thing I am resolved on – I will visit little – I will do <u>something</u> – no matter what – I will not christen my indolence Melancholy, Despondency, Lack of Motive – I will employ this very evening well if possible – busily at least – so goodbye.

At the end of January Derwent is in despair, believing that Mary is engaged to C. G., an older man who seems to have been regarded as a good match by the Pridhams. 'So she is gone. C— proposed and accepted – by the mother at least, and by implication by M—.' The poem on the last page of the book was probably written at this time:

> We meet no more – the die is cast
> I may not see thy face again:
> My hope is gone – it was my last,
> Thy looks, thy words are all too plain . . .

The following Thursday at the Athenaeum Mr Pridham told him that Mrs Pridham wanted him to call. He sent his picture a few hours before he called and found Mary copying it. Mama shed tears and left him with Mary . . . 'She alluded to her previous assurance that C. visited the house out of <u>brotherly</u> love solely, giving me her word that she thought so when she said it. I believe her from my soul.' In February 'she is not to be his!' Her mother communicated the circumstances to him. 'I hear that she has also been engaged to a youth in <u>Bath</u>, and that his claims were thrust aside to make way for this more advantageous connection. Why it did not take place I have yet to learn. I apprehend that the pecuniary and other advantages which he had to offer were found to be insufficient to compensate for his inequality of age etc.'

On Tuesday 15 March Derwent wrote that he had had 'a succession of vague and variable feelings, irresolute, desponding, wild with sorrow, dizzy with joy, cheerful, content, determined, my mind has gone through all these phases in the last few days'. On

53

Thursday last he called at 12 Frankfurt Street at 1 p.m. 'I shall never express how beautiful M. looked in her morning dress, her cap carelessly thrown on, almost dropping off her dark curls, and her face glowing, glowing!' They were left alone without Mary's younger sister, Sara. 'She held my hand. She spoke of pure thoughts, and said I must be happy if I entertained none but such as these: and diffidently strove to make me connect to religious feeling, with my dreams of bliss.'

Soon they went to see some pictures together: 'she conjured me to rest satisfied with "pure and noble friendship", which was all she could give me, "to await the effect of time". I promised her to follow her bidding, be it what it might ... While she spoke, I held her hand – she kept her face turned from me, nor could I induce her with all the asking of look and gesture to give me more than a glance. But suddenly ... she turned round – I felt her lips upon mine – I pressed them, long – I clasped her in my arms ... I have had many sweet kisses but never one like this.'

On 20 March they walked to Greenbank in a family party to see Mr Prideaux's gallery.

> We fell together – she leant upon my arm and I kept her hand pressed against my heart – and then I told her in plain terms that I loved her – not as a friend – that I could not bear to see her given to another – I spoke of what I had felt when I first lost her and how unwise it was to expose myself to a second such feeling a second time ... Among other things she said she had suffered so much from her matrimonial engagements that she looked upon them almost with disgust – that her home was happy to her, so happy that she did not wish to change her way of life in any single respect. I cannot fully interpret her meaning: perhaps she has not made it very clear to herself.

A perceptive remark. One can imagine Mary, a romantic girl of 17, sickened by the eighteenth-century idea of marriage as a business arrangement, aware of the fact that her father, a banker, would not look kindly on her engagement to a young poet with no prospects, standing on the threshold of womanhood but clinging to the security of her childhood home.

On 23 March Derwent writes his last reverie for some time, '... having to write for the *Quarterly* in a very limited time. The course of yesterday however must not go unrecorded – or the feelings of today – of today? – of today, and forever! Is it thus? Experience says no – but something within me seems to whisper that my roving days are over and my mind, slower to form, will be firmer to retain the good intention – I have arranged my rooms with a sort of solemn cheerfulness – as if I were about to begin a new era, with a new stock of hope – yet where it comes from is difficult to say.'

Yesterday he had called by appointment to walk to Compton with Mrs Pridham and the family. Mary took his arm.

She spoke for the first time of her Father, with whom it appeared she had had some conversation respecting my frequent appearances at South View, in which he expressed a natural apprehension that we might mutually find each other's society too agreeable. She merely requested me not to come at night for the sake of appearances ... She assured me that she could not dispense with my Friendship – that it would be heartbreaking to her. And when we had I fallen so far back as to be quite alone she led me down to a little waterfall which I shall love forever, and there after many silent entreaties she at length permitted me to clasp her in my arms and press her to my heart and press my lips to hers. In this little Jordan, she proposed that we should christen each other: and so we did. It was a pretty little rite, conceived in the gentlest spirit of Paganism, when Idolatory was young and spoke the meaning of the heart in the language of the eyes. Did not our souls, Mary, in this baptism of love, promise everything to each other? ... We christened each other – and she said she could not bear to wipe the water off which I had sprinkled on her face. As I crossed her lovely brow her lips floated a while over my hand, which she gently kissed – so gently! It cannot be but in that moment she loved

55

me – yet awhile her cooler mind seemed to return, and she became circumspect in the confessions which she allowed to be extorted from her.

I drank tea there, by invitation, and oh! how happily did I spend that evening, with her by my side, guiding her savant mind, conscious that I was successfully and not ungracefully exerting that superiority of intellect which enabled and entitled me to guide her perceptions and for the time to lift them to the level of my own . . .

Mrs Pridham was all kindness . . . at parting she gave me a number of little presents, increasing marks of respect which seemed to indicate that this was a sort of farewell evening and that I must make my visits, very like the Angels, few and far between – indeed she hinted something of the sort in her playful manner.

It sounds as though Mama, at least, was won over.

Next day he took Mary and her cousin Caroline violet-gathering in Mutley Fields. 'How very beautiful she looked, with her bonnet back, her curls flying – laughing in the sun and wind.'

On Tuesday, 29 March:

From 1 till 3 this morning I was with Mary – reading *La Nouvelle Heloise*. She let me hold her hand and surely I could not be mistaken in the attendrissement of her manner.

Good Friday – shall I indeed call thee good in this calendar of my feelings? Yes – I will call it good to feel my passion strengthened if possible in a tenfold degree – to have made up my mind to love – my heart has long been made up – to love, and be loved again? Indeed I cannot but hope it.

The record ends on Monday night, 11 April. 'It is evident that Mary has yielded at least for a time, to feelings similar to my own . . . even to me she does not expressly declare them. Mr P. is partially awake to the dangers of our intercourse: Mrs Pridham apparently not so. The necessity if we are to see each other at all of Mary's playing a part is among the most unpleasant circumstances attending our interviews.' The previous week had been a holiday when he had seen much of Mary. On Tuesday they had gone in a family party to Compton. Before the rest of the family arrived Mary, Sara (her little sister) and Derwent went to the orchard; 'we lay for an hour in the sun on faint primrose beds. Her cheek rested on mine . . . I may truly say that the reality of life can hardly furnish a situation more truly paradisical – I kissed her and her face flushed with delicious trouble . . . We walked home together in the twilight with many a stolen look and word of love and spent the evening together at South View.'

At the end of July 1825, Derwent gave up working with Macaulay and went to teach at the school conducted by the Reverend Lowndes in his vicarage at Buckfastleigh, a small village in a wooded valley on the edge of Dartmoor, some 20 miles from Plymouth. It is not clear why he made the move, but perhaps he was trying to improve his prospects, as he was to receive £150 p.a. and free board and lodging in the vicarage. His salary at Plymouth was £150 p.a. but he had to keep himself out of this. He remained friendly with J. H. Macaulay and stayed with him the following Christmas.

On 4 August Mary wrote to Derwent: 'The scene of your departure from Gloucester Place, my dear Derwent, was well pictured to me by Charles Whiteford, and his excellent description of our much regretted Poet wheeled off by the side of good Mrs Kibby served to draw a smile from lips which still hung down with melancholy at his loss.' She goes on to describe how Macaulay accompanied the family on a picnic to Bickleigh Vale and gives a lively account of how he went with them next day, together with her cousin Caroline, Charles Whiteford, Bezzi and Ball, on board the *Brunswick* to see the Eddystone. 'Scarcely had we lost sight of the Breakwater when almost all our party were stretched out in a state of utter helplessness saving Mac and myself . . . we still continued well and cruelly laughed at the unfortunate. We repeated "Beauty" together with many other things until at length by slow degrees we too sank into the most sleepy quietness, repulsing with the little remaining strength the tedious offers of

Brandy and Biscuit and praying for silence as the greatest favour that could be given.'[1]

On 25 August Derwent sent Mary thirteen pages 'On Intellectual Development and mental training – a letter of advice and counsel'.[2] He said it was 'the substance of several conversations in which I have endeavoured to point out to you the desirableness of intellectual cultivation and the best methods of intellectual culture – drawn up at your own request and intended for your actual use.' He began with a report on Mary's present condition: 'Though warmly alive to intellectual pleasure you are not <u>very studious</u> in my sense of the term. The susceptibility of your feelings, united to the ebullience of your animal spirits tends to withdraw you from the calm enjoyments of the patient Muse, while a slight shade of constitutional indolence renders you somewhat averse to that labour by which alone what is really good can be purchased.' This letter contains the hard core of his educational philosophy – the need really to master something difficult, the need for real understanding of whatever is learnt, the dangers of mere verbalism and superficiality. The aim of all teachers should be to prepare the taught for their own self-education.

Above all, moral and intellectual education are inseparable.

I reflect how much the moral as well as intellectual being may be strengthened by proceeding on this only legitimate course – how directly it leads to habits of patience, firmness, independence, fortitude, nay honesty itself. (For Virtue is closely allied to reason, and right feeling to right thinking). It is by education alone, in its highest sense, that the mind attains to that intense sympathy with the Good, the Great and the Beautiful, alike in the visible and in the invisible world.

It was this conviction that later led him to adopt a Latin tag he found in Bacon's essay 'Of Studies' as the St Mark's College motto: *Abeunt studia in mores.*[3]

[1] Derwent Coleridge MSS. HRC, Texas.
[2] Ibid.
[3] Studies are changed into morals.

58

Derwent continues:

> I utterly dissent from the doctrine of certain old-fashioned virgins, and vulgar-minded men, who would confine a woman's education to sitting in a backboard and working her sampler, as if she were only fit to dance before marriage and to sew after it ... Moreover it is to be observed that all domestic arts, of any real use, may be acquired without the least sacrifice of intellectual culture ... I am thus averse to the substitution of satin stitch for thought − at open war with that string of nameless and unaccountable <u>nothings</u> in which so large a portion of a domestic day is usually spent.

He went on to give Mary some sound advice on studying − on the need for

> devoting with severe and scrupulous strictness, a <u>certain</u> number of hours to the object you have in view. Plan each day in the morning and compare at night the intention with the achievement. Set a minimum below which only necessity will make you fall, which you will normally exceed − I suggest 3 hours a day, one before breakfast (as being the only time you can certainly depend on) and the rest directly after it ... Read systematically; that is for a determinate object, steadily pursued on a pre-arranged plan; not from occasional impulse, to gratify the whim of the moment. Finish what you begin. Distrust your own knowledge − examine yourself often and carefully, and do not distrust the most elementary books unless you are really in possession of all they can teach.

Derwent suggested that while Mary had the benefit of Bezzi's instruction she should learn enough French and Italian grammar and idiom to be able to read any classical author in these languages and she should try to learn enough French and Italian pronunciation to be able to read aloud 'with pleasure to yourself and an English hearer'. She should study Adams' *Summary of Geography and History*, which would take her half a year to digest. She should then read Rollin's *History of Greece* in French, Goldsmith's *Roman History*,

Gibbon's *Decline and Fall of the Roman Empire*, and Hume's *History of England*. She ought to complete this course before she was twenty-one – 'you might compass it in half the time'. This might be followed by Southey's Memoirs, Voltaire and an abridged account of the French Revolution, Clarendon, Burnet and Sismondi. The staple of her English reading must be Spenser, Milton and above all Shakespeare – if she must read a novel (unless Sir Walter Scott) let it be in French. 'Read no magazines', he concluded, 'except *Knight's Quarterly*, and very little of that.'

On 11 September William Ball, the artist, sent Derwent a portrait of Mary 'at the request of Miss Mary so that you might receive it on Wednesday being your birthday'. The bearer of the portrait was Mrs Pridham herself, visiting by the mail coach her son John, who was a pupil at the Buckfastleigh Vicarage. Derwent wrote to Mary: 'My five and twentieth birthday will be marked by me in a very solemn and peculiar manner. I shall on that day hang up the portrait you have given me which will ever be for me a talisman of memory and admonishment – I shall see in it at once a breviary of my past and a revelation of my future life.' He continues: 'You rejoice me exceedingly by the account you give of your studies: persevere, after Adams everything will be smooth and easy ... As you are so good about the Adams and the Italian I do not at all disapprove of learning the guitar – it is very kind of Bezzi to teach you.'

On 9 November Derwent wrote to Mary: 'I direct it to Mama for the sake of propriety. Please give to my dear, dear Mary.' He referred to the 'kind and generous parents to whom I owe the liberty I now enjoy of letting my pen follow the guidance of my heart', so it appears that Mr Pridham also was won over. He spoke of his earnest spirit of devotion and high strung resolve which would find a language in deeds. 'Your picture hangs before me over the mantelpiece.' He needed the inspiration it provided for he was far from happy at the Vicarage. 'My boys have given me so much trouble ... a lot of dirty, disagreeable boys, from morning to night.' It was not a very comfortable house, especially in winter. His bedroom fire smoked and he longed for Mama to come and turn everything at Buckfastleigh upside down.

Derwent sent Mary some letters from his former correspondents, including one from Sebe, pointing out that Mary had had her Sprys and Gandys and 'my amoretti would fill a folio' but adding: 'No, Mary, I knew love but by guess till I saw thee.'

While at Buckfastleigh Derwent bought a horse, which he named Camilla. His mother wrote with strong disapproval of the expense involved. On Christmas Day 1825, she wrote: 'You wish, my dear son that your poor Mother would forget you were in existence "for one short year" – Ah, that is impossible! In other words, you wish to still the warning – the enquiring voice.' She concluded with what must have been a most irritating P.S. 'I hope Derwent you a horseman enough to be a safe rider: I cannot say I am easy on that account.'

During 1825 Derwent still seems to have hoped for a literary career. On 24 February he lectured at the Athenaeum on the poetry of Wordsworth, and later on 'The Nature of Poetry'. He wrote to Edward Calvert, the artist, 'My subject nominally is Poetry, but nearly as much about Painting as about anything else. The real subject is what is common to all the fine arts as such . . .' During the year he had much correspondence with his old Cambridge friend Henry Malden, who wrote on 14 April that Knight was to publish a new magazine with himself and St Leger as the editors. Derwent provided nearly eighteen pages of articles by August and his lecture on Wordsworth for the second issue; he hoped that Knight would also publish a small volume of poetry for him. However, on 9 December Malden wrote to Derwent that Knight was not to continue the Magazine, and by February 1826, Praed was writing that he had met Knight, who was 'in a pretty bad way . . . your poems will not get hard cash in that quarter'. Derwent had reviewed one or two books for the *Quarterly Review* under the editorship of his cousin John Taylor Coleridge, but his literary aspirations received a further blow when Lockhart took over the editorship in December 1825.

While he was at Buckfastleigh Derwent was still struggling with the loss of faith which he had undergone during his last year at Cambridge. Mary was a devoutly religious girl and was perturbed by his loss of religious convictions. There is a long undated letter from Derwent to Mary which reveals much of his inner conflict:

My dear, dear girl! Tho I have written to you so lately yet I cannot suffer your beautiful and affecting appeal to remain another day unanswered. Yet what shall I say that every word, look, action of my life has not at least begun to demonstrate – that no hand but that of Destiny shall pluck thee from me; – that I will perform every act, undergo every suffrance, will every volition, that may in any way tend to your happiness, if it be possible, in me, – if not, to your welfare without me: – that I will not long keep you in suspense, that within the ensuing year, at farthest, – but, I trust, within a few months, every doubt, every fear of your heart, shall end in certainty; – and that thus, if, as I confidently hope, it may be permitted to me to call thee mine, my whole life shall be a tissue of endeavours from the moment that Heaven shall unite, to that in which Heaven shall divide us ... Believe me I have read and read again, and shall continue to read the sweet breathings of your pious love – read them with tears, read them, Mary, with the humblest, heart: believe me, I yield meekly, almost reverently, to your gentle admonition ...

When I write to you – and how can I forbear – in admiration of that spirit, of which you are the gracious vessel, – that inner heart of goodness, which is, you know and feel, but an emanation from the source of all being, then Mary, guide of my way! I know that this will humble, not exalt thee, in thine own conceit – and will only make thee bow, in lowlier prostration, before the Giver of Every good and perfect gift. – 'Tis true – I am proud, because I am conscious of greater powers, than will probably ever be made to appear – except to few, but I am not stubborn. Believe I am guided by nothing but love, and a sense of right when I say it is not right that you should be made acquainted with the dark and perilous struggles of my intellectual being in the pursuit of Truth ... Moreover I am conscious of greater logical powers, and greater use in the handling of ratiocinative weapons, than any clergyman I ever met with, and an apparent victory, anything that I should deem a conquest would be worse than no engagement ...

I write these words in pain of heart, Mary, and in perfect sincerity. Alone, silent, uncommunicating, unsupported, unflattered, unsympathised with, think you then that is Vanity which could make me <u>wish</u> to overcome, in a contest, in which the victor's reward is – gloom here, and darkness hereafter – to be troubled and then be still – to grieve and then only sleep! ... Think you I would not rather court a defeat which would give me Paradise here Heaven hereafter? But it is neither from Books or Men that <u>I</u> am to seek conviction – where I find little but the *ipsedixits* of self-elected Doctors – self-hypocrisy – faithless power, – or imbecile amiability, – In my Father's writings, – by far the most powerful on the side of religion, – I find, when I find anything tangible, a bold, and as seems to me intolerant assumption of Data, professedly incapable of proof, but affirmed to exist in every good man's nature – which yet I find not in mine – and know not to have been found by others. (These however I will re-examine with impartial, and willing attention.) <u>My</u> convictions must be the natural growth of my own mind: of what nature they may be let none enquire. I must be here my own confessor. I have given proof that I shall act in honour and love: hereafter I hope to give fresh ones. To make my fellow-creatures happy, to do good according to the measure of strength, – above all to make thee happy, my only-beloved, as the duty imposed on me from on High – Your last letter has called for this reply, which is not in strain wh. I wd. most willingly pursue: but I wish to avoid even the <u>appearance</u> of evasion. Indeed, indeed I write in the spirit of meekness. More I cannot add but that I love thee, Oh! But believe – my brain is whirling round, and my hand trembling, so I must fly to the open air and to gayer thoughts; when I return I will add a few words.

This is a very honest letter. Derwent loved Mary deeply and admired her religious faith but he was not prepared to perjure himself intellectually in order to retain her love. In his love for her he found a new sense of purpose and a gradual awareness of ultimate meaning in life. He eventually became able to appreciate his father's religious ideas. The essence of Coleridge's religious teaching, based on a lifetime of voracious reading, deep thinking and intense inner struggle, was that the truths of religion are evolved from within, in man's need for a God who comes to meet and redeem him. 'My metaphysics are merely the referring of the mind to its own consciousness for truths indispensable to its own happiness.'[1] Faith, in other words, involves believing where we cannot prove; it means embracing on trust a belief in the existence of God; a belief which is reinforced by experience. Coleridge's religion was founded on Faith that his response to truth, beauty, goodness and a sense of duty was response to a higher reality discerned by Reason in his sense of the eye of the spirit, rather than by logical demonstration.

> If the mere intellect could make no certain discovery of a holy and intelligent first cause, it might yet supply a demonstration, that no legitimate argument could be drawn from the intellect against its truth. And what is this more than St Paul's assertion, that by wisdom (more properly translated by the powers of reasoning) no man ever arrived at the knowledge of God? ... I became convinced that religion, as both the cornerstone and the key-stone of morality, must have a moral origin; so far at least that the evidence of its doctrines could not, like the truths of abstract science, be wholly independent of the will.[2]

By 5 November Derwent was writing to Mary:

> A month to Christmas. I trust I shall do a month's work, with which for my credentials I shall fly to thee and tell thee ... that I am not far from the right way. Thou shalt see this, even in my writings – my Essays, you will find, embued with what I hope is the spirit of Religion – with Love and Truth, contemplated as living powers indwelling for ever in Man's heart – two phases of the same moon, answering to and

[1] Samuel Taylor Coleridge. *The Friend.* p. 67.
[2] Samuel Taylor Coleridge. *Biographia Literaria* (Shawcross) Vol. I, pp. 134–5.

explaining each other – I am so unaccountably nervous today, I must not write any more.
Your devoted, aye Mary, <u>dedicated</u>
D. C.
Write, write, write, write, write, please, pray, do, I ask, entreat, conjure, soon, immediately, now!

On 16 November Derwent wrote a long letter to his friend Henry Malden in Cambridge. He asked him to try and find out how Praed had applied Mrs Coleridge's money and what debts remained. He concluded: 'As soon as I am clear of encumbrances, which I hope to do in less than twelve months, I purpose making a strenuous effort to enter some profession – <u>if it be possible</u> <u>the sacred one</u>; with this vantage gained I might pursue, with leisurely but careful steps, that literary career which I believe is given me to run.' Derwent had resolved his intellectual struggles and had decided to make the leap of faith, and even to go into the Church. He evidently thought that work as a clergyman might be combined with literary pursuits (a lingering ambition which he never fully realised), but there is no doubt that his spiritual conversion was genuine.

I am in many respects a Changed Being – indeed I have [been] subjected, during the last twelve months, to such influence, from without and within – have been made the vessel of such heart-awing emotions – that not to have suffered change would have been to have been God or Devil or Dead Matter – mere clay.

Malden replied on 14 December: 'Congratulations with all my heart, my dear Derwent, on the change which you describe yourself to have undergone. It will give the sincerest pleasure to learn that your principles and opinions have settled where I always believed they would settle, and I shall rejoice to see you a member of a regular Profession, whether the sacred, or any other, but especially the first, for I think you would make a good clergyman if you once entered into Holy Orders with fixed opinions and purposes.'

In December, Derwent included in a letter to Mary a day-dream of himself as a country parson, married to Mary '... home we walk amid the grateful looks of nodding and curtseying rustics, far better pleased with such homage than with the admiration of evening congregations in a crowded London chapel. But the Praise most valued after the satisfaction springing from a good conscience is that which I earn from her in whose hands all my earthly Happiness is placed'.

Later he wrote to Mary: 'Will you read with me, love, this Christmas – write with me – will you let me intermingle my intellectual being with thine, so that thou inbreathe thy gracious soul into mine – till I cease to feel save with thy heart? Is it arrogance in me thus to claim the task of lifting thy character to what I believe to be the level of mine (when I am myself) – or furnishing forth thy spirit with all that I know, or think I know, of great and beautiful – true and fit – and graceful – while I deliver myself to thee, to be purified and chastened – nay, in a far higher sense – strengthened and exalted? Sweet, I know this seconds thy own aims.'

At Christmas Derwent's mind was made up. The Reverend Lowndes had suddenly discharged him from the school at Buckfastleigh. Derwent decided to return to Cambridge and read for Orders. He would then look for a curacy. This made possible his official engagement to Mary.

His father wrote to Derwent on 4 January 1826:

My dearest Derwent,
   Mr Edward Lowndes has just brought me your letter ... From what I had before heard of Mr M. Lowndes I was a little shocked but not at all surprized at his abrupt discharge. But had I considered this as a misfortune it would have been swallowed up in the Comfort and gladness which your determination to prepare yourself in good earnest for Orders has given me. I never indeed could fear that a young man of your acuteness and habits of reflecting on what goes on around and within you should fail to see that in certain points there must be an act of the Will, a hoc credam, as well as an acknowledgement of insight ... I send the *Aids of Reflection* by Mr Edward Lowndes

– The Father, and not the Author, earnestly entreats that you will give a fair and (as far as is in your own power) an unprejudiced attention to its contents...

Mr E. Lowndes does ample Justice to your conduct and character at Buckfastleigh – He supposes that his Brother must suddenly have met with some Clergyman who it was necessary to engage at once or lose –.[1]

Coleridge was prompted to write *Aids to Reflection* (published 1825) by his distress over Derwent's atheism when he came down from Cambridge. He sought to show 'that the Christian Faith is the perfection of human intelligence'. It was 'especially designed for the studious young at the close of their education or on their first entrance into the duties of manhood'.[2]

The lovers parted on Thursday, 19 January 1826 when Derwent left Plymouth at 9 a.m. by the Regulator Coach, arriving in London at 5 p.m. the next evening.[3] He stayed with Charles Whiteford in Bedford Square and sent Mary a note 'by private hand' saying that he was as well and happy as he could be without her, that he had had the inside of the coach to himself all the way except from Ashburton to Axminster 'where I had to entertain a Miss Fanshaw – an agreeable and tolerably pretty girl, who being on the point of fainting all the way called on me for a degree of exertion which perhaps did me good'. He spent the rest of the journey 'thinking of you, sleeping and studying the *Aids to Reflection*'.

Fortified by the company of Charles Whiteford, Derwent went to Highgate to break the news of his engagement to his father. On 22 January he wrote to Mary:

My dearest love,

My meeting with my Father has been of the most happy kind – he is on the whole well, and in good spirits: and (to come to the point at once) received the news of our engagement with the utmost kindness and acquiescence ... I

[1] Collected Letters of Samuel Taylor Coleridge. Ed. E. L. Griggs. OUP.

[2] Samuel Taylor Coleridge. *Aids to Reflection*, Moxon. 1854. Preface p. XIV.

[3] Derwent Coleridge. Notebook 1826. Derwent Coleridge MSS. HRC, Texas.

never, no never, can look upon my Father, his beautiful white locks, his beaming affectionate face, without conjuring up your dear beauty and setting you in Fancy before him. I transfer my filial rights in him to you – hear him call you daughter – and bless you, and take you forward with the holy circle of his fraternity – you kiss, you love him, – I know you will – you drink in his eloquent words. . .

The postscript to this letter adds 'My father likes your drawing very much – but cannot discern the likeness.'[1] This was a copy Mary had made of Ball's portrait of Derwent, described by Coleridge in very unflattering terms in a letter to his nephew Edward Coleridge, 'I having objected that it was no more like him, than a wig-block to a Jew's harp.'[2]

When Derwent had departed on Saturday evening by the Mail to Cambridge from the Saracen's Head, Coleridge, assailed by all the feelings of guilt and misery associated with his own marriage, wrote to his son:

My dearest Derwent! *Experto credes*? – That the most heart-withering sorrow that can betide a high, honorable, morally sensitive and affectionate-natured Man . . . is: to have placed himself incautiously in such a relation to a Young Woman as neither to have it in his power to discontinue his attentions without dishonour and remorse, nor to continue them without inward repugnance, and a future <u>life</u> of Discomfort, of vain Heart-yearnings and remediless Heart-wastings distinctly before his eye – as the alternative! – Either Misery of Remorse, or Misery of Regret! . . . For God's sake, think and think again before you give the least portion of your own free agency out of your power! You give away more than Life—

This is a case in which with my principles I can only give the general Rule – the application of it to persons and particulars I must ever leave to yourself—[3]

[1] Derwent Coleridge MSS. HRC, Texas.

[2] Collected Letters of Samuel Taylor Coleridge. No. 1521. Ed. E. L. Griggs. OUP.

[3] Collected Letters of Samuel Taylor Coleridge. Ed. E. L. Griggs. OUP.

However, Coleridge was overjoyed by Derwent's decision to take Orders. He wrote to George Skinner, Fellow of Jesus College: 'My son Derwent Coleridge having (as indeed I never doubted that he would) sloughed the last skin of his Caterpillarage has made the first use of his eyes and wings into which he has unfolded by returning to Cambridge in order to prepare himself in good earnest for taking Orders. He hopes to be able to maintain himself during the time, in part by pupils – If it should be in your power to serve him in this respect, I intreat you to confer this additional obligation on me – and I trust that the wrigglings of the larva will be forgotten by you in the present <u>Psyche</u>, which I believe to be the very <u>Imago Sui</u>.'[1]

In a long letter to his nephew, the Reverend Edward Coleridge, housemaster at Eton, Coleridge said of Derwent –

> ... his present plans and intentions are a great relief to my mind ... He professes – and to the extent of his own consciousness most sincerely, I doubt not – to be convinced that the first great Premise, in which all his legitimate conclusions will lie as an Oak in an Acorn, must be a <u>Postulate</u> – and the Concession a Choice, and Act of Moral Election ... I see no reason to fear a <u>relapse</u>, but whether Derwent will press forward to the Goal, and have that <u>within</u> which will render him in tone and manners, as well as life and doctrine, an <u>exemplary</u> Clergyman, will, I suspect, depend (humanly speaking) on circumstances – perhaps, on afflictions. He has a very fertile but somewhat shallow surface-soil – below, I hope and I believe, there is rock and springs of pure water; but between, and as the <u>immediate</u> subsoil, there is a stratum of blue clay, abundant in wild waters, strongly impregnated with earthy iron vanities and self-regards, and an unfit menstruum for the <u>preparation</u> of nutritious substances... He has many good points in his character – ex. gr. he is kindly natured, open, unsuspecting, and you never hear from him – any more than from Hartley – an unkind word, or aught that borders

---

[1] Collected Letters of Samuel Taylor Coleridge. 26 January 1826. Ed. E. L. Griggs. OUP.

69

on detraction — and if I could keep the Press, and Critical Essays out of his head, I trust, he will be a comfort to me on the whole.

Mrs Coleridge wrote to Derwent on 30 January, before she heard of his engagement: 'I hope no child of mine will marry without a good certainty of supporting a family. I have known so many difficulties myself that I have reason to warn my children!'[1] She was pleased at the change in his opinions and his decision to enter the church, but, as ever, feared that he would not keep himself out of debt.

Derwent wrote his mother an unusually long letter on 30 February telling her of his engagement to Mary. She replied that she would try to hope that all would be well in the end, but two young people without fortune, and with expensive tastes, should never marry. She feared that Mr Pridham might go bankrupt like so many bankers of the day. In fact, during the national financial crisis of 1825–6, the Naval Bank in Whimple Street, of which Mary's father was director, of all the Plymouth banks alone remained solvent.

Mary wrote to Derwent on the Saturday, two days after his departure, telling him how she had fallen asleep on the Thursday

> determined to rise the next day a very Stoic — terrible was the vacuum of the next morning — but a good resolution seldom fails, and I found my task less difficult every hour — in the middle of the day arrived your little note for which accept my best thanks — it came like a reward from you for my good conduct.
>
> I have your Picture that I copied from Ball's over the chimney-piece and now you are gone it looks very like you . . . My mind is overcome with thankfulness, to behold that darling wish which I have so long cherished likely to be realised, to see you going through the straight path which is sure to lead you right — [it] renders my spirits so very happy and tranquil that when I am once settled into a regular form of study and discipline my days will flow away almost imperceptibly . . . I

[1] Mrs Samuel Taylor Coleridge. MSS. HRC, Texas.

intend to commence on Monday ... and I will tell you from time to time my progress. You must scold me for every fault – it is for you that I am to improve myself...

She wrote out for herself 'Laws to be strictly attended to during the next half-year.' She drew up a timetable running from 7.30 a.m. to 10.30 p.m., starting with psalms before breakfast and continuing with music, Italian or French, and Hume's *History of Great Britain* until lunch-time, drawing in the afternoon and light reading, followed by work, reading or writing, 'whichever is most proper or convenient', for the remainder of the day. She also noted: 'When I walk out, must leave the Drawing ... or between dinner and tea, attend to Hume at that hour instead. Writing to Derwent must never occupy a whole morning, he would not like this I am sure – so I must fill my letters by degrees, which will be much the pleasanter, as nearly every day I may communicate with him for a while...'

Her diary shows that Mary kept to her laws with remarkable self-discipline. Her light reading included Walter Scott, *A Midsummer Night's Dream*, and Samuel Taylor Coleridge's *Aids to Reflection* 'beautifully written but very hard to understand'!

On 22 February she was down very late and received a serious scolding from her mother 'for not doing more things in a domestic way ... I am not idle, I employ all the day in the best way that I possibly can. Oh Derwent, I want you sadly now and then – the least thing upsets me now that you are away'. On 24 February Mary brought in 'the first cup and saucer of flowers from the garden for the parlour – Oh, that I could send one to Derwent'. The 'unaccountable nothings' of the domestic day interfered sorely with Mary's stern resolve to improve herself intellectually. On 23 February she had begun her Italian when she was 'called away by Mama to put cuffs into my plum coloured frock'. On 23 March 'after dinner Mama talked about my stays – had them made tighter'.

Mary was cheered by frequent letters from Derwent who arrived in Cambridge at 2 a.m. on Sunday, 22 January. His first letter, written from Malden's house in Emmanuel Close on 25 January, was addressed like the subsequent ones, to Mama, with the superscription 'Mama will please to give this letter to her beloved daughter and accept the true and grateful love of her affectionate

Derwent'. He says that his pleasure at finding his father not averse to his engagement compensated for the time for the loss of Mary's society.

> But I have now been three evenings alone – when I am fully and regularly employed I shall feel it less i.e. I shall bear it better – and in the meantime I make whatever I do a true act of homage to my earthly divinity ... I shall henceforth speak less of those emotions which as a lover – a fond and passionate lover, Mary, I am sometimes exposed, first, because my feelings battle with my words, and getting the better in the strife, return into my bosom, flushed with the victory, and more unmanageable than they were before – and secondly because for your dear sake, my letters ought to have a calming rather than a perturbing influence, and be indeed the harbingers of Peace and Quiet, and Cheerful Hope and Patient Resignation ... I will make my letters journals of what I am doing, thinking and intending rather than of what I feel – which indeed you may best learn from your own breast.

He goes on to give an account of his doings since arriving in Cambridge. He has already attended three Divinity lectures and begun reading Pierson on the Creeds. In London he asked his Father to begin looking out for a curacy for him. 'He wishes me to get a Chapel in town, that I may get known.' He concluded by asking Mary to open 'the little blue box' and send him the hair it contained. 'I wish you would also beg a lock of Caroline's hair, to plait with yours and mine into a ring, in Commemoration of Compton.' The baptism at Compton evidently symbolised for Derwent the turning point in his life. 'I am fond of all the little superstitions of love – The locket is quite invaluable to me – and never leaves my neck – day or night. The rings are part of my finger.'

Derwent only stayed a short while at Malden's house, then moved into lodgings with Mrs Barron, his landlady when he was an undergraduate, who was then in Petty Cury but now in Eden Terrace, 'a little out of Cambridge' and therefore cheaper.

Derwent like Mary, was full of earnest intentions. His notebook for 1826 records that he was attending Professor Hollingworth's Divinity lectures three times a week.[1] His tutor, Reverend Ralph Tatham, got him a pupil – Pratt, 'a medical gentleman about 30'. The notebook continues: '30th January. Commenced bathing in a tub every morning. 1st February £21 in hand; 10th February, began reading for Orders.' He wrote to Mary on 2 February 'I have commenced a very regular, methodical life' and went on to describe how he arose as soon as it was light, spent three-quarters of an hour dressing 'as I have a sort of bathe', breakfasted at half-past eight, reading at the same time, and attended Divinity lectures at 12 three days a week. His pupil came at 1, at 2.15 he walked out, he dined at 3.30, and went back to his rooms at 4. He was 'occasionally hoisted out to Chapel'. When the days were longer he would walk before breakfast. 'I shall be capable of taking orders in about seven weeks but should not like to do so for three months – a good deal of reading is necessary to pass your exam with credit.' He went on to say how anxious he was to get clear of debt. He had lost nearly £100 through his failure to obtain the Exhibition money from the Mercers' Company and was now owed £25 for his writings (presumably by Knight, the publisher), 'which I know not how to get – perhaps I never shall get it. However, I am determined to make a vigorous effort to clear myself this quarter.' He was not anxious to have another pupil as 'I can easily supply the want by my pen'. Various editors of the Metropolitan Press were 'prowling about in quest of my Essay on Wordsworth, of which they have got scent'. He had told them he wanted 15 guineas for it.

In the same long letter Derwent continues: 'I too brood over anticipation of summer days, when we shall wander together over those hallowed green fields – wiser, better, happier beings than when we last made them our sanctuary, loving each other yet more fervently. I picture us sitting together in some of our old haunts – I read to you as you draw, or hear you read – Spenser or Milton or sweetest Shakespeare – who often saw us in his gentle vision and read our hearts – or I expound to you the sage cantos of the Florentines – or hear you translate Tasso – which, with my assistance, you will I hope be able to do then. Lay up a rich store of

[1] Derwent Coleridge MSS. HRC, Texas.

things to repeat, for I am never happier than when I hear the golden words of immortality in your sweet tones...' Mary was the fulfilment of Derwent's *Dream Love* giving him the spiritual and intellectual communion he yearned for as well as being beautiful.

Though full of good intentions, when left on his own Derwent lacked Mary's powers of self-discipline. His volatile temperament swung easily from elation to sadness; in his letters to Mary at this period and others written at Buckfastleigh he referred several times to his sleepless nights and headaches. He craved for good company and conversation and he knew that he had to find influential friends if he was to get a curacy, so he soon became involved in social life in Cambridge. He could not narrow his lively mind down to the exclusive study of divinity and he rapidly developed other intellectual pursuits. He was also very busy with his pupils and with 'writing for my bread', and had begun to learn German again since 'almost everything that is of value in modern literature, for the last 30 years, at least as far as learning is concerned, has come from the German press.'

His letter to Mary of 16 February was begun in the morning when he said: 'I am well and in excellent spirits ... I know not which way to turn I have so much to do ... I have also much on my hands in the way of authorship, besides letters innumerable'. He had just sent off to Colburn, for the New Monthly, a short article entitled *Reverie No. 1*. On the evening of the same day he wrote that he was sitting by the fire in a large grey woollen dressing gown with his books, including folios, and quartos 'containing Divinity enough to make a bench of Bishops', and described himself as 'pale faced and white-handed with study and want of sleep' and having 'a little too much to do'. He went on to describe how Mrs Barron, his landlady, 'has a party this evening – a congregation, I suppose I may call it – they have finished their tea and nice buttered toast – and have passed from earthly to spiritual things. One of the number, evidently an old hand, is delivering a rousing discourse, and has been this hour, with a stentorian voice and a rich evangelico-provincial twang. Praise-God Barebones was a fool to him! I hear all his serious points through the party wall. There goes his fist – there again! – take care of the table – *Dieu Merci!* he's done, and they seem likely to withdraw. I might as well be in a congregation of Preacher Monkeys, or in Charles

Church, Plymouth. Mary has just come in with some seed cake to propitiate me. I have given her an assurance "I am not in the least disturbed".'

Derwent had recently received and returned a call from a new friend of Praed's – Fitzgerald, 'a wild, good-natured, romancing, hyperbolical little Irishman, with <u>extremely</u> elegant manners and appearance, and much given to <u>serenading</u> – author of some very clever verses – he is generally either enraptured or horror-struck'. He fought duels, took opium, locked up the night watchmen in their own watch-houses, 'a decided Character – the only man whom I have heard of here since our Set broke up, that deserves the name.'

Mama Pridham was evidently alarmed at Derwent's liking for Fitzgerald. His next letter (still addressed to Mrs Pridham) reassured Mary that he had been for a walk with the Reverend Thomas Tylecote, Fellow of St John's, and after hall read a little Italian and drank a little port with him till Chapel time. At 6 he went to his rooms and as he was now having German lessons with H. D. Oppenheim on alternate afternoons, he was not likely to see much of Fitzgerald. 'Kiss Mama for me and say I am a very good boy and am everyday to be a better one'. Mrs Pridham, a lady of strong character and great self-confidence, exerted more influence over Derwent at this stage of his life than his own mother whom he referred to as 'the Mamalet'. He wrote to Mary from Buckfastleigh, 'Tell Mama to send me a scolding letter every week to keep me in order – and that I mean to do everything she bids'.[1] He was aware of his need for discipline from outside. Mrs Pridham, against all the dictates of prudence so dear to his own mother, had made possible his engagement to Mary. She had allowed the Romantic ideal to triumph over the notions of the eighteenth century. He wrote from Cambridge, 'Oh Mary, how dearly, how dutifully ought we not to love her, who has shown such love for us!'[2]

On 10 March Derwent wrote that poor Fitzgerald had been rusticated for three terms (no doubt to the relief of Mama) – it was

[1] 5 November 1825. Derwent Coleridge MSS. HRC, Texas.
[2] 10 February 1826. Ibid.

'iniquitously unjust', he had been mixed up in the aftermath of a dinner party when drunk and the Bulldog swore he had beat him about the head with a stick, though he had only a Turkish tobacco pipe in his hand. In 1859 he published *Omar Khayyam*.

Throughout this period Derwent was 'anxiously looking' for a Title. He gathered that a chapel in town was rarely given to one newly ordained: 'I must make my début in the country.' He frequently dined out in the hope of making the necessary contacts. On 16 March he dined at Trinity with Knowles and met Lord Charles Wellesley. More than one curacy was mentioned as to be had 'with the proper interest', but that was what Derwent lacked. Knowles, however, promised to write to his uncle about it.

Derwent spent much of his spare time at Cambridge in the company of Tylecote, a clergyman 'quite untainted with the loveless and joyless philosophy, which is playing such havoc with the hearts and heads of many of my old acquaintances'. He was 'passionately fond of music and a very tolerable performer on the flute'. They walked to Madingley together, and he wrote 'Tylecote and I often go out on fine days a-steeple-hunting on foot, leaping over all the gates and fences that cross our path'.[1] 'I have fairly beaten him; tho' on one occasion a spike catching on my inferior habiliments rent them from top to bottom'.[2] He was also reading Schlegel's translation of *A Midsummer Night's Dream* with Tylecote and found it twelve times as difficult as French. Even so, Samuel Taylor Coleridge had learned his German by reading Burger's translation of *Macbeth*.[3]

On 20 March Derwent wrote to Mary: 'I shall think with feelings of peculiar awe next Sunday [Easter Sunday] when I take the sacrament: and during the intervening days would abstract my mind, as far as in me lies, from every care and anxiety except that of fitting myself for worthy participation in this holy rite. I look upon it as a sort of aera in my life: it is now 7 years since I last ventured to avail myself of this means of grace and tho' it is indeed a humiliating reflection to consider that during seven years I have made no advance in moral excellence, and that it is

[1] 20 March 1826. Ibid.
[2] 17 March 1826. Ibid.
[3] K. Coburn. *In pursuit of Coleridge*. Bodley Head, 1977. p. 136.

well if I recover all that I then possessed, yet it is a truth that I dare not conceal from myself or from you. The next 7 years will I trust, with God's help, afford me at their close a very different retrospect.'

Derwent went to Highgate on Easter Monday and wrote to Mary 'in capital spirits'. He had dined with his cousin Edward, master at Eton, and Charles Lamb 'who rivalled Mr Pridham in the number and badness of his puns'. He continued 'Why cannot you come to town this Spring? I do long to see you in London and to introduce you to my Father. You would love him so entirely. His mind seems growing more heavenly-minded every year. His countenance now is of perfect goodness – on the whole, his health is better than I have ever known it.'

On 4 April Derwent wrote: 'I have seen Moultrie. We have met once more, I trust under happy auspices; we are friends again, and shall never more, I hope and believe, cease to be so.' Derwent had heard from Charles Knight, the publisher, that Moultrie was looking for him. He wrote to him and next morning Moultrie came to Highgate. 'We did not say much but it was evidently a reunion of hearts, as complete as could be desired.' He returned with Moultrie to London to meet his wife and two days later they all went to the National Gallery together. Moultrie had married Margaret Ferguson, daughter of a retired Army doctor living at Windsor. Mary wrote in her diary 'He is reconciled to Moultrie – what unspeakable pleasure does this reunion of hearts give me. May they never again be separated.'

Derwent bid adieu to London's gaieties by dining with Praed and Ord, the meal including turtle soup, cold punch and claret, after which they went to see Weber's *Oberon* at Drury Lane and on to a Masquerade at the Opera House, leaving after five in the morning. He had a very long conversation with Mrs Gillman about Mary. 'The great requisite, she affirms, in the person destined to share my fortunes, is an affectionate heart.' In a postscript he added 'My Father has read my essay on Wordsworth[1] thrice, and is much pleased with it.' However, his father wrote to him on 15 July 1826 '...I would have given a finger-joint to

---

[1] Published in the *Metropolitan Quarterly Magazine*. 1826. pp. 457–479.

have prevented the composition and not merely the publication of the whole passage on Wordsworth's later poems.'[1] Samuel Taylor Coleridge particularly objected to Derwent's quotation from the *Edinburgh Review* – 'whose whole literary existence has been marked with the most assassin-like hate and slander of every Man of Genius, whose names must be sacred to you by private affection...'

On 11 April Derwent wrote to Mary from Cambridge that he 'was resolved to go to bed, and to get up early, to cut parties, as far as possible (for dissipation kills me) and to be in every respect in the same state of mind as if I had only to get ready, and to come down to you from Mrs Kibby's'. But he must go to Eton as Praed, Fitzgerald, Hawkins, Ord etc, were there, 'a complete congregation of a certain set of whom you have heard me speak in terms of such praise. I foresee much unavoidable claret. Praed has just cellared a dozen bottles of *Crême du Noyau*, and another dozen of *Marasquino* (tipples of unspeakable merit) for mine and Fitzgerald's especial drinking – however I will be as cautious as possible.' He goes on to say that he had had a letter from his mother. 'She does think us a little rash ... she conjectures that if you were a year or so older you would have made a wiser choice ... but she is pretty well reconciled to the thing.' He had started attending lectures on chemistry and enquired about the progress of Mary's studies.

On 20 April Derwent wrote that Mary was 'not so happy as you promised to be. The terms of our engagement included the expectation of difficulty and delay – nothing has occurred worse than we anticipated.'

She was evidently upset by his mother's reception of their engagement. He told her that his mother had 'a timid anxious temper, naturally the opposite to sanguine, and rendered still more so by continued advertsity'. He tried to comfort her – 'it will not be many months before you address your letter to the Reverend Derwent Coleridge'. Charles Taylor was hopeful of getting him a Title in Kent. He would see her the second week in June, when he would be 'completely free and unencumbered'. He assured her that the visit to Eton was partly prudential, as he had many friends there

---

[1] Collected Letters of Samuel Taylor Coleridge. Ed. E. L. Griggs. OUP.

with whom it was expedient to keep in touch, including his cousin Edward, who was shortly to be son-in-law to Dr Keate (Headmaster of Eton) 'and who knows what may turn up'. Mary had clearly been somewhat worried by the visit to Eton and recorded in her diary on 17 April: 'Letter from Derwent – not a very satisfactory one'. He went on to tell her that he had walked out early that morning – 'how lovely and how happy-making everything appeared' – and had swum in the river near a grove of willows, full of nightingales and linnets. On 8 May Derwent wrote that he had been up before seven and bathed in the river. 'There is a freshness and a poignancy in the air for a couple of hours after sunrise in Spring and Summer which you never find afterwards. All Nature seems twice alive, yet man perversely cleaves to oblivion and the image of death in this season of double life, in order to walk like an apparition at midnight.'

In April and May Derwent was much preoccupied with writing a review of Shelley's Poetical Works for the *Metropolitan Magazine*. (Shelley had drowned in the Bay of Spezzia four years previously.) After spending a week in Eton, he arrived back in Plymouth on Friday, 2 June, having been away four and a half months.

Derwent's father made strenuous but fruitless attempts to get him a curacy. Samuel Taylor Coleridge's liberal religious views coupled with his unconventional life had scandalised the rest of the Coleridge clan, with their customary devotion to the Church, the Law and the Army. Samuel applied to Lady Beaumont, whose son was married to the daughter of the Bishop of London, but gathered that his nephew, William Hart Coleridge, Bishop of Barbados 'has done everything in his power to injure me'. Samuel wrote: 'Besides this, I have spoken or got offers to speak to all I could think of, with whom I had any acquaintance.'[1]

It was Derwent's respectable cousin, James Duke Coleridge, who came to his rescue. James was the son of Colonel James Coleridge of Heath Court, Ottery St Mary, and the elder brother of John Taylor Coleridge, of Edward Coleridge (Master at Eton), and of Henry Nelson Coleridge. He was Chaplain to the Bishop of Exeter in 1825 and Vicar of the parishes of Kenwyn and Kea in Cornwall, adjoining

[1] Collected Letters of Samuel Taylor Coleridge Vol. VI. 15 July 1826. Ed. E. L. Griggs. OUP.

Truro, in 1826. In the summer of 1826 Derwent went to Truro to see him, and he promised to appoint him his curate after he was ordained. Mrs Coleridge wrote to express her satisfaction at this and to urge Derwent not on any account to argue with James. She could not forbear from pointing out that Derwent should have saved when he was earning, and she begged Derwent not to think of marrying until he could provide Mary with a comfortable home.

Derwent had a pupil but depended heavily on the kindness of the Pridhams. He slept at Mrs Kibby's but probably had most of his meals with the Pridham family. He was extremely short of money and wrote to Praed on 12 October for the balance owing to him. Praed wrote from Eton on 14 October his most formal and dispirited letter to Derwent. 'I am sorry to hear you are in the difficulties you describe.' He had been unable to send the money he hoped to in June and July:

> Touching your cash in my hands, you are of course aware that you have received from me more than was committed to me, and you will easily perceive that the property upon which my profit has been or is to be made is not at every moment or under all circumstances convertible ... I am indebted to you in more, perhaps in more than double the sum you ask for, but it must be said for me at the same time that this increase has not been obtained for you by a conjuror's wand, nor without more trouble and perplexity than I at first calculated upon ... Today being Sunday I cannot get at any bankers. Tomorrow I will supply you with the loan of £10.7s.6d of which your want seems to be most pressing. When I go to town I will make arrangements if I possibly can without any material sacrifice on your own part for the payment of the balance due to you. I shall be heartily glad to put an end to an affair of which I should not complain because it has been somewhat onerous to myself if it had not also been tantalising and distressing to you.[1]

Derwent was ordained Deacon at Exeter Cathedral on Sunday,

---

[1] Derwent Coleridge MSS. HRC, Texas.

29 October 1826. He had to borrow money from Mrs Pridham to go to Exeter. He wrote to Mary on Friday 27 October that he had just left Dr Bull's after an examination of five hours. 'I have passed muster, I hope, tolerably well.' On the Wednesday night he had been up till one, read six chapters of the Acts, had gone to bed before two and got up again at five to get the coach at a quarter past six. He sat up till one the next morning, looking over a number of Articles. 'I got up this morning at a quarter before seven, and felt as if I did not know one single thing about it. I never was so nervous in my life.' He went to Dr Bull and 'found I could answer all the questions – doctrinal and historical. I had not half finished the historical when Dr Bull came up and told me I'd done quite enough of that sort and must go with all speed to the others: I was rather short and sweet in answering these, however we had it all out when I came downstairs. I construed my Grotius and Greek Testament and Dr Bull said everything was very right: that he could not look over my historical papers yet, they were so long, but from the glance he had had he was assured they would do, and told me to go to the Bishop and present myself to him – we talked a little about my cousin, whom I am to meet at the Palace tomorrow.' Derwent evidently took this examination more seriously than Dr Bull had bargained for.

He did not enjoy the ordinands' dinner with the Bishop, who, he told Mary 'confined his conversation to the son of Sir James Williams from Clovelly, whom he visits – talking exclusively of great people and their houses – anything but apostolical'. But he was clearly impressed by the ordination service. He wrote to Mary on 29 October from Streets' Hotel, Exeter: 'I am thoroughly exhausted with the long and aweful ceremony which I have gone through this morning . . . I have thought of you a great deal today, I hope in a manner not unsuitable to the occasion . . . It is the most important day of my life – it has invested me with a new character, accompanied with many difficult and important duties. My character I feel requires a good deal of change, more than I have ever before been aware of. Let us unite our prayers that this change, through the blessed influence of the Holy Spirit, may progressively be effected.'

Derwent did not go to Kenwyn after all. On 9 October his cousin Edwin Ellis Coleridge (son of Samuel Taylor Coleridge's brother

Edward, who was Vicar of Buckerell, and kept a private school at Rock House, Ottery St Mary) invited Derwent to come and stay for a few weeks with them at Ottery St Mary. He continued: 'Congratulations on entering into Orders under such favourable auspices as curate to that most excellent of men our cousin James Coleridge.' Ottery St Mary was the heartland of the Coleridge family – Samuel Taylor Coleridge's father had been Vicar there and headmaster of the King's School, which was taken over by Samuel Taylor Coleridge's brother, the Reverend George Coleridge. Samuel Taylor Coleridge had scandalised his family at Ottery by his irregular way of life. His son Derwent was now summoned to be inspected by them, as a brand plucked from the burning.

On 23 November Derwent wrote from Ottery St Mary to Mrs Pridham:

My dear Mama.

By the advice and with the all powerful recommendation of my cousin James, I have consented to become a candidate for the Foundation Grammar School and Lectureship of Helston near Penzance, Cornwall. The sum insured to me (independent of boarders) is £130 p.a. ... but if I become popular as preacher, it will be considerably more. My name, moreover, and connections, especially James,(who has had the nomination almost put into his hands) will assure me scholars, – so that if I am not wanting to myself, a fair prospect seems opening before me of an early independence.

It will perhaps be necessary for me to go down to Helston next Monday morning – if so, what am I to do? You know the length of my purse. Had I better ask my Uncle Edward to lend me a few sovereigns or not? The time is not far distant, I trust, when these borrowings will be no longer necessary.

Derwent went on to say that cousin James was now staying at Combe Tatchfield, eleven miles from Ottery, and he rode there this morning on Uncle's old hack.

Let me know Mr Pridham's, yours and my beloved Mary's opinion respecting this arrangement by return of post, and tell

the latter not to repine if an event apparently so fortunate takes me away from her a week or two earlier than she expects at present ... My Uncle Edward's recommendations will be of great avail, especially with Sir Richard Vivian. Love and kisses
Your most affectionate son,
Derwent Coleridge

The following day, 24 November, Derwent wrote to Mary:

I proceed to give you the few particulars which I possess respecting Helston. The last lecturer was a strong Calvinist – a very ignorant fellow to boot: so much so that my cousin James was obliged to refuse him Priest's orders, on both scores ... The respectable portion of the Helstonites, being thoroughly sick of this fellow and nevertheless being anxious to obtain a zealous and stirring person, tho' of sane doctrines and practical views, apply to James as an individual whose recommendation seems most likely to ensure them such a character. After some time he bethinks himself of his cousin Derwent, and writes to Mr Grills, the rector, a man of large fortune and influence, whose son now assists at Kenwyn, to know whether a person of his name and family if so disposed would be acceptable to them. He replies that nothing would give them so much pleasure and requests to know whether Mr Derwent Coleridge 'would condescend to undertake the school'. On receiving this answer, James sends for me, and puts me in possession of the particulars which I have here detailed.
Now he says that there is at present no good school in Cornwall; Falmouth being unfavourable on account of its situation and all the other schools being absolutely contemptible. My name will do something – James's interest more, and my Uncle Edward's a good deal. I am the only Coleridge, except Edward, employed in tuition, so that he thinks it only depends upon myself to establish the best school in Cornwall, to become independent and to marry. The sum assured is as I have before said £130, with the prospect of its becoming much more, if I made myself popular. Under these circumstances I said that I would certainly accede to the proposal and would

commit the business to James's management. I am now anxious for a letter from Mama to know her opinion, and also from Mr Grylls.

From his rooms at the Angel Inn, Helston, Derwent wrote in quiet triumph to Mary on Christmas Eve, 1826: 'I have accepted the cure of Helston, I have accepted the school.' He went on 'A late Master, Mr Stabback, made a large fortune in the place, but Mr Daniel has reduced the school to nothing and I shall probably commence with two boys only ... There is an excellent school room and play yard.'

Derwent was received very hospitably, dining on Christmas Eve with Mr Humphrey M. Grylls, who was 'most kind', on Christmas Day with Mr Borlase, an alderman, and next day with Mr Grylls, the Mayor. 'Mrs H. M. Grylls undertakes to manage everything in the way of lodgings, washing, etc.' Mr Grylls, the Mayor, was the Reverend Richard Gerveys Grylls, then aged 68, described by Derwent as 'a tall thin, kind, shy, ugly, gentlemanly old clergyman of fortune, with a dark brown bulbous-headed nose.' Mr Humphrey Grylls was his nephew, then aged 37, who became Mayor in 1827. Derwent's pen-picture for Mary was of 'a short, round, ruddy, smiling, well-bred, semi-sportsman man of fortune, who looks like anything but a solicitor, and certainly does not wear himself to a thread about his bank'.

Derwent had a sermon to prepare for next day (Christmas Day) and had done 'two full duties today. The chapel is by no means so agreeable to my voice as that of St Andrews, but I was heard – and I believe have given satisfaction.' He went on: 'Tell Mama it certainly was as well she did not come with me, as I have not had one moment to spare since I arrived.' Mrs Pridham's interest in Derwent's career had evidently needed tactful restraint.

Derwent told Mary he was 'principally induced by the character of the inhabitants to accept the curacy, as I shall explain when we meet. The situation is most promising.' Although he was hardly in a position to pick and choose, Derwent's poetic, sociable, enthusiastic nature must have warmed to the Celtic temperament of the Cornish people who entertained him.

One of his first sermons was on the text 'Then answered Peter ...

84

Behold we have forsaken all and followed thee: what shall we have therefore?' For Derwent the answer was plain and satisfying – to be his own master, to run his own school, to pay off his considerable debts and to marry Mary Pridham.

PART IV
Helston 1827–40

Chapter 1
The First Year – 1827

Helston was a small market town seventeen miles south-west of Truro, with a population of 2,671 in 1821. It lay three miles inland from Mount's Bay, the great sweep of wild coastline extending from the headland of Carn-du, beyond Mousehole, in the west to the Lizard Point in the east. North of the town, granite moors rose to over 800 feet at Carnmellis. The River Cober flowed from the moors along the western boundary of Helston into the Loe Pool, a mile to the south. This beautiful narrow lake, over a mile long, was surrounded by woods of pine and oak, underlaid with primroses, violets and rushes at the lake margin. The seventeenth-century mansion of Penrose lay at the head of one creek. Between the Loe Pool and the sea was the Loe Bar – a great bank of shingle a quarter of a mile long. In a south-westerly gale there was a fine contrast between the peaceful woodland walk beside the waters of the Pool, and the mighty waves crashing on the Bar.

In the early nineteenth century the tin and copper mines on the fringes of the moors were at the peak of their activity. The fortunes of the local gentry were founded on the labour of the poorly-paid miners. Wesley had preached among the miners and converted thousands to Methodism. To the south and east of the town was a rich farming area, while the coastal villages depended for their livelihood on fishing.

Helston was ruled as a close corporation by a small group of inter-marrying families. The Common Council consisted of the Mayor and four aldermen, co-opted for life from the freemen, who were elected by the Mayor and aldermen. The First Report of the Municipal Corporations Commission, 1835, stated: 'The influence is chiefly vested in one family.'[1]

The most influential family in Helston in the early nineteenth century was the Grylls family. The Reverend Richard Gerveys Grylls (1758–1841) was vicar and patron of St Neot, curate of Helston at one time and nine times mayor of Helston. His brother Thomas Grylls (1760–1813) was an attorney, who lived at Bosahan and Helston, where he was three times mayor. Thomas had two sons, Humphrey Millett Grylls (1789–1834) who was a banker and solicitor and four times mayor of Helston, and Glynn Grylls (1800–1866) who was a solicitor and seven times mayor. The mayor and aldermen were patrons of the Grammar School and appointed Derwent to the headship. It was therefore essential for him to be on good terms with them. In fact he soon became a popular visitor in the large houses in Cross Street which they occupied. A little plan which he sent Mary[2] showed that Mr Grylls (presumably Rev. R. G. Grylls) lived in a handsome house opposite the end of Cross Street. Mrs T. Grylls lived in the beautiful white villa with the Ionic portico standing on a little hill on the right going down Cross Street towards the river, and Mr Glyn Grylls lived in the fine house which is now the Vicarage.

With regard to parliamentary representation, Helston was a 'pocket borough', under the patronage of the Duke of Leeds, whose grandfather had married the daughter of the Earl of Godolphin. The Godolphins had been patrons of the borough for many generations but had no more male heirs. The patron chose the two MPs for Helston. In return for this privilege the Earl of Godolphin rebuilt the church in 1761 and rebuilt the Market House, and he and subsequent patrons maintained all the poor so that no poor rate was ever levied, and paid all the church rates, the Lecturer's salary and the Organist's salary, at an estimated cost in 1812 of £1,600 p.a.[3] In

[1]Appendix 1. pp.511–14.
[2]21 May 1827. Derwent Coleridge MSS. HRC, Texas.
[3]H. Spencer Toy. The History of Helston. OUP, 1936. pp.283–4.

1813 there was a debate in the House of Commons on the system of election of MPs in Helston, in which Swann, MP for Penryn, stated that the Helston seats were sold for 5,000 guineas each. He stated that the Duke derived a profit of £800 a year from the patronage of the borough. The rest of the money was distributed as patronage by the leading members of the Corporation to the Freemen, who were the voters, 'in such a way as to preserve their own consequence in the borough and to render the voters dependent on themselves alone'.[1]

The working population of the borough was largely Methodist. Derwent started a little notebook entitled 'Parochial Minister's Assistant' in which he set out to record the names of the householders at each house in every street, their occupation and the number of boys and girls in the family. He did not get further than Meneage Street, with 190 families including 47 families in back courts, and Church Street with 75 families.[2] He wrote on the fly-leaf 'Derwent Coleridge: curate of Helston – February 8th 1827.'

> Of the inhabitants of Helston it may be affirmed in general, (I do not include the gentle folk, or their servants,) that they attend Chur:[ch] very irregularly, and the Sacrament never: that they none of them use family devotion, (except on dissenting principles, and very rarely in any way): that they have almost all a Bible or Testament; a much smaller, but still a considerable proportion have prayer books: and that they all attend other places of worship.
>
> The majority of the people are everythingarians, with Methodism 'in excess'. The Methodist and Baptist congregations are also pretty strong, especially the former. There is a large Methodist and small Baptist chapel, several private rooms in the different parts of the town, are also made use of at stated times, by the dissenters, for religious purposes. There is a sprinkling of Brionites, sufficient to do a good deal of mischief, but no Brionite chapel: I believe they meet somewhere in a private room: –

[1] Summarised from H. Spencer Toy. Op. cit. p.297.
[2] This notebook is now in the possession of Mrs Mary Coleridge.

The local gentry however were largely Anglican, and Helston, although remote from London, was by no means cut off from the world of ideas and literature which Derwent craved. Truro was a fashionable centre for the county families and had its Philharmonic Society and the Royal Institution of Cornwall was founded there in 1818. There were a considerable number of clergy and gentry with cultivated tastes and well-stocked libraries. Falmouth, thirteen miles from Helston, was the home port for forty packet services to foreign countries, carrying the mails and passengers, and was also a health resort for Londoners seeking a milder winter climate. It was thus the centre of a vigorous social and intellectual life, to which much was contributed by the various branches of the Fox family of Quakers who lived in and around Falmouth.

Derwent left Plymouth on Thursday, 11 January 1827 to take up his new duties at Helston. He wrote to Mary on the following Sunday afternoon that he had travelled on top of the coach in hail, rain and wind, which blew a hurricane coming over Lostwithiel Downs.[1] He had a kind reception at Kenwyn from cousin James and his wife. They had much talk on clerical matters – 'he has a great hope that we shall succeed in making Helston a perpetual curacy'. At Helston he stayed at first with Mr H. M. Grylls, who also received him kindly. 'I hope my sermons today went off tolerably well ... I feel the loss of your Society as much as I can feel any worldly privation ... I want Mama too very much to cheer me up and tell me how I've done. I have been sadly spoilt ... I feel the awful responsibility of my situation, daily more and more so – and more as I become acquainted with its importance and its difficulties.'

The following Wednesday Derwent told Mary he had read prayers in church for an hour to one old gentleman, Miss Emily Trevenen and two girls in black – 'a large congregation'. On five weekdays out of six there was no one present in church, so no prayers were read, 'but it shall be different'. He was very busy meeting people and trying to write his sermon with many interruptions. The Trevenen family had been particularly kind. Mrs Mary Trevenen, widow of John Trevenen, alderman, and mother-

[1]15 January 1827. Derwent Coleridge MSS. HRC, Texas.

in-law of H. M. Grylls, admitted him to her excellent library at her house and told him he could borrow what he wanted. Miss Emily Trevenen, first cousin to Mrs H. M. Grylls, offered him the use of her library and told him that on parish visits he could 'command her purse' for temporal relief.

Miss Emily Trevenen, then aged 41, was to become a life-long friend of Derwent and Mary. A wealthy spinster, she was the only daughter of the Reverend Thomas Trevenen (rector of Mawgan-in-Meneage), the grand-daughter of the Reverend R. G. Grylls, and cousin to H. M. Grylls. She lived, of course, in Cross Street. Her portrait[1] shows her with rather a thin face and dark hair drawn back loosely at the nape of the neck, a long nose, a small serious mouth and large grey eyes with rather a sad expression. At this early meeting Derwent described her to Mary as 'one of the humblest and most pious and most beneficial persons (without the least ostentation – but on the contrary an almost painful degree of retiringness) I ever met in my life'.

Derwent began to devote all his energies to building up his run down parish and the nearly defunct Grammar School. He described to Mary on 29 January how he was compiling his notebook of the parish.[2] 'In this way I make myself known to about 10 families daily ... and I discover my sick and bed-lying parishioners, who for some time have been without spiritual assistance ... I now visit 4 daily or every other day.' He went on to describe how the previous week he had conducted his first service in the workhouse. Owing to his necessary calls and visits and business letters he did not begin writing his first sermon until Friday. He completed it before dinner on Saturday. After dinner he visited sick people and then fell asleep from weariness, so that he did not complete his second sermon until the clock struck two on Sunday morning. After church he was too exhausted to do anything until six, then visited a poor family in a hamlet just outside Helston where the mother had been killed by a fall on the stairs.

Derwent no longer had the time he had had at Cambridge for

[1]In the possession of Mrs Mary Coleridge.
[2]Derwent Coleridge MSS. HRC, Texas.

Emily Trevenen, oil painting, artist unknown.
(By permission of Mrs Mary Coleridge)

writing long letters. On 30 January Mary wrote a somewhat petulant complaint at Derwent's failure to satisfy her desire to know all that he was doing. He replied that she evidently did not realise the nature of his present situation. Mary replied:

> I reconciled it pretty well till you say that you <u>expected</u> me to be querulous and dissatisfied when you were straining every nerve for both our sakes – Oh Derwent my heart felt cutting to pieces – then I was hurt – but what touched its very core and affected me more than <u>all besides</u> was when you became your very <u>dear self</u> again and longed to see me in my black dress – it seemed to bring you to my side once more, the same being that you left it. Some bitter tears were shed – Oh my dearest D – if you knew how earnestly I have prayed daily for the last year and a half that you might be a clergy ... you could then believe what joy I feel ... to know that you are doing your duty to God and to your fellow creatures.

Derwent moved into lodgings on 2 February at Mr Woolcock's in Meneage Street at ten shillings per week, though Mr and Mrs H. M. Grylls begged him to use their house as he pleased and he accepted a general invitation to dine with them on Sundays.

The old schoolroom being 'horribly neglected', Derwent commenced his school at his lodgings on Monday 5 February with two boys, for whom the Corporation paid £13 6s 8d a year. This was the Helston Grammar School, which had been rebuilt in 1610 and was endowed with the sum of 20 marks a year. Derwent stated years later in an article in the *Saturday Magazine*[1] that the date of its foundation and its early history were unknown. Derwent's first two pupils were James Henwood, aged 13, the son of a surgeon apothecary, and John Vivian, aged eight, the son of Mr Vivian of Nanslo (one of the local gentry), 'a nice genteel little boy'. On 19 February Derwent wrote to Mary: 'they are doing up the schoolroom and play yard very nicely but I shall not alter the present arrangement until I have another pupil or two'.

[1]Vol. VII, No. 222, 19 December 1835. p.236.

Derwent worked hard to establish himself as a clergyman. He wrote to Mary on 5 February that he had a respectable attendance at weekday prayers the previous Friday for the first time and an increased congregation on Sunday, when Mr Grylls thought he had preached 'two excellent sermons'. 'My labour in Helston itself has been most gratifying: the upper class express themselves highly pleased with my exertions and I am gradually getting loved and respected by the lower. On Saturday I had two applications to visit sick people.' But six days later he wrote 'I have an uphill game to play – Almost every individual of the lower and middle classes are estranged from the Church, and I find I make little impression upon them.'

He took enormous pains with his sermons. On Sunday evening, 11 February, he wrote that he had started his second sermon at H. M. Grylls' the previous night and had spent an hour writing the first sentence. He had not finished it till 2 a.m. on Sunday morning. Mary had sent him her drawing of the Magdalene, which he had hung over the mantelpiece in his room. 'The Magdalene is an infinite comfort to me – I was looking at it at 2 last night with my feet on the table and a pipe of Persian in my mouth for 20 minutes before bed – thinking of the dear hand which had been at work on it.' The following week he wrote: 'I have just finished a sermon on Truth (Col. iii, 9) which I like as well as any I have written – I began it for the third time yesterday morning. It is nearly 6 o'clock and I have another sermon to write ... I believe I toil as hard every Friday, Saturday and Sunday as any man in England.' This letter was delayed in being posted as on Sunday 'when nearly dressed for Church (about 10) I heard of a most alarming fire that had broken out in Wendron Street. I immediately gave orders that the bells should be stopped, slipped on an old coat, went to the place and found two houses in flames and the whole town in an uproar. Mr Grylls (the Mayor) was almost blinded with the smoke, which blew down the street ... I immediately called Mr John Borlase ... to assist Mr Grylls – the other gentlemen and their servants were already there – collected all the buckets which I could lay my hands on, and was there in the lines until the fire was got under, which was happily effected in about two hours ... two tenements only suffering much damage, but had it happened in the night or on any other day than Sunday the destruction of the whole street, which is full of thatched houses, would have been inevitable. I then returned, took off my wet clothes, sat down, and wrote a complete sermon on the occasion ... beginning a few minutes before 12 and finishing a quarter after 3.' He went to Church to preach the sermon and then had to conduct a funeral 'in bitter weather'.

On 10 March Derwent wrote to Mary that he had begun three sermons but could not please himself in any. 'I am very fastidious: I want my sermons to be plain, striking, impassioned and scholarlike, not that I value anyone's criticism but my own a single button, but I can't put down and deliver a commonplace, disjointed piece of rigmarole – it turns my stomach: I want to get at people's consciences, and to do this in a dignified and masterly kind of way, equally remote from genteel slip slop, and vulgar storming.' He went on to observe 'people had rather be told that there is no soundness in them, that their souls are a putrefying sore, that they are wicked to the last degree of wickedness etc. – than that they are required to alter one single particular in their condition'.

Derwent dined out frequently with the gentry of Helston but he continued his visiting of the working classes and there are frequent references in his letters to his new experiences of real poverty and distress, attendance at death beds and the baptism of dying infants. He ran a Sunday School which started at 9.0 a.m. and on 14 March wrote to Mary that next week the Sunday School was moving to the Town Hall as the room was not big enough. He had a master and mistress to help with the Sunday School 'and to sit with the urchins in Church'.

On 5 February Derwent had tea with Miss Emily Trevenen and discussed with her starting a school under the auspices of the National Society for promoting the education of the Poor in the principles of the Established Church. 'She says I may command her purse.'[1] On 16 March he wrote that Miss Emily Trevenen had bought four little houses adjoining the Churchyard, which were to be pulled down 'to give a plot for our schoolroom'.[2]

[1]Derwent Coleridge MSS. HRC, Texas.
[2]Ibid.

Derwent was certainly trying to mend his ways in the management of his own finances. He wrote to Mary on 5 February: 'You cant think how well my first "<u>Rec'd</u>" looks – the first column of the little pocket book in which I keep my accounts. I mean to pay my household expenses, postage, washing etc., etc., every Saturday night.' On 19 February he wrote: 'I keep my accounts with the accuracy of a cashier ... I pay everything weekly and I am trying how low I can bring my expenditure.'

Until 1865 the borough of Helston formed part of the ecclesiastical parish of Wendron. By the end of the eighteenth century Queen's College, Oxford, had purchased the patronage of Helston. Derwent was appointed as Lecturer, but he hoped to persuade Queen's College to convert this post into a perpetual curacy. The elderly Mr Trevethan was curate but seems to have done little. He resigned three weeks before Easter but wished to claim the Easter offerings for himself. The Corporation however refused him any share in the offerings which were given to Derwent. Derwent was anxious to be ordained priest as soon as possible and at Easter he went to Wells for that purpose, but the trip was abortive as the Bishop of Exeter failed to send on the necessary papers. However, Derwent was able to visit Plymouth and to see Mary on his way back to Helston.

His first three months at Helston show Derwent throwing himself into his clerical vocation with dedication and energy. He wrote to Mary on 31 January 1827: 'It is my fixed resolution to suffer no labour, however severe, no worldly hopes however inviting, no worldly affection, however tender, to withdraw me from doing the Lord's works to the utmost of my limited ability.' On 19 February he wrote

> ... when I compare what I am now in mind, body and estate, with what I was even one year ago I feel myself under especial obligation to express my gratitude by every means in my power, one of which I trust will be that I shall never give you reason to doubt that I love you with all my heart and with all my mind – you who have been in the hands of Providence the earthly means of bringing me to myself – when far astray – you, in the first instance, and

with you your dear Father and Mother to whom I trust I shall always feel and affirm myself as deeply indebted as one human being can be to another.

Derwent's efforts at Helston were rewarded. He returned there on 21 April from Plymouth and wrote that night triumphantly to Mary: 'The Duke of Leeds has attached to the school an old but excellent house with garden, tenements and blacksmith's shop attached to it – the two latter let at £13 to £14. I shall furnish two rooms for myself, look out for a steady house-keeper, and advertise for pupils.' He went on to say that the Corporation had absolutely refused Mr Trevethan any share in the Easter offerings. Mr George Borlase had collected Church and Cross Street himself and there was 'already £18 in the book without Mr Grylls'. H. M. Grylls and Borlase had 'abstracted the whole of £7 10s 0d from Trevethan.' The total collected for Trevethan last year was only £5 10s 0d. Finally, 'Mr Stabback intends to yield a considerable part of his school into my hands if treated with civility i.e. if I do not refuse to meet Mr Grylls once or twice a year at his house to dinner.'

Mr Stabback had fallen from grace seven years before. The nature of his offence is not made clear. Derwent said: 'His offence was committed years ago ... a difference of opinion exists as to the degree of notice which ought now to be taken of him – he will never be readmitted into general society, but perhaps a formal visit twice a year is not too much to bestow on a clergy, after 7 years expiation and now ostensibly penitent.' However, by September Stabback was helping Derwent in the school from 9.15 to 12.0 noon so that he could leave the boys with him on prayer days for an hour.[1]

The following Monday, 23 April, Derwent wrote gleefully that he had been 'looking at our house' and 'talking to my tenants'. He described the house as 'a queer old everlasting passagy, odds and endsy, roomy, stairsy, straggling, incomprehensible dwelling, with offices innumerable and an under-cellar capable of holding 500 dozen of wine'. There was 'a tapestry bedroom, the hangings in

[1] 1 September 1827. Ibid.

excellent preservation and very curious. They were wrought by the nuns and cost, they said, £100 ... The garden is a delightful little spot, full of currant and gooseberry bushes with a strawberry bed and a little wall fruit, also one standard apple tree in the midst of a little grass plot.' There was a view of the Church and 'a pretty prospect'. It was Mrs Borlase's – 'dear good old honey-vending Mrs Borlase's' – idea to apply to the Duke of Leeds for the house. There was going to be a sale of furniture at the house of the deceased John Borlase (no relation) and Mrs Borlase would advise him what to buy.

Derwent made careful financial calculations. He tabulated his income:

£120 from the Chapel −£30 from Vicar
                          £30 surplice fees
                          £10 Duke of Leeds
                          £10 from the Members
                          £5 from Mr Rogers
                          (presumably from Mr John Rogers
                          of Penrose)
                          £35 Easter offerings
£26 from the School
£25 rent from the house
£16 from two pupils

'If I was clear of the world', (i.e. clear of his debts) 'I should now be very comfortably off,' he wrote. He went on to reckon that if he could get seven day-scholars he would have £200 clear income and if he got six boarders he would have £300 clear. The house was in Wendron Street and Derwent drew a plan of the ground floor (see page 99).

A few days later he wrote that he had bought a mahogany four-poster bed with dimity hangings for £4, 'the pillars a good deal carved, rather old-fashioned'. He had bought £44 worth of furniture altogether, including six mahogany chairs and two elbow chairs, eleven cane bottom chairs with white cushions, crocks, china, cutlery, tables, fire irons, a rosewood cabinet, and a Brussels carpet, which would be £14 new, for £9. He had engaged a

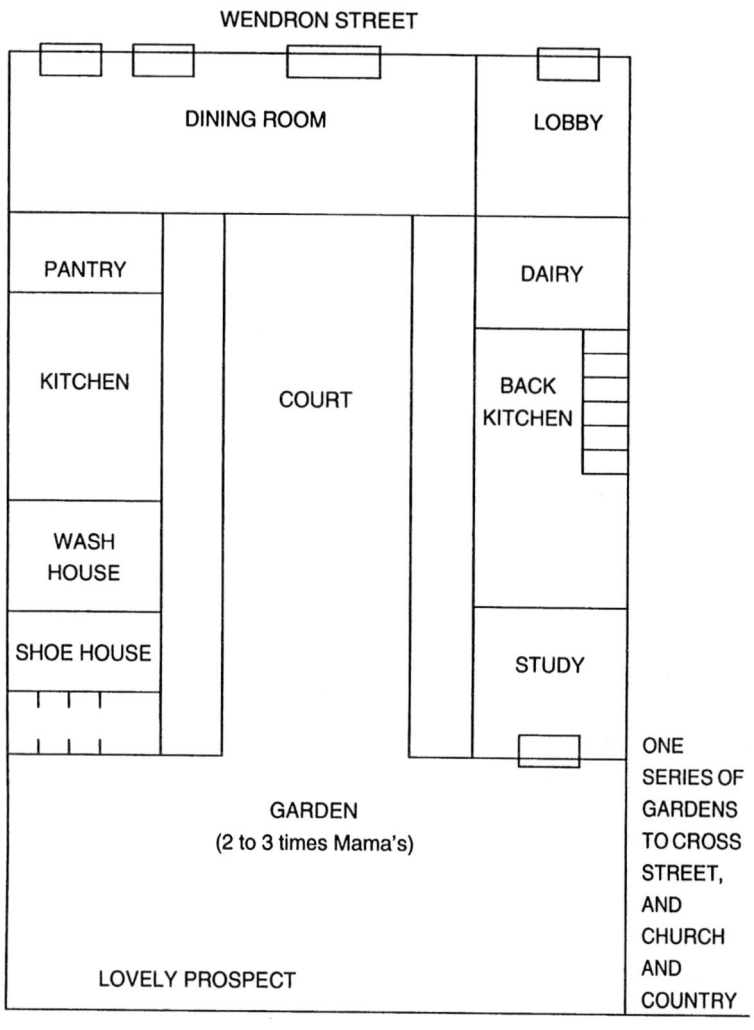

WENDRON STREET

DINING ROOM

LOBBY

PANTRY

DAIRY

KITCHEN

COURT

BACK
KITCHEN

WASH
HOUSE

SHOE HOUSE

STUDY

GARDEN
(2 to 3 times Mama's)

ONE
SERIES OF
GARDENS
TO CROSS
STREET,
AND
CHURCH
AND
COUNTRY

LOVELY PROSPECT

LANE 8–10 ft down below

Derwent Coleridge's house in Helston – plan of ground floor.

housekeeper, Betsy, an old servant at present with Miss Emily Trevenen, well-known to her and Mrs Grylls. 'You can't think what a superior looking sort of person she is – she has been a housemaid but can cook plain things, understands the whole art and mystery of washing, breadmaking etc. and is a good sempstress.' He warned Mary: 'You mustn't run away with too high an idea of the house – it is an old ramshackly place, and will take more money to put it in order than I shall expend without having it assured to the School, and the School to me, in perpetuo – and not then without I have a good prospect of success.' There were nineteen rooms in all, including the offices, and some rooms needed considerable building works.

On Monday 7 May Derwent wrote that he would get into the house on Saturday fortnight, i.e. 26 May. He had been with Miss Emily Trevenen to the ironmongers and had bought kettles, pans, mops, brooms and a boiler. Mrs Grylls and Miss Trevenen had bought bed linen and Betsy was making them up. He had had the recess in the dining parlour fitted with shelves for 'the gayer part of my books'. In the garden there were 'enough lilies of the valley for a nosegay'. The Bishop of Exeter ordained on 15 July and Derwent determined to take his priest's orders then. He had decided to call the house 'The Parsonage'.

On 12 June Derwent wrote making plans for Mama Pridham to visit Helston. She would not see Miss Emily Trevenen who was going away for the summer. She had had much annoyance about the National School, for which she had given £670, owing to 'the jealous fear of her relations that she would confine the business to my management and keep them out'. However, this was overcome by her asking H. M. Grylls, who had married her cousin, to take charge, and the previous Saturday the gentlemen met at Derwent's house to set up a Committee of Management.

On the 15 July 1827 Derwent was ordained Priest at Exeter and licensed to the free and endowed school of Helston on the nomination of the Mayor and Aldermen of the Borough of Helston. He visited Plymouth on his way back from Exeter and on 18 July Mama Pridham and Mary's younger brother John returned with him to Helston to stay until 1 August. The previous year a steamship service had been opened between Plymouth and Falmouth, so they travelled in the *Sir Francis Drake*, a little wooden paddle steamer of 113 tons. Derwent reported to Mary,

Mama found the packet very agreeable for the first hour, but soon began to feel herself ill enough for the purposes of vituperation, in which she displayed all that variety and effect of which she is so perfect a mistress – Papa (for allowing), me (for advising), herself (for consenting) – all came under her ban, especially the last personage, whom she consigned to sundry diseases and divers kinds of death if ever her foot was found in a steam vessel again. Thus the noise, the company, the motion, suggested to her imagination such a store of comparisons and pleasant hyperboles that I was prevented from illness by dint of sheer laughing. Jack was doubled up in one of the cabin boxes, where for some hours he continued giving us the converse of his last week's eating – beginning with 3 pennyworth of black cherries and ending with heaven knows what. For a long while Mama was bent upon landing at Fowey, but on learning that there were no post-chaises to be had there she resigned herself to her fate – the angry sea smoothed its rugged brow – and we all grew hourly better. Mama lay and sat alternately on the cabin sofa – with the men – having been propelled from the female compartment like an arrow out of a bow by the sight of three sick women. Jack crawled out of his hole – and got hungry – a lamb chop was produced of which John made a complete example – Mama had a couple of slices, cut up for her, which she handed into her mouth with a silver knife. We did not arrive at Falmouth until near 11 o'clock, too late to proceed, so we had some tea and went to bed, where Mama and I spent the night in a state of the most restless inquietude – unable to make up our minds whether we had caught the itch, or were being devoured by fleas – but I believe it was only the nettlerash.

Mary wanted to know more: 'You describe your voyage in the steam vessel in the most lively terms imaginable. I can almost see Mama stretched on the sofa – looking very solemn, and being not in her most amiable mood. I can imagine you trying to comfort her by every little means in your power, but I cannot answer the important question which everybody asks – was Mama actually sick? In good earnest? Or only qualmish?'

Mama wrote to Mary: 'I thank my Stars we are out of that filthy steamer'. Her letter was full of enthusiasm for the parsonage house. 'What a house – it is really truly and positively one of the most comfortable, convenient, respectable, roomy, cupboardsy, staircasy houses I ever met with ... and very well calculated for a school.' Betsy she found to have 'respectability written on her forehead'.

Derwent wrote that he had three sermons to write, including one for the Friendly Society on 26 July. 'I have offered to preach to all the different clubs at their several anniversaries if they will come to Church – to give me a guinea for my sermons and I shall become a member – it will do good, at least I hope it will, to connect their establishments as much as possible with the Church, – I have reason to believe the principal club – that of the tradesmen – will accept my offer – there's never no knowing: 3 out of 4 are Methodies or Baptists – and 9/10 of the remainder no religion at all.' He was writing his sermons through the night, going on until 2.0 a.m. and getting up again at 5.0 a.m.

On 3 August Derwent wrote to Mary that Mr H. M. Grylls had recommended to him a pupil, Mr Kendal of Llanlivery, who wished to be prepared for entry to Oxford at Michaelmas 1828 and who was prepared to pay £100 p.a. as a boarder at the Parsonage. This added to Derwent's financial prospects, though Mr T. Grylls said 'no wine at that price'.

In August Derwent's old friend John Moultrie, still lecturing at Eton but soon to become Rector of Rugby, came to stay with Derwent at Helston. Moultrie wrote to his mother from Helston on 22 August 1827 that he and his wife Maggie had stayed ten days with the Pridhams and he had left Maggie at Frankfurt Street for the seabathing. He described Mary as 'one of the most beautiful and charming girls I have ever seen – she has been passionately attached to Derwent these 3 years and a half, during 2 of which they have been avowedly engaged – I hope in no distant time to have the pleasure of marrying them. Derwent's prospects are brightening daily – he is an active and excellent parish priest and preaches eloquently, he superintends a grammar school. In the very stronghold of Methodism he succeeds in making himself universally popular. He is at least ten times happier than he ever was in his life before.'

When Derwent had time, he and Moultrie walked down past the Loe Pool to the sea and swam off the Loe Bar. Moultrie wrote to his wife: 'The walk to the sea continues to improve on acquaintance. It is so beautiful that I can't understand how Derwent could have kept poor Mrs Pridham here for a fortnight and never shown her any part of it.' Perhaps he felt that after her passage on the *Sir Francis Drake* the less she saw of the sea the better, with her return passage already booked. 'We continue to enjoy our dips', wrote the somewhat prosaic Moultrie to his wife. By the same post Derwent wrote to Mary: '... conceive the Atlantic come swelling in upon an open coast with a fine sandy beach and us, watching for a smooth, in order to plunge through the breakers into the waves, which, though rather high, were as gentle and tractable as could be desired, and bore us up and let us down, like a managed horse, prancing obediently to his rider's wish'.[1]

Derwent and Moultrie stayed overnight with Mr and Mrs H. M. Grylls at Bosahan (near Helford) before Moultrie proceeded to Falmouth and so by steamer to Plymouth. On his return to Helston Derwent reported to Mary a conversation with Betsy, his housekeeper, who was disgusted with the state of Moultrie's linen and thought little of his wife – 'to push them out to wash, down here, among strangers! I'm sure she cant be no relation of Mrs Pridham's ... If folks be never so poor, they try to be a little bit whole and daycent when they go <u>abroad</u>!'

On Sunday evening 2 September Derwent, overjoyed at the news that they were to be married two weeks sooner than planned, wrote Mary a long extravaganza:

Dated from the Desk which I value as the gift of my fond Mary;

[1] 22 August 1827. Ibid.

—at the Table which will soon be all the distance between me and my bonny Mary,

—in the Library, where I shall spend my long Xmas evenings with my lively Mary

—in the Parsonage, soon to be kept in order, so tidy! by my notable Mary.

—in Wendron St where everybody will try to live, that they may be near my Mary

—in Helston, where the folks are all agog, wondring when ye Parson will bring home his Mary

—in Cornwall, which has its diamonds, but the *real* Cornish diamond will be my Mary

—in England, the only land that cd have produced my English-hearted Mary,

—in Europe, where ye men have broad foreheads, like me, and ye women white and red cheeks like my blooming Mary,

—in the Planet Earth, – little, round, landy, seaey, – hilly, daly, woody, rocky, laky, greeny, browny, blacky, whity, hotty, coldy, sandy, snowy, grassy, heathy, stony knob – subject to hurricanes, earthquakes, volcanic eruptions, snowfalls, stone-showers, land-slips, water-spouts, sand-winds, malarias, and such like, – so that if one was looking out for a planet one might not consider it quite so eligible as the advertisements in the Solar system Gazette (published at the Sun-office, a few doors from Sirius) wd have us believe – and between ourselves (for I [wouldn't] have it known out of the system, tho' the fact's notorious) of late years, the place has been over-run with a small biped – of all the queer, naked, odd-shaped, straddling, dirty, noisy, quarrelsome, mischievous, offensive vermin, – that ever were pro-duced, – the most detestable; – now where I live, Sir, in Saturn's ring – things may go on much better I daresay, – but I'm used to it, you see, and really don't find the place so bad, (for a few years, I mean) especially when my pleasures are doubled, and all my pains divided by my own dear, good Mary. –

Sunday Evening, 2nd September 1827 – And so, dearest love, we are to be made happy a fortnight earlier than we looked for? – and Mama approves – if I quite like it – know then that I QUITE like it – that I am delighted, – dizzy, shaky, nervous, unquiet with pleasure at the thoughts of it – but I need not attempt to describe my feelings to you – and as it wd be profane to expose them to anyone else I shall communicate with you, on this subject, only by winged thoughts...

On 9 September Derwent wrote to Mary agreeing that Ball should paint her picture, but he had 'faint hopes that Ball will make anything of you', on condition 'that you neither see nor are seen by anyone while there on any excuse or pretext whatever – I wd not on any consideration have you mixed up with B's in and outers and if possible still less with his in and outresses – his playmates, I mean. I was never jealous of your affections for a moment – but I have been a little afraid of your facility and good nature, and unsuspectness ... I have sometimes been grievously annoyed – when it would have been wicked to be angry with you – Mama may perhaps understand my feelings ... I have but one caution to give you with regard to your conduct at Helston, and that is to keep Stabback at least as far from you as the Equator from the Pole – you being the Pole, understand me – freezing – distantly civil and civilly distant...'

On his birthday, 14 September, Derwent wrote: 'I pray for the success of Ball's brush in his hazardous attempt to limn your pretty visage – he may hit the figure off – but I tremble for the face. The chalk drawing has no pretensions to a likeness whatsoever.'[1]

Two months later Mary wrote to Derwent that 'my picture is hung up in the Drawing Room over the chimneypiece'. It showed 'a warm romantic face, and looks more as if she was sighing in the groves of Arcadia than your own happy Mary – still it is not an Arcadian beauty, for it is not very pretty, only rich'. The portrait in oils[2] shows Mary in a black tight-bodiced dress, with white edging

[1] This must be the drawing Mary sent Derwent on his birthday at Buckfastleigh of which he wrote irreverently 'I wish to goodness Tipsey up here over the mantelpiece was more like you.'
[2] Now in the possession of Capt. G. P. D. Coleridge.

Mary Pridham, 1827, aged 20, painted by William Ball.
(By permission of Capt. Gerard Peter Derwent Coleridge)

to the neckline, and a white blouse with short puffed sleeves and transparent long white oversleeves. She has black ringlets curling over her high brow and down to her shoulders[1] and a long graceful neck. She has a pointed chin, a small rosebud mouth, a long straight nose, and a high colour in her cheeks. She has well-marked, strongly arched dark eyebrows and black eyes. One feels that Ball has not captured the expression of the eyes, but the general effect is of a strikingly handsome girl.

Derwent reported to Mary his mother's growing approval of their plans: 'she is much better satisfied with our marriage – more convinced of its <u>prudence</u> than I ever dared to anticipate'. She spoke in the highest terms of <u>Mama</u> – her letters had been read by the Southeys and the Wordsworths and were 'highly approved of'.

The next day, Sunday, Derwent was up at 6.30, conducted a funeral at 7 and another at 8 and was incessantly occupied until 5.0 p.m. He cried off an evening with George Borlase and his wife ('Emily my dear') and walked through 'Gouella's fields' with a beautiful view of the Loe Valley and the sea and the Helston moors. The night before he had been called out to baptise the child of a carpenter called Badcock 'said to be an infidel ... a clever well-informed man – served on the Peninsula through the war, sergeant major for eight years. I am a good deal interested about him. Whatever sceptical notions he may have picked up must have been confirmed, rather than weakened, in a shrewd half-informed way, by the rant and absurdity of Cornish Methodism.'

On 26 September Derwent held his first School Meeting. At 9.30 the boys rehearsed at the house in Wendron Street. At 11.30 they went to church and at 1.30 they went down to the school, which was at 47 Coinagehall Street. The school was crowded with visitors. The boys gave recitations. Kendal 'spoke *Cephalus and Procris* beautifully, *Alexander's Feast* as well as I think it deserves to be spoken', and the visitors expressed the highest satisfaction. These proceedings were followed by a dinner, at which Derwent made a speech, which was 'a <u>new</u> thing' but 'it went off capitally'. H. M.

---

[1] In fact at the age of 44 Mary's hair was very dark brown. Mrs Mary Coleridge has a lock in her possession.

Grylls, the Mayor, returned thanks in the name of the Corporation, alluding to the ruin of the school, and saying they had at length succeeded in putting it in the way of being re-established on a permanent footing, as they could judge from what they had heard from the pupils and from Mr Coleridge's speech. There were thirty-one at the dinner, including Sir Richard Vivian, the county member, 'a very agreeable young man', who had heard of Derwent from his brother Mr Vivian of Nanslo (whose son Derwent taught), and Sir Christopher Hawkins, who was rival to the Duke of Leeds as patron of Helston.

The previous Monday Derwent had been to a sale of furniture and bought a four-poster bed which 'looks very grand and will suit the Tapestry exactly'. The posts were very massive and carved with a sort of leaf, there were six gilt pineapples on top, and the whole was trimmed with black velvet. However, when the bed was put up Derwent found it 'not such a bargain as I was led to suppose' – the folds were not sufficiently full. 'I anticipate Mama's remarks ... her triumph over me at my being deceived in a piece of furniture – and her reprobation of my grandee notions.' However, the bed suited the room and 'it only cost £16 for the two bedrooms'.

With the house Derwent had inherited Oates, the gardener, and his son. After consultations with Derwent they had sown a lawn, which made the garden look bigger and showed off the landscape beyond. By the end of September the grass was coming up but the slugs 'were thinning it in many places lamentably'. Oates comforted Derwent by telling him the roots remained but he refused to take any more steps about the garden until '"the Lady comes – if we should do wrong, sir" – he means Mama (you are Mrs Coleridge).'[1] Mrs Pridham had evidently impressed her personality on Oates.

At the end of October Derwent gave a supper for the workmen and gardener ('11 stout hungry young fellows') to celebrate the completion of work on the house. Betsy and her assistant cook, Dolly, prepared 32lb of boiled beef and 'two thundering plum puddings'. At the right moment Derwent bore in a brimming bowl

[1] 16 October 1827. Derwent Coleridge MSS. HRC, Texas.

of punch and called for a song. 'Isaac the bellringer led off – a very fine voice he has – and 3 struck up with Sweet Home ... I then proposed a toast, the single married and the married happy.' After another song, Mr Polkinghorne, the plasterer, proposed the toast of Mr Coleridge, which was drunk standing. With another bowl of punch they drank the healths of Mrs Pridham and Miss Pridham. The total cost of the party was £1 15s 0d and there was 'beef enough left for a whole week'.[1]

Derwent was a popular member of Helston upper-class society. He told Mary that after the School Meeting on 26 September: 'I shall have no occasion to have recourse to my own cellar or larder for the rest of the winter.' Sir Richard Vivian called and admired the clouds being painted on the drawing room ceiling in the Parsonage. Derwent returned his call at Trelowarren and was full of enthusiasm for his library. He dined out frequently with the Vivians at Nanslo, the various branches of the Grylls family, including Humphrey Grylls the mayor, now living a good deal at his country seat at Bosahan, George Borlase and his wife Emily, and Miss Emily Trevenen.

On 16 October Derwent calculated that his average outlay since he had set up house twenty weeks ago was seventeen shillings per week. He thought in their first year of married life they ought to save at least £50 out of the £250 which he expected his income to be.

Derwent and Mary were planning to marry on 6 December. On 15 November Derwent wrote that Stabback had told him it was impossible to break up so early as 1 December, but Stabback would take the school that week. The following week Derwent would have to return to school, after which they would have the Christmas holiday.

Praed, who had just been elected to a Fellowship at Trinity College, Cambridge, wrote to congratulate him on his forthcoming wedding: 'I suppose that you have in yourself a vaster capacity for very intense happiness than ninety-nine bards in a hundred; and inasmuch as your acuteness of sensation has wrought you no small pain it is only fair that it should produce for you proportionate gratification: which I am sure it will.'

S. T. Coleridge had sent Mary a poem on 16 October 1827:

[1] 29 October 1827. Ibid.

To Mary S. Pridham.

Dear tho' unseen! tho' I have left behind
Life's gayer views and all that stir the mind,
Now I revive, Hope making a new Start,
Since I have heard with most believing heart,
That all, my glad eyes would grow bright to see,
My Derwent hath found realiz'd in Thee!
The Boon prefigur'd in His earliest Wish;
Crown of his Cup, and Garnish of his Dish;
The fair Fulfilment of his Poesy,
When his young Heart first yearned for Sympathy!
Dear tho' unseen! Unseen yet long portrayed!
A Father's blessings on thee, gentle Maid![1]

On Tuesday evening, 27 November Derwent sent Mary his last letter before their wedding headed 'DONT TURN OVER but read what follows beneath'.

My dearest, dearest love –
Hand over this letter to Mama, without reading any more than what you see on this page:– you see the confidence which I place in your discretion, and I am sure you will not abuse it. Time will clear up every mystery; for the present be content to know that I am very well, and most happy; and that, if nothing falls out contrary to my expectations, I shall be at your side, on Monday next, before five o'clock. Now be a good child, and love your constantly attached, and fondly devoted
                    Derwent Coleridge
N.B. Ask no questions and remember Mrs Bluebeard.

On the next page:

My dearest Mama –
Friday is a holiday – I have written to Tom Sheephanks to

[1]Copied into Mary's leather-bound locked commonplace book. Derwent Coleridge MSS. HRC, Texas.

come over and do my duty next Sunday morning – J. Trevenen will take it in the afternoon – If this arrangement can be managed I shall leave Helston on Thursday – and shall be with [you] the day after you receive this – burn this letter. Do not tell Mary (unless you think it best so to do) and believe me ever underlining and forever your truly affectionate
                    Derwent Coleridge
Best love and duty to Mr P.—

Derwent and Mary were married on Thursday, 6 December, at St Andrew's Church, Plymouth, by John Moultrie, who was now Rector of Rugby. Derwent is described in the marriage register as curate of Helston. He was twenty-seven and Mary was twenty.

The married couple returned to Helston in time for Derwent to resume school the week after the wedding. They probably stayed a day or two at Lostwithiel on the way. The next week Moultrie spent three days with them at Helston before returning to his wife, who was staying with her parents at Windsor. Over the Christmas holiday there were no doubt many callers and visits paid in return. Mrs Pridham came to stay and Mrs Samuel Taylor Coleridge wrote affectionately to wish them well, regretting her inability to be present at the marriage. It was five years since she had seen Derwent for a few days at Cambridge.

It was five years also since Derwent had seen his sister Sara, on the same occasion at Cambridge. In the spring of 1823, during her first visit to London with her mother, she had become clandestinely engaged to her cousin, Henry Nelson Coleridge, a struggling young barrister. When Colonel James Coleridge in 1824 became aware of the engagement of his son to the penniless daughter of his ne'er-do-well brother Samuel, he demanded the engagement be broken off. However, the lovers remained unshakeably faithful to each other, although they did not meet again until Sara visited London late in 1826, and by 1827 the Colonel had capitulated and given them his blessing, although they were not able to marry until September 1829. In April 1828 Sara sent Mary a poem of eighteen verses, inscribed in Mary's leather-bound locked commonplace book:[1]

[1]Derwent Coleridge MSS. HRC, Texas.

111

Epistle from Sara to her sister Mary, whom she has never yet seen – her Yarrow unvisited April 27th 1828.

Now Mary, Winter's reign suspended
Our Mountains doff their hoods of snow,
Rich purple tints of heath are blended
With green, and furze's golden glow.
Yon Lake, whose name thy Derwent bears,
No more of dusk and steely hue,
Now glitters silver bright, now wears
The Heav'n's reflected azure blue . . .
. . .
Mary, 'twere sweet but long to tell
How dear thy Derwent was to me,
By knoll and wood and rocky dell
How blithe we wandered, fancy free;
How o'er the stream to safe dry land
His 'sylph-like Sister' oft he bore
And guided her with gentlest hand
Thro' flowery fields of classic lore . . .
. . .
His life's horizon seemed to lie
Immers'd in gloom and misty fears,
When thitherward I bend my eye
No hope, no joy my bosom cheers.
But soon the darkness and the storm
Seem'd chased away by magic sleight
My spirit sees an Angel form
Arising bathe the scene in light . . .
. . .
Mary! I ne'er beheld thy face
And cold and vain description's art
A breathing portraiture to trace
Such as can satisfy the heart
Thine eyes, the colour of thy hair
Each feature told me o'er and o'er
I know them all – how sweet, how fair –
Methinks a Sister should know more! . . .

The liveliest image of thy mind
I see in lines thyself has trac'd
These show thee tender and refined
With purity and meekness grac'd
In these the welcome warranty
Of deeply cherish'd hope I view,
That thou and I may live to be
Dear friends affectionate and true...

S. C.

So began the life-long friendship between Sara and Mary.[1]

---

[1]Of Sara Coleridge's surviving 1,400 letters in the HRC, University of Texas, 468 are addressed to Derwent or Mary, and of these 312 letters are to Mary.

Chapter 2

Early Married Life and School Problems (1828–34)

Derwent and Mary worked hard to build up the school at Helston. Now that Derwent had a house and a wife he could take boarders; the organisation of the domestic arrangements of the school was Mary's responsibility.

Mary had a good deal of ill-health, which dated from the birth of their first child, Derwent Moultrie Coleridge, on 17 October 1828. On 6 November Derwent wrote to his cousin, Henry Nelson Coleridge, 'dearest Mary, after a most excellent time, and a fortnight's rapid recovery and apparent convalescence has, I grieve to say, had a most serious attack, first in her bowels, narrowly escaping inflammation, and now in her limbs ... but for this unfortunate pain in her legs, which we <u>hope</u> is rheumatism, she would again be a convalescent. You may suppose how anxious I am.'

However, in July 1829 Derwent and Mary were able to go to London and visited Samuel Taylor Coleridge at Highgate, to his great pleasure. He wrote to Derwent[1] enclosing £10 which Mr Sotheby sent as a 'Little Friendship offering in his name to you or your "lovely Wife"'. He was longing to go to Helston ('I am in a

---

[1]Collected Letters of Samuel Taylor Coleridge. 28 August 1829. Ed. E. L. Griggs. OUP.

degree very unusual for me fidgetty to see and kiss my little Derwent') but his medical advisers forbade it. He concluded: 'Tell my dearest Mary that she has left a genial life on the whole state of my thought and feelings, has shed in upon my spirit a new light of Love, and Hope and cheerful Purposes, which I could not have anticipated and for which, I trust, that God will bless the thanksgiving, which I offer him in my morning and evening Prayers – and often too in the watches of the Night.'

Sara Coleridge married her cousin Henry at last on 3 September 1829. It had previously been arranged that after the wedding Mrs S. T. Coleridge would leave Greta Hall, her home for twenty-nine years, and go to Helston – as she wrote to her old friend Thomas Poole: 'for a long visit – where I shall finally settle I know not yet; D. and his wife say my natural home is with them – time will shew...'[1] Derwent, to his deep regret, could not afford the long journey to the wedding, but Miss Emily Trevenen, who had family links with the Lake District, was there and Mrs Samuel Taylor Coleridge travelled back to Helston with her. Derwent wrote to his mother on 6 September:[2] 'Dear, dear Sara! What would I not have given to have seen her in her gay bridal dress, attended by such a train of bridesmaids and youthful friends! Yet my heart was most with the homebiders; and well I know what a trial it must have been for you all – for you, dearest Mother, above all – but be of good cheer, your sorrow-ful parting will, there is every reason to hope, be the occasion of many merry meetings ... I feel assured that you will find with your other daughter, a little Zoar, where you may still set up your rest in an hour of sunshine, and with a cheerful prospect.'

Derwent continued: 'Miss Emily Trevenen will be interested in the following piece of tidings ... I have got rid of Stabback!' They had signed an agreement that Stabback was to get 'a moiety of the Profits, during the unexpired remainder of the 7 years (4¼ years)' and was 'to have nothing to say to the School – never to show his nose inside it'. Stabback was free to take pupils outside Cornwall

[1]Ed. S. Potter. *Minnow among Tritons.*
[2]Derwent Coleridge MSS. HRC, Texas.

115

now, and after seven years anywhere except within a ten-mile circuit of Helston.

Mary added a postscript:

Dearest Mother,
    Only time to add how fully I participate in dearest Sara's happiness, and how delightedly I look forward to receiving and welcoming you under our roof where I sincerely hope that you will find a happy home with
    Yr. affectionately attached children
    Derwent and Mary Coleridge.

Mrs Coleridge was happy in Helston, but in the summer of 1830 Sara and Henry moved to Hampstead, where they had more room, and Sara, expecting her first child, sent for her mother. Mrs Coleridge, who had become very close to Sara during their many years together at Greta Hall, was glad to rejoin her daughter and to help with her family, and spent the remaining fifteen years of her life with Sara.

Mary continued to have trouble with her leg. She wrote to Derwent at Highgate on 13 January 1830 that 'Dr Cookworthy (the Pridhams' family doctor in Plymouth) saw my leg today'. He recommended cold water rags on it to relieve the pain at night, adhesive plasters and a calico bandage. In June 1830 Mary was again staying in Plymouth with the baby while Derwent was writing to her every few days from Helston with concern and orders about her health. He wrote frequently of the pains of separation – 'your society has certainly become since our marriage daily more and more indispensable'.[1]

Derwent was particularly worried about the behaviour of one of his private pupils, Frederick Montagu, son of Samuel Taylor Coleridge's old acquaintance Basil Montagu, a lawyer of Lincoln's Inn. On 1 June Derwent wrote to Mary that Montagu had broken Daintry's collarbone wrestling. On 6 June he wrote that Montagu had fought three times 'with a drunken, half-witted wretch of a cobbler' and had injured the man. Derwent awarded retribution. 'I gave it him within an inch of his life – my Mother being present. He

---

[1] 10 June 1830. Derwent Coleridge MSS. HRC, Texas.

is completely silenced now.' On 8 June Montagu walked to Falmouth and boarded the London packet. Derwent sent his father his account – £91 due to Derwent and £54 due to tradesmen – and on 18 June Derwent wrote to Mary that Mr Montagu was refusing to pay his son's debts. Derwent evidently took Montagu back at Helston, as on 4 December 1830, Mrs D. B. Montagu wrote to Derwent from Bedford Square: 'Mr Montagu will cast Frederick off entirely if he reads your statement of his conduct.' He was a sickly child removed from home in infancy to be placed under medical care which alienated his father; he had been to sea and his mother wrote: 'I see no prospect for this unhappy boy but returning once more to sea.' She sent Derwent 'a thousand thanks for all your forbearance and to your sweet wife also – who has had no doubt her full share of vexation'. She asked Derwent to send the account again to Mr Montagu:'I beg you to state that the Tradesmen's bills are approved by you – Mr M. will not pay any debts he has incurred that you do not approve' – and she would say that Derwent felt 'that College would be ruinous to him and to his Father'. She concluded: 'I shall write to Frederick to ensure such behaviour as may render him less obnoxious to you and your family.'[1]

Derwent's financial position was precarious. On 24 April 1830 Praed wrote to him: 'I fear I can point to no means of coming at so large sum as £500, but my name is quite at your service as security for you in any way, if your own speculations can devise any.' He went on to say he had hopes of being able to help with £100 or £200 'by and bye'.[2] In January 1831 Derwent went to London for a short stay to see his father and Sara. Mary wrote to him 'Do not spend your money, there's a dear boy – remember the Christmas bills at Helston – and what a large family we shall have to provide for next half year.' She finished this letter with 'don't expose your ragged night-shirt on any account'.[3] Moultrie, now Vicar of Rugby, had been urging Derwent to apply for an assistant mastership at Rugby, under Thomas Arnold. Derwent wrote him a long letter saying it was 'utterly inexpedient and indeed not morally possible for me to quit Helleston for Rugby ... The question does not turn on

[1]Derwent Coleridge MSS. HRC, Texas.
[2]MS at Cornell University.
[3]12 January 1831. Derwent Coleridge MSS. HRC, Texas.

the comparative advantages of Rugby and Helleston ... but whether being at Helleston happy and prosperous beyond my hopes, and almost to the extent of my wishes, with a sphere of usefulness before me for which I believe myself better calculated than for almost any other – I should run the risk of a change leaving a load of debt behind me...[1] He went on to say that his present income was between £800 and £900 p.a. '... With every prospect of increase, and this in a few years will be without incumbrance', and that the cost of living was cheap in Helston. It must be remembered that he was under contract to make over half the profits from the school to Stabback for another three years. Derwent told Moultrie that his hopes of being offered a good permanent living had been dashed by the change of Government, but he met this situation with Christian fortitude.

Derwent went on to say that his chief temptations were 'a disproportionate love of reading, a want of sympathy amounting to impatience with vulgar minds, and a painful sense of the half-hypocrisy and covert selfishness which disfigures the religious profession of our times'. He found himself out of sympathy with most of the Evangelical ministers. 'The truth is their (intellectual) views of things are little higher than those whom they address, and so they speak right on with prevailing fervour: while I am continually haunted with what I believe to be a deeper truth ... than I can venture to announce, and thus am forced to speak an accommodated language, clogged with restrictions, which few, if any, apprehend, and which in fact are mere sacrifices to my own truthfulness...'

In 1832 Mary had further serious ill-health. On 18 January Praed wrote to Derwent commiserating with him on Mary's illness. Praed had spent the previous summer at his family home in Bitton giving support to his father while his elder sister, Elizabeth, was dying of consumption. In his previous letters to Derwent Praed had expressed agnosticism, but in this letter he says that the death of his sister strengthened his faith and concludes: 'I pray for Mary and you daily: and yet more for myself that I may be fit to love you hereafter.'[2]

[1] 6 February 1831. Ibid.
[2] MS at Cornell University.

On 13 January Sara Coleridge wrote to Miss Emily Trevenen saying what a shock 'her dear sister's danger' had been to her.[1] 'This tendency to inflammation is very alarming.' She anticipated a long convalescence would be necessary. Mrs Pridham was in Helston nursing Mary and Miss Trevenen had been very helpful and attentive. Mary evidently had all her hair cut off. She wrote to Derwent from Plymouth on 8 June: 'I fear my hair is growing but slowly.' She added: 'I seldom feel my throat now – it is quite strong again.'[2]

In April Mary went to Plymouth to convalesce for seven and a half weeks, leaving little Derwent Moultrie in Helston with his nurse. Derwent wrote that he was looking forward to rejoining her on 14 June, but he was anxious that she should consult Dr Cookworthy before they resumed co-habitation.[3] Mary wrote that Mama had talked to Dr Cookworthy: 'I believe he thinks it better to be prudent for a little while longer.' Derwent made up his mind that they must sleep apart.[4] Mary took the matter more lightly and hoped there was no occasion for any further fuss 'but that we might return at once to our proper and natural way of going on',[5] but on Derwent's insistence he was given a separate room when he arrived in Plymouth.

During Mary's absence Derwent was busy with the school and his clerical duties, and when he had time he went for long walks in the surrounding countryside. He generally wrote cheerfully to Mary but on 25 May, when he had been kept awake by noise in the street, he confessed that 'your continued delicacy of health as a married woman – the state of our affairs, which though not gloomy yet taken in conjunction with the great uncertainties of a school, demands just at present the most watchful attention – the situation of my Father and Brother – these and a host of lesser grievances <u>sometimes</u> press heavy on me. I thank God however for all.'[6]

[1]Sara Coleridge. Letters, 1339. HRC, Texas.
[2]Derwent Coleridge MSS. HRC, Texas.
[3]19 May 1832. Derwent Coleridge MSS. HRC, Texas.
[4]29 May 1832. Ibid.
[5]8 June 1832. Ibid.
[6]Ibid.

One of the minor irritations was that Canon Rogers of Penrose withdrew his five guineas subscription to Derwent as Lecturer. He told Derwent that he thought Ministers of religion ought not to be dependent on non-residents for their support, or on their congregations. He said he would give £100 towards making the situation independent, i.e. setting up a perpetual curacy, and he had communicated with the Bishop about it. Derwent told Mary this was just what he should like, to be an independent beneficed clergyman – 'a salary of not less than £100 which with the day school would be a provision for life . . . But I have no expectation that the scheme will be accomplished.'[1]

Conscious both of the remoteness of Helston school and the uncertainty of his income both from the school and as an unbeneficed curate, Derwent started applying for headmasterships in other schools. On 24 December 1832, he wrote to Robert Southey, saying that he had read that the headmastership of Stamford School was now vacant and requesting a testimonial.[2] The income of the Headmaster from freehold estates alone was £600 p.a. with the prospect of an increase as leases fell in, 'which would be a comfortable independence for life, and free from the anxieties inseparable from a fluctuating and precarious income . . .'

Derwent spent much time and energy collecting testimonials for this position but then began to have grave doubts about it. The Mayor of Stamford wanted to appoint an English master, who would share the income, and would teach reading, writing and arithmetic, without Latin, free to all the tradesmen's sons in the borough. Derwent thought free scholars should be taught Grammar (i.e. Latin and Greek) which would enable them to go to University. He thought the Mayor's scheme would degrade the ancient Grammar School to a free commercial academy. In any case, on 18 April 1833 the Mayor of Stamford wrote to Derwent informing him that he had appointed the Reverend J. R. Major, MA of Trinity College, Cambridge and Assistant Master of King's College School, London, to the vacant mastership.

After this disappointment Derwent made enquiries about the

[1]4 June 1832. Ibid.
[2]Ibid.

possibility of a Head Master's post at Coventry, where the elderly holder of the post, with a salary of £600 p.a., had only one scholar. The Corporation were trying to get him to resign but it seems they did not succeed.[1] At all events Derwent does not seem to have pursued the application.

In June 1833 Derwent went to Cambridge and attended a literary meeting, where he met his father for the last time. In a letter to Mary[2] he described how, after dining at St John's, he went with Praed to Thirlwall's, 'where Father was keeping a large party of young fellows in alternate peals of laughter and mazes of astonishment – all of them appearing to eat him with their eyes'. It is pleasing to know that Samuel Taylor Coleridge in his old age was received back with respect in his own university. He had left Jesus College under a cloud in 1794 without taking a degree. He was suspected of Jacobinism, having enlisted in the Army under the assumed name of Silas Tomkyns Comberbache to escape from his debts, but after four months he was bought out by his elder brother George. He had for a long period been enslaved by opium until rescued by Dr Gillman. He had for years been ruthlessly slated by the critics for his works of genius and foresight. Mrs Coleridge wrote to Thomas Poole: 'Samuel was most highly gratified with his reception, and pleased to see his College and old haunts once more.'[3]

Despite financial uncertainties, Derwent was gradually increasing the numbers and reputation of the school at Helston. Writing to Mary on 4 June 1832, he mentioned 13 boys. To the Dean of Ely on 30 January 1833 he wrote that he had over 20 boarders and a considerable number of day boys. The boys were examined annually in September by a visiting examiner, after which they attended a service in church, and later a dinner was held at the *Angel* for the Corporation, distinguished visitors and old scholars. The sermon Derwent preached on 26 September, 1832, on the occasion of the School Meeting, and subsequently had printed, gives a summary of his educational philosophy at this time.

[1]S. B. Singleton and Sons to J. H. Macaulay. 7th May 1833. Derwent Coleridge MSS. HRC, Texas.

[2]29 May 1833. Derwent Coleridge MSS. HRC, Texas.

[3] Ed. S. Potter. *Minnow among Tritons*, p. 176. 24th July 1833.

The pulpit was in the middle of the nave, a third of the way from the back of the church. Derwent stood beneath the great brass Godolphin candelabra, hanging from the oval panel in its plaster-moulded ceiling. The church, with its classical interior, was bathed in light from the clear rounded windows. His text was from Ephesians vi.4: 'And ye Fathers, provoke not your children to wrath, but bring them up in the nurture and admonition of the Lord.'

He began by emphasising the need to implant from the start deep religious knowledge and habitual reverence and faith. 'Only with many tears and prayers, only with spiritual exercises, long and painful, shall we regain, in after years, the sweet serenity of that early faith, that sense of the liveliness of virtue.' He spoke of the need in the home for example, but emphasized that home education alone was not adequate – a well-conducted school fostered self-dependence.

He argued that physical science in all its branches was sure to meet with ample encouragement in the world '—whatever promises to assist in the production of wealth ... is sure to be praised and rewarded ... Not so with those pursuits which bear directly upon the mind itself – mental philosophy, including logic and philosophical grammar, are regarded as serving only to the entertainment of the idle learned.' Derwent saw this view as leading 'to the wild and increasing extravagance which characterises the religious opinions of this day' and 'the lack of the governing principles of thought which it should be the first object of all education to elicit'.

In schools where the higher and middle ranks are trained for the performance of their various duties the main attention should be to grammatical studies, especially 'the ancient languages to which we owe the civilisation of modern Europe', to theories of abstract, and mathematical science, and above all to 'sound, rational and truly spiritual Theology'.

In March 1831 Derwent appointed as Assistant Master Charles Alexander Johns, a young man of 19, from Plymouth. His father, Henry Incledon Johns, had been co-partner in a Devonport bank, but when the bank failed in the general financial crisis of 1825 he had taken up a position as Drawing Master in the New Grammar School in Plymouth. There was no money to send his son to university but

122

he wrote to Derwent on 19 March that his son had given much time to botany 'which shows that he is studious'. In fact in 1837 C. A. Johns entered for a degree course at Trinity College, Dublin, where he did not have to be resident except (with Derwent's permission) for two fortnights a year. In 1840 he obtained his BA and was ordained Deacon, and was ordained Priest in 1841.

He had a lifelong interest in botany and wild life. His book *Flowers of the Field*, published in 1853, remained in print until 1949, and his *British Birds in their Haunts*, published in 1862, was in print until 1948. He was Headmaster of Helston Grammar School, after Derwent had left, from 1843–47. In 1848 he became a Vicar in Berkshire and in 1863 opened a private school at Winton House in Winchester. He kept a journal during the period 1832–36 which throws some light on the school and the Coleridge family at that time.[1]

On 20 February 1833 (Ash Wednesday) Johns recorded that he walked with Derwent to the Loe Bar – Wednesday afternoon was a half-holiday. There was a storm, with mountainous seas. They were surprised by the waves and got wet up to the knees several times; this must have been a refreshing antidote to Derwent's desperate pleas for preferment.

A few months later, on 30 October 1833 Johns recorded the arrival of two new pupils: 'Mr Coleridge went to Penryn and left me to act as guide to Mr Kingsley, a clergyman from Clovelly who had brought two sons to school. A lovely day, Mr Kingsley and his sons very fond of Natural History with every branch of which they had some acquaintance without being adepts in either one. Returned to dine with Mrs Coleridge . . .'

These boys were Charles Kingsley, future author of *The Water Babies, Alton Locke* and *Westward Ho!*, then aged 14, and his brother Herbert, then aged 13. On 2 December Johns recorded that Kingsley Major had violent English cholera, which caused alarm – he was ill for a week and Johns sat up with him half of three nights.

On 8 March 1834 Derwent wrote to Mary from Exeter, where he had gone to make enquiries about a new job. Dr Colyer was

[1]Now in the County Records Office, Truro. DD X. II.

proposing to make him 'Master of the Lower School' but there was no certainty of his succeeding to the headmastership.

On 29 March 1834 Derwent wrote a long letter to his brother-in-law Henry Nelson Coleridge, which reveals the full extent of his worries about Helston.[1] He had given up all thought of the Exeter business. 'I am too sensible of the many inconveniences which must attend removal from this place.' Presumably Derwent meant that he did not know how he could pay off his debts in Helston, as he went on to say he could not look for pecuniary assistance from his own family, from his wife's, from the Bankers there, from any private friend – 'for where could I apply without risking the mortification of a refusal?'

His fears about Helston, he said, were partly general and partly particular. The catchment area of the school was very small, so the least accident could convert success to failure – 'add to which that I have to beat up against a constant Tradewind setting N. E. – and which not only prevents my ships from coming to harbour, but is forever carrying them from their moorings when they are there, and in the event of mishap might sweep off the whole fleet'. In other words Helston School, in the remote south-west peninsula, was ill-placed to compete with schools like Harrow, Eton, Rugby and Repton in much more populated and accessible parts of the country. Johns in his diary for 3 April 1833 mentions Vivian, an old pupil now at Harrow.

Derwent went on to detail the particular worries which had beset him of late. 'At the beginning of last half the younger Wright brought from his father's ship an inveterate species of Itch or Scurvy'. The disease was confined to the Wright brothers and the younger Treweek in school, but

> I can find no words to express the vexation, loss and inconvenience which have flowed from this source. The two Wrights have left school. Two of the servants caught the infection – we had to send them to Falmouth for sulphur baths about 2 weeks ago. It would take a little volume to describe what we have gone thro – the purifications, the correspond-

---

[1] Derwent Coleridge MSS. HRC, Texas.

ence, the medical consultations, the visits ... Our loss, to say nothing of anxiety, is most serious, nor are we able to calculate the extent of the mischief which it has done.

Then comes a new light on the Kingsley brothers.

This is not all. The Clovelly connection from which we expected so much has proved hitherto a source of annoyance scarcely exceeded by what I have just detailed. The elder Kingsley is a sort of Montagu, without however his fierceness – in short, half mad. The younger is a thief and a liar, and a runaway. He stole two silver spoons, battered them and sold them to different silver smiths, and on being detected, took himself off, and was within an ace of getting aboard one of Don Pedro's recruiting vessels. He was out all night: and three people after him. His Mother instantly came down, and as it appeared that expulsion would not merely have ruined the boy for life but killed his Father (who is subject to perilous attacks in his head) I was obliged to accept his submission and provide for him as I best cd by confinement, heavy impositions etc.

This letter is an interesting supplement to the idyllic account of Charles Kingsley's schooldays at Helston given by his wife in *Charles Kingsley: His Letters and Memories of his Life* published in 1876. She does however quote a letter from Charles Kingsley's old school friend at Helston, the Reverend R. C. Powles, in which he recalls that one of Charles' favourite performances was to jump from the playground wall across the deep lane to the wall opposite. 'The walls, which were not quite on a level, were rounded at the top, and a fall into the deep lane must have involved broken bones.'[1]

Luckily young Charles had a passion for botany and geology and Derwent largely kept him out of mischief by sending him off with C. A. Johns on long plant-hunting expeditions in the Lizard peninsula. According to his friend Cowley Powles, Charles also had

[1]Op. Cit. Vol. I p. 25.

a passion for art. He wrote to a friend at the age of 16: 'I love painting. They and poetry are identical – the one the figures, the other the names of beauty and feeling of every kind.' One is reminded of Derwent's lecture to the Athenaeum in 1825 on the Nature of Poetry – 'My subject nominally is Poetry, but nearly as much about painting as about anything else. The real subject is what is common to all the fine arts.'[1]

While at Helston Charles Kingsley wrote poetry and stories based on his love of nature and of the surrounding countryside; the encouragement he received from Derwent and C. A. Johns to appreciate the natural world was deeply formative. He wrote to his mother frequently that he was very happy at Helston. In 1836 his father was appointed Rector of St Luke's Chelsea, and Charles had to leave Helston at the age of 17 and was sent to King's College, London for two years before going up to Cambridge. In 1876 his widow wrote: 'It was a great grief to Charles to leave the West Country and the society of those who were all ready to help him in his botanical and geological studies, and in picking up the old traditions of the neighbourhood. The parting with his dear friend Cowley Powles, the loss of the intellectual atmosphere of Mr Coleridge's house and his valuable library, and, above all, of the beautiful natural surroundings of both Helston and Clovelly, was bitterly felt.'[2] Derwent had given him a good grounding. At the end of his first year at Cambridge he was first in classics and mathematics and chose as his prize 'a fine edition of Plato in eleven volumes'.[3]

In 1864 Charles Kingsley wrote to Mary Coleridge:

But I feel more and more how much I owe to you and Mr Coleridge; for your human kindness and forbearance at a time when I needed them very much: and for his [tact] in putting me in the way of books and thoughts which I could not have fallen in with at a common school, and which have been of quite inestimable use to me, as putting me, from the time I was 17, before the thought of my generation instead of behind it, like

[1]v. supra page 61.
[2]Op. Cit. Vol. I p. 37.
[3]Op. Cit. vol. I p. 43.

most public school boys. Believe me, I shall ever look back with gratitude on the years which I spent under your roof.[1]

In a letter to Mrs Kingsley in 1874 Derwent recalled that when he last saw Charles Kingsley in 1874 'he flung his arms about my neck, exclaiming, 'Oh! my dear old master! – my dear old master!' nor was he less affected at the sight of Mrs Coleridge'.[2] Kingsley's lifelong friend Cowley Powles afterwards became Fellow and Tutor of Exeter College, Oxford.

The unfortunate Herbert Kingsley died at school on 19 May 1834 from heart failure. In the words of R. C. Powles: 'Herbert had had an attack of rheumatic fever, but was supposed to be recovering and nearly convalescent, when one afternoon he suddenly passed away.'[3] He is buried in Helston Churchyard.

Derwent's letter of 29 March 1834 to cousin Henry concluded on a sombre note: 'other boys have left – the numbers diminish – the rumour gets abroad that the school is declining. Boys themselves feel inclined to rat etc. etc. – and all this without the smallest power on our part either to prevent or to check the evil. Against this I have to set the probable effect of the New Buildings, which will be truly beautiful and which will enable me as it were to begin again and this is at present the sheet anchor of our hopes.'

[1]Op. Cit. p. 24.
[2]12 December 1874. MS at Cornell University.
[3]Op. Cit. p. 26.

Chapter 3
The New School and Family Life 1834–39

The new buildings, completed at the end of 1834, were a gamble which, for the time being, retrieved the fortunes of the school. The plans[1] were drawn up by George Wightwick, the Plymouth architect, with much consultation and advice from Derwent. Instead of the old school building at 47 Coinagehall Street, a new schoolroom was built attached to the Master's house and lying back from Wendron Street, with a large Tudor Gothic porch and 'shoe house' adjoining. A school library was built, leading out of the schoolroom, and next to this a porch which opened onto the school dining-room. Over the new school-room, two new dormitories were built, and an assistant's room over the school library and an oriel room next door. The master's house was also enlarged, with two new bedrooms and a dressing-room, and downstairs an entrance-hall, second kitchen, butler's room and store-room. There is an undated letter from Derwent to Wightwick, saying he is 'mightily puzzled in regard to this Inscription – where to set it up . . . Also, whether to have the two parts of the Inscription on the same, or on separate slabs . . .'[2] He goes on to give pencil sketches of Tudor

---

[1]Now in the possession of Mrs Mary Coleridge.
[2]Derwent Coleridge MSS. HRC, Texas.

chimney-pieces and says in the P.S.: 'That my chimney-piece shd have formed the groundwork of your working drawings, I consider a compliment, being a first attempt...'

The inscription in Latin was eventually put on separate slabs, which are still to be seen on the walls of the old building, now the Godolphin Club. Only the entrance porch of the school (which is now used as a beer-cellar by the club) and the two side walls remain. The building has been gutted and reconstructed inside. The first tablet, being translated, states:

> The Helston Grammar School, endowed with the annual sum of twenty marks through the past centuries, has revealed the name of its founder in no records, as it seems. Let us honour the unknown founder with due reverence.[1]

This tablet is on the wall of the main room of the club, which is the site of the school dining-hall. The second tablet may be translated as:

> The Town Council, in whose hands lie the patronage and preservation of the school, in conjunction with a large number of old pupils and supporters of the school, who contributed to the expenses, ordered to be erected, in the year of our Lord 1834, this building intended for the purpose of educating boys in Greek and Latin literature, and in all other subjects that pertain to a pious, happy and cultured life, when the old building, situated for a long time in the lower part of the town, seemed too small for the number of pupils.[2]

This tablet is on the wall of the lounge bar of the club, which is the site of the school-room.

Henry Nelson Coleridge was able to visit Helston from time to time, as a barrister on the Western circuit. On 5 September 1834, he wrote to Sara from Helston: 'Mary is looking delicate – active and in

---

[1]H. Spencer Toy. The History of Helston. OUP, 1936. p. 356.
[2]Op. Cit. p. 358.

good spirits, but without proper colour and her face is thinner and more trenchant than it used to be. Derwent is not looking delicate and fragile at all but he is dull and out of order. He is full of the details and final effect of his new erections, all of which seem very well arranged and likely to give a totally new character to his school.'[1] Derwent had 23 boarders and hoped to increase this to 33. 'Today I was hearing 2 classes in Greek – they did exceedingly well – the first class quite equal to their co-equals at Eton. He sat with me and I could see that his tuition is very searching and accurate . . . I like little Derwent much . . . broad and stout and very active and, speaks excellent Cornish.'

He had a long walk the day before with Derwent to the bar and back via Porthleven. He felt that the distance seemed no complete objection to their sending their son Herbert (then four years) to school in Helston at about eight years old – 'the advantage of Derwent's tuition would be very great and some sacrifice might be made for it', though he expected he would feel differently about the distance in London.

> Derwent wishes to have the names of some of his family amongst the benefactors of the school, to be inscribed in the school room – I think I shall give something to gratify him. What a pity it is that the distance takes from him the chance of the boys of the third generation being sent to him, as they wd be otherwise.

Henry resumed on 7 September: 'The town have forced him to put the ornamental stone-cutting into the hands of some people of the place – inadequate workmen – after dinner yesterday we were called out to see an almost finished spandrel of an arch – cracked right thro. D. says it is all on him and he worries himself more than enough, I think, about it . . . I think he might be content with less exquisiteness of execution, but he thinks his reputation as an architect is at stake.' Derwent's enthusiasm for all he undertook had been transferred to architecture and he was quite incapable of economising when his enthusiasm was aroused. 'D. spends money

---

[1]Coleridge papers. HRC, Texas.

liberally in books and his other elegant pursuits,' Henry continued, 'but I think as he has no patrimony – nor his wife – he ought to try to diminish the capital of his debts and to insure a small sum for his wife and child – happy for him that he has not had a child per annum.'

Henry concluded that he began to think differently of the scheme of asking Hartley to Helston. 'Derwent would assign him a nice room in the new building and on occasion he might help greatly in polishing up a boy's scholarship – and this wd take off a sense of dependency. I really think it might be tried, if D. can go for him...' Since the departure of Sara and his Mother from the Lake District Hartley had at first turned increasingly to alcohol and to a wandering life and then after a year in Leeds, where he produced a volume of poetry and a series of biographies of northern worthies, he returned to Grasmere in 1833, where he lodged with a kindly widow and led an aimless life writing occasionally and largely dependent on contributions from his mother and the charity of friends. Sara and Derwent worried a great deal about him. When Samuel Taylor Coleridge died on 25 July, he enjoined them in his will: 'My dear children, love one another!'

In August 1834 Mary invited Hartley to visit them for a few months 'in the spring of next year', but the scheme was not carried out, possibly because Derwent could not 'go for him'. He had been longing for years to revisit the Lake District, but could not afford the time or the money. It may well be that Hartley, pathetically lacking in self-esteem, refused the offer. He received no encouragement to accept from Sara or his mother. Sara wrote to him: 'goodbye my dear brother. I wish we had a chance of seeing you soon. But I think of you with pleasure in that lovely vale, sometimes with more pleasure than of dear D. – whose twofold profession with its twofold anxiety and demand upon the sensibility sometimes gives me anxious thoughts.'[1] Mrs Coleridge added, 'Mary calls your letter to Derwent "A deeply affecting, heart-softening Letter" – she talks of asking you in the spring, of going down to Helleston – but I think I am happier when you [are] at Grasmere, considering all things.' Despite Mary's many responsibilities in the domestic arrangements

---

[1] Quoted in Blunden E. and Griggs E. L. Coleridge 1934. p.231.

of the school, the care of her husband and son, and the entertaining of visitors, she sewed shirts for Hartley, using measurements received from Sara.

Sara wrote disapprovingly to Henry: 'Dear Derwent's anxiety about architecture is a pity – he divides his energies into two [sic] many channels instead of bringing them into one grand reservoir where they may both present a more imposing aspect and possess a greater force. Persons who succeed in the world without moulding themselves on the world's model are those who command attention by doing some particular thing thoroughly well: a crowd of minor achievements pass for nothing, or convey only the notion of a studious idler.'[1] Derwent, however, found that architecture fascinated him and he followed this interest with his usual enthusiasm.

Towards the end of 1834, he sent Wightwick a carefully drawn detailed plan for a complete reconstruction of the Master's House as a Gothic miniature mansion with vaulted ceilings and a grand library, with shafts supporting the groining ribs and arched recesses for books all around the walls.[2] 'I have completed a formidable sheet of drawings for your inspection', he wrote, '– some of which I think you will honour with a nod of approbation – I do not however intend to [be] my own Architect in any degree, even if I could flatter myself that I had partially succeeded ... I do not regret what I have done, as it has amused me for the time and given me, I think I may say, considerable insight into a very elegant and interesting branch of art ... The most creditable course for a person of Architectural taste is always and in all cases to employ an architect...'[3]

A drawing of a new elevation for the Wendron Street frontage of the Master's House in a modified Tudor Gothic style is labelled 'Helleston – April 20th 1837. Geo. Wightwick and Derwent Coleridge Arch'...'[4] There are panels over the windows framing the Coleridge family motto 'Time Deum – Cole Regem' and the date MDCCCXXXIX in the middle. There is no evidence that this

---

[1]Coleridge papers. HRC, Texas.
[2]Now in the possession of Mrs Mary Coleridge.
[3]Undated. Derwent Coleridge MSS. HRC, Texas.
[4]Now in the possession of Mrs Mary Coleridge.

was ever built – funds would not run to it. Derwent also used the family motto on his seal at Helston – an indication of his pride in his father's name.

Derwent certainly made the best of what life allotted to him. Sara, writing to Miss Emily Trevenen in the summer of 1833 remarked: 'His accounts of everything belonging to him, both external circumstances and his own state of mind are very gratifying to us – and the more so as he is not without his crosses and anxieties. If his state had been unusual prosperity and exemption from care we might have feared a turn of the wheel. But now we see that his felicity is chiefly owing to his happy temper and the wise regulation of his mind and these will avail him come what may.'[1]

A letter to Southey on 11 September is on a double page spread of which one page is the programme of the annual school meeting:

Helleston Grammar School
School-Meeting September 24th, 1834.
Examiner – Winthrop M. Praed, Esq. M.A., Late Fellow of Trinity College, Cambridge.

Subjects for examination on 23 September included works of Greek and Latin classical authors. On 24 September, immediately after divine service, 22 boys gave recitations, including passages from Æschylus, Cicero and *Julius Caesar* (Act I, Scene ii) by Kingsley, and passages from Horace, Theocritus and *Paradise Lost* by Powles. The recitations were given in the upper room of the National School, which still stands at the churchyard gate.

On 8 November 1834 Mrs S. T. Coleridge wrote to Thomas Poole: 'Derwent is delighted at having 2 London Boys in his school – a brother of the Judge's[2] is about to send a Boy of 14 – in consequence of the report of Mr and Miss Powles – who have visited Helleston this last summer, and have a big Boy in the school.'[3]

At the close of 1835 the *Saturday Magazine* (published by the

[1]9 June 1833. Coleridge papers. HRC, Texas.
[2]i.e. Judge Patteson who was married to H. N. Coleridge's sister Frances.
[3]Ed. S. Potter. *Minnow among Tritons.* p. 183.

133

S.P.C.K.) carried an article on 'Grammar Schools in England' by 'C', written by Derwent.[1] He spoke of the need for more attention to the ancient grammar schools as a means of promoting the education of *all* classes – middle and lower. Their tradition was a source of strength even if in decay at present. Local association attracted local involvement and support, e.g. the loyalty of past pupils. The greatest general improvement was to be anticipated 'from the efforts of local people interested in the welfare of the school, rather than from state laws, which can never meet the varying needs of particular cases'. Their decay and misuse of their funds was not inevitable, but the result of public neglect. What was needed was to make the existing machinery work properly 'as in several of the most important corporation schools in recent years'.

He illustrated his points by reference to Helleston Grammar School. Derwent describes how the school has now been rebuilt 'in a very superior style' by Mr George Nightwick.[2] He described Helston as 'a clean, quiet and highly respectable town ... the remarkable salubrity of the climate may occasionally draw pupils from a distance'. There is a meeting of 'gentlemen who have derived any part of their education from this school' annually on the first Wednesday after St Matthew and it is 'very largely attended'. At the same time the pupils undergo public examination and prizes are awarded.

W. F. Collier, who entered Helleston School as a pupil in 1836, wrote an article for *The Cornish Magazine* in 1899, entitled 'Helleston Grammar School under Derwent Coleridge'.[3] He recalled Derwent as a staunch advocate of Latin in mental training. He described him as 'a handsome, brisk little man, with a fine head and face, and a good manly figure'. There were no class rooms, but a large school-room, with oak desks, and a small library attached to the school-room – 'not his own well-furnished library' – where he took his own classes, his 'den' ... 'I well remember really enjoying lessons in Homer and Virgil with him', though the writer was no scholar, except in mathematics. The cane was a 'formidable weapon

[1] *Sat. Mag.* 19 December 1835. No. 222.
[2] Evidently a misprint.
[3] *The Cornish Magazine.* Feb. 1899. Ed. A. T. Quiller-Couch.

Helston Grammar School, 1835.
(By permission of Mrs Mary Coleridge)

of large size' but Derwent seemed to dislike using it 'and struck all the harder on that account'. He used to leave it on the chimney-piece in the school-room. Boys cut off ends 'to smoke' until it became so short that it was replaced by a new one, without comment – 'he hated the sight of it'. His wife was 'a fine, handsome, clever woman'.

The house was linked with the school-house by a small court, and there were guests of repute, of whom the boys heard. C. A. Johns was second master and was devoted to botany and natural history. The writer thought he was not a good teacher – his lessons were not as interesting as Derwent Coleridge's. He took the older boys out for field-work on holidays and half-holidays. There was a third master – a local man who taught writing and mathematics – 'quite an inferior person, of a benevolent and fine temper, kind and gentle'. The boys went to church services on Sundays.

Collier went on to recall that the boys had much freedom, with half-holidays on Wednesday and Saturday, and whole holidays on Saints' days. They went out in pairs – never singly – and had to put their names and destination on a slate. They played cricket on Helston Downs and Canon Rogers of Penrose House allowed them access to the Loe Pool where they went fishing.

The eighth of May is still observed in Helston as 'Flora Day', an eighteenth-century refinement of the medieval 'Furry Day', probably derived from the old Cornish word 'fer' meaning 'a fair'. In the Middle Ages Furry Day was a people's religious festival, the eighth of May being the Feast of the Apparition of St Michael the Archangel, who is the patron saint of Helston. W. F. Collier tells us that when he was a boy at Helston School in 1836 the boys went out early on Flora Day to fetch branches in leaf and spring flowers to decorate the school-room and the playground. Later in the day the boys joined the dance of the gentry through the town, through the front door of Derwent Coleridge's house, through the playground and the school-room and out at the school entrance. The same dance was performed later by first the tradespeople and finally the working class. In the evening there was a ball at the Angel for the gentry and visitors.

Soon after Derwent had arrived in Helston he wrote to Mary about Flora Day: 'The Methodists here lock up their doors and the children are bribed with dainties to stay all day in the meeting house: Mr Daniel[1] (a puritanical vagabond, as James calls him) used to lock up his boys or carry them out of town during the festival, than which ... nothing can be more innocent. I like these celebrations; they tend to soften the asperities of life, with music and good humour, and to connect the present with the past.'[2]

W. F. Collier concluded his account of his school-days at Helston by describing the examination every year; the visiting examiners included Kenneth Macaulay (brother of J. H. Macaulay). He described the prize-giving and speeches, including an acting by the senior boys of a House of Commons debate, in which they played the parts of Fox, Pitt, Sheridan and Burke, trained by Derwent Coleridge. Collier said they had visiting teachers of French and dancing and also mentioned that boys came to Derwent Coleridge from London and other distant parts.

Sarah Fox, wife of the Quaker Charles Fox of Perran, who herself came from Ulverston and who knew Hartley Coleridge well, wrote to him in 1833: 'Thy Brother seems to be prospering in all his undertakings – he is admired and beloved and his school is in great repute. His beautiful taste, and his bright and varied mind make even drudgery charming.'[3]

The demands of the school had become so great that Derwent was obliged to give up the curacy. He wrote to Moultrie on 2 November 1834: 'I am completely detached from the Pastorate, having resigned all the emoluments, and with them the name and responsibility of this part of the clerical office. A lectureship, which I retain, is fully as much as I can render compatible with my other avocations ... I can do little more than communicate the common truths of Christianity, as they are commonly represented.'[4] He was delighted that Moultrie had returned to writing poetry; his own busy life had left him no time for versifying. 'I believe myself contrary to what is usually thought of me to be a man of more judgement than fancy, of more logic than invention, of more taste than genius.'

[1]Derwent's predecessor as Lecturer and Schoolmaster.
[2]19 February 1827. Derwent Coleridge MSS. HRC, Texas.
[3]1 September 1833. Derwent Coleridge MSS. HRC, Texas.
[4]Derwent Coleridge MSS. HRC, Texas.

At the age of 34 Derwent had achieved a fair degree of self-knowledge. From infancy he had been encouraged to believe that to be a poet should be his highest aspiration, but his experience as a clergyman and schoolmaster had taught him that his talents were of a more practical kind.

Henry Coleridge was at Helston again in October 1835. He wrote to Sara[1] that the boys had given Derwent a very handsome silver salver, two feet in diameter, with a free-standing border of leaves and daffodils. It was engraved with the Coleridge crest and with the inscription:

Reverendo Viro

Derwent Coleridge M.A.

Scholae Hellestoniensis

Magistro

Ingenii Morum Curae

Non Immemores

Magni Amoris manus exiguum

Discipuli

Gratis Animis

Dant

M.D.CCCXXXV

This may be translated as: 'To the Reverend Derwent Coleridge, Master of Helston School, his pupils, not forgetful of his talents, goodness and solicitude, with thankful hearts give this small

---

[1] Coleridge papers. HRC, Texas.

present of great love, 1835.' Henry wrote to his wife, 'The inscription reads well, although there is a little ambiguity in one word, as I felt when composing it.' The pupils had evidently let Henry in on their secret.

In April 1836 Derwent was involved in some negotiation regarding Harrow School – possibly with regard to running a house there – but he wrote to Henry Coleridge that he was not sorry that it fell through – 'I am indeed perfectly comfortable, and like my mode of life quite as much as any other which is at all likely to fall to my lot'.[1] Henry had written to Sara from Helston in December that the school was clearly prosperous, with several boys coming and none going. The new buildings had, for the time being, made the school successful. Derwent continued: 'My real motive for looking out for change is that the profits are not large enough to save from to any considerable extent, and that it offers nothing to fall back upon in the event of broken health and declining strength.' That year he hoped to make £1150 after paying the masters and other school expenses, insurance and interest. If his present income continued he would be able to liquidate his debts in a few years ... For many years he had had to pay £100–150 p.a. to his predecessor (presumably Stabback) so had 'a great deal of leeway to make up'.

Derwent stressed that they were economising – he had sold his horse and cart, they had no piano, Mary had no watch. 'In books I have been more dispendious – but less than you may imagine.' He laid out £8–10 p.a. on books for the School. They saw no company and had scarcely even a glass of wine or spirits, though the former was daily on the table for his private pupils. 'I mention these facts, not merely in answer to your remark, but because I know that I have not so high a character for prudence, with some of my best friends, as I think I deserve.' The establishment was of necessity exceedingly expensive – a large house 'almost entirely to rebuild' and to paint, repair and furnish for a large family. Whereas the corporation and subscribers paid for the new school buildings, presumably Derwent had to pay for the additions to the Master's House. 'I am not very strong but never so far invalided as to absent myself from School or Church. At

[1] 10 April 1836. Derwent Coleridge MSS. HRC, Texas.

this moment I am very sick. What I suffer from is weakness of stomach, indicated by permanent apthae on my tongue, gums, lips and palate. Any uneasiness of mind brings them on at once.'

On 9 August 1837 Derwent wrote to his mother and Sara, 'The School is full beyond example – there are 31 in the House, besides our own family.' There were four pupils – Vivian, Tonkin Major and Minor and Damain (a Frenchman from Mauritius). These were young men whom Derwent was coaching privately for university. There were five 'parlour boarders' – Powles Major and Minor, Penrose, Paul and Elliot (a relation of Lord Minto's) – and 22 boys besides. Vivian and Powles were to leave at Michaelmas.

The pupils had their own rooms to sleep and sit in. The Coleridges' own son Derwent slept in his father's dressing-room. 20 boys slept in three dormitories, one in the portress's cottage and one at Mr Johns' lodgings. It had been necessary to make all the arrangements in the time since Derwent and Mary returned from their summer visit to London – 'what it has cost Mary in thought and labour I leave you to guess ... My time is overengaged – Damain, the Tonkins and Vivian require separate attention in addition to the School ... and the Exam is coming on ... Unluckily too I have had a worse feverish attack than I have had for many years, and narrowly escaped bleeding for the pain in my back, sides and epigastric region.' Young Derwent was well and growing fast – 'but poor fellow! I can do nothing for him at present, and he is obliged to take the run of the school.'

Sara, in her reply, said with reference to 'Dervy': 'Cannot you find someone to come and give him some special lessons in writing, arithmetic, Latin and the Greek grammar? Is he the youngest boy in the school? I believe you said he was.'[1]

Henry Coleridge was at Helston again that autumn and commented to Sara about Derwent: 'He seems much overworked.'[2] Derwent told Southey, 'I have to recommence teaching after tea, which exhausts all my remaining strength ... the absolute want of leisure must always be to me a serious deprivation.' He described the seventeen-year-old Auguste Damain from Mauritius – 'He is

[1]Coleridge papers. HRC, Texas.
[2]1 September 1837. Coleridge papers. HRC, Texas.

upwards of a hundred days' sail from his parents and has not a friend in England or indeed in Europe but ourselves … He is extremely intelligent and amiable … it is rather a delight to me to translate Horace and Virgil into <u>French</u>, when I am thoroughly wearied with their English travesty … I have introduced him to his own literature as well as ours, and have witnessed a Frenchman's first love for Racine.' Derwent went on to say: 'I have unguardedly engaged with Parker to bring out a volume of Sermons, for which he is to give me £75 – a serious undertaking under all the circumstances.'[1]

On 30 September 1837 Sara Coleridge wrote to her husband: 'A nice note from Mr Powles, but no letters from H. [i.e. Helston]. He gives a <u>most flourishing</u> account of the school. <u>Eton</u> and <u>Winchester</u> men who were present declared the school not [at] all inferior to those in which they were bred. School dinner attended by 61 persons, six more than were ever assembled before. Among them was Sir C. Lemon,[2] who expressed himself to Mr P— as well as publicly, quite surprised at the state of advancement in which he found the school. It was a brilliant affair altogether. Cowley comes tomorrow to King's College and will [ever re]member with gratitude his days at H.'[3]

On 27 September Henry Nelson Coleridge wrote to Sara that he would regret Derwent's ceasing to be Lecturer at Helston but at the same time he was not altogether surprised that the Vicar took exception to the appointment. 'Many clergymen dislike such appointments (emanating as they do from the parish only) as virtual interferences with their monarchy.'[4] This is a further illustration of the precariousness of Derwent's position at Helston.

Derwent gave up the lectureship in the autumn of 1837. On 13 November he received a parchment[5] with 169 signatures, including those of R. G. Grylls, H. Borlase, Jas Plomer, Glynn Grylls and Emily Trevenen stating:

We the undersigned Inhabitants of the Borough of Helleston

[1] 18 October 1837. Derwent Coleridge MSS. HRC, Texas.
[2] The County MP.
[3] Coleridge papers. HRC, Texas.
[4] Coleridge papers. HRC, Texas.
[5] Now in the possession of Mrs Mary Coleridge.

justly sensible of the manifold and great advantages derived to this Place from the abilities and exertions of the Reverend Derwent Coleridge since his residence amongst us cannot forbear to express our unfeigned regret and concern that any circumstances should have arisen to deprive us of his wonted valuable services in the Church.

These our sentiments we should have taken an earlier opportunity of manifesting to him, but for the Hope and expectation that something might have occurred which would have enabled him to resume his usual Duties among us. We now beg him to accept our best thanks for all his past Services, and to express our hope that he will continue them in future on every occasion which may present itself, tending to the Utility of the Borough or its Individual Inhabitants.

Dated Helleston 13th November 1837.

Derwent had certainly done a great deal in 11 years to build up the congregation in the church. The plan of the church in 1838[1] shows that at that time there were 445 appropriated sittings and 490 free sittings. Some of these sittings were in three galleries, one of which was built in 1837 to accommodate additional congregation.

This period had its family joys and sorrows. On 6 July 1835 Mary gave birth to a daughter – Emily Frances Gillman Coleridge. When she was five months old Henry Coleridge told Sara, 'She is one of the 2 or 3 really rememberably pretty babies of my experience.' Derwent wrote to Henry Coleridge on 10 April 1836[2]: 'As for that concretion of honey dew, whom I love and call by my own daughter's name, she is nectar and ambrosia to my soul. You shd see her sitting in her chair with her crub alias crust – a glorious benumblement! Or when she is put into her crib to go to sleep, willee, nillee – then when a well-known face peeps over, down goes the counter-pane and she bursts into a laugh of resolute wakefulness – or in the interregnum between waking and sleeping, with her little subucula[3] and nothing else on – but this is a father's talk.' Alas! baby Emily died two months later, on 13 June 1836. Mary's sorrow was

---

[1]Hanging in the north transept.
[2]Coleridge papers. HRC, Texas.
[3]Vest.

compounded by a miscarriage four months afterwards, on 14 October.

Robert Southey paid his long-awaited visit to Helston, together with his daughter Edith and his son Cuthbert in December 1836. Derwent wrote to Southey on 28 October about Mary: 'Her nerves have been much affected – her recent sorrow having been renewed in all its bitterness by the last event. She possesses however very considerable elasticity of mind and I am in hopes that your visit will be of great service to her.'[1]

Two days before Emily died, Derwent was writing to Joseph Cottle, the Bristol bookseller, having just heard that he proposed to publish a memoir of STC with letters from STC about his opium-taking. 'It cannot surely be necessary – it cannot I think be useful, or in any wise desirable – wd it even be delicate or proper – just to the sacred memory of the departed – kind to the feelings of the surviving relatives – that these letters shd be made public, more particularly in a Memoir referring to so small a portion of my Father's life, in which this feature must obtain so much more than its due relief?'[2] On 28 October Derwent wrote to Southey when he was staying with Joseph Cottle on his journey westwards, asking him to intervene with Cottle. Whatever the conversation they had, Cottle published in 1837 his *Early Recollections: Chiefly relating to the late Samuel Taylor Coleridge* in which he told the story of Coleridge's opium habit, which he regarded as moral cowardice, scorning James Gillman's view that it was Coleridge's chronic rheumatism which had led him into opium taking.

Southey and his children, Edith and Cuthbert, stayed with Derwent and Mary from about 16 to 23 December 1836. Southey had undertaken this journey to obtain some relief from the terrible strain of his wife's prolonged insanity and Mary wrote to Derwent's mother on 3 January 1837 after Southey had departed: 'always excepting Derwent's revered and saint-like Father he is the most striking man I ever saw – his noble form, his white hair, and the pathos in his voice was most touching. He was deeply affected at seeing Derwent.'[3]

[1]Derwent Coleridge MSS. HRC, Texas.
[2]Ibid.
[3]Derwent Coleridge MSS. HRC, Texas.

Despite their preoccupation with the school, Derwent and Mary had many social contacts. Their closest friend was Miss Emily Trevenen; Sara Coleridge wrote frequently to her, discussing Derwent and Mary as if she were a member of the family, and assuming she would pass on her letters to them. In 1835 Emily Trevenen wrote an improving book of verse for 'Dervy', entitled *Little Derwent's Breakfast*, subsequently published in 1839. It begins with a verse on

> Early Rising
> Up, up with the cock when he cheerily crows,
> When Nature awakes from her night's repose,
> He calls the farmer – 'Come guide the plough' –
> He calls the maiden – 'Come milk the cow'
> Up, little Derwent, away, away!

There are verses on all the ingredients of the breakfast table and their origins, with morals drawn from them. The book concludes:

> To D.M.C. on his Birthday
> I've loved little Derwent through many a year,
> Since first a blithe prattler he sat on my knee,
> And asked a new tale or a story to hear
> And he was a dear little Derwent to me,
> Oh may I but see him repay the fond care
> By parents now lavished to guide him aright,
> May he merit their love, and respond to their prayer,
> Then Derwent will ever his parents delight.

Besides dinners with Emily Trevenen and the various members of the Corporation, there were many exchanges of visits with various branches of the Fox family, Quakers who lived in and around Falmouth and who had intellectual and cultured interests. Caroline Fox, who kept a remarkable journal, visited the Coleridges in 1835, when she was 16. 'Papa and I', she wrote, 'spent the evening at the "Derwent Coleridges" at Helston. It left a beautiful impression on us, and we visited the lovely little sleepers, Derwent and Lily, saw the library, and the silver salver presented by his boys, and, best of all, listened to his reading of passages from *Christabel* and other of his father's poems, with his own rare felicity ... Mary Coleridge was in all her beauty, and ministered to a bevy of schoolboys at supper with characteristic energy.'[1]

In 1839 Caroline recorded another visit to Helston when Derwent gave them some of his views on education. Derwent deplored the monitorial systems of Bell and Lancaster.[2] 'All mechanical systems he holds as bad: wherever they appear to act well it is from the influence of individual minds, which makes them succeed in spite of the system. To build up the intellectual man is the purpose of education.' He thought this was not effected by teaching science 'though he hopes he can appreciate this branch of knowledge too'. People must be taught to think. 'For instance, let him, instead of being taught the meaning of a word, search the lexicon and select from a number of synonyms the particular word which best suits his purpose.' Derwent's educational philosophy and devotion to the classics are evident in this description.

Derwent went on to criticise the Plymouth Brethren 'amongst whom, to his great vexation and grief, are many of his friends ... He spoke very civilly of modern Quakerdom.' He congratulated them on 'their preference for cultivation of the intellect', on their rejection of Puritanism and 'their peculiar appreciation of the good and beautiful in others'. She finished her account of the evening – 'He took us into his library, a most fascinating room, heated by a mild fire, just up to the temperature of our poet's imagination; coffee for one on a little table, a reading desk for the lexicon to rest on, and near it a little table covered with classic lore; in the centre the easy-chair of our intellectual man.'[3]

In 1840, at the home of her uncle and aunt, Charles and Sarah Fox, Caroline met Moultrie. 'Went to Perran to breakfast and found we had been preceded about five minutes by Derwent Coleridge and his friend John Moultrie ... Moultrie is not a prepossessing-looking personage – a large, broad-shouldered, athletic man, if he had but energy enough to develop his power ... but his countenance grows on you amazingly. J. Moultrie wrote a sonnet for me, illustrating the

[1] Caroline Fox. *Memories of Old Friends.* i.4.
[2] See pages 165, 166.
[3] Op. Cit. i.78.

145

difference between the sister arts of Poetry and Painting, and read it; his voice and reading a painful contrast to the almost too dulcet strains of his beloved friend.'

In July 1837 and again in July 1838 Derwent and Mary and young Dervy visited London. Derwent wrote to Moultrie in 1837 that he was hoping to meet him at Windsor or in London.[1] They were planning to stay for a week with Henry Nelson Coleridge and Sara at their new abode, 10 Chester Place, Regent's Park, and to spend the rest of their stay with J. W. Powles at New Bank Buildings, Princes Street, Bank. 'Our calls to London are those of duty, necessity and prudence – otherwise we shd stay at home for economy.' However, Derwent admitted: 'London has many attractions for me – Books, Pictures, Statues, Antiquities, Architecture, Intellectual Conversation – above all, kind and intelligent sympathies, old familiarities, and near and dear affinities – such are its charms for me – and they hold good in a measure for Mary.'

Sara Coleridge's letters to Emily Trevenen contain many references to Mary's beauty and goodness. In 1834 she wrote: 'Nothing but miserable illness could prevent Mary from appearing what nature originally [intended] her to be – a fine and brilliant creature ... She is more like the pretty Scotchwomen that I have seen than the English – And the handsome among the Scotch are very handsome indeed; she is a Highland Chieftain's daughter.'[2]

There had been a coolness between Derwent and John Moultrie, owing to a letter which Derwent wrote to Moultrie in 1834 after the death of Moultrie's infant daughter.[3] Derwent said that he had not written earlier because he felt it his duty to say things which might hurt, especially Margaret but 'I must adventure ... speaking as a parent I have felt that your grief has been excessive ... more particularly with regard to your Xtn profession. One of your cherubs is removed to a better world – the Lord who gave, hath taken away – it is a case of simple bereavement ... and this of an infant – an event so commonly attached to the married Life, as almost to be considered a natural contingent of that state ... Yet by

[1]11 June 1837. Derwent Coleridge MSS. HRC, Texas.
[2]Letters of Sara Coleridge, 1343. 27 April 1834. HRC, Texas.
[3]Derwent Coleridge MSS. HRC, Texas.

this single touch of affliction you say the whole course of your future years is darkened. Is this faith?' Religion above all 'is that which takes the sting from Death. If it does not this, it is nothing. You have the character of being decidedly religious people. Oh friends, show it now ... Forgive me this lecture ... I may not refrain from an unworthy fearfulness of giving offence.'

Evidently the letter did give offence. Writing to Moultrie on 11 June 1837, saying that he hoped to meet him in London, Derwent said: 'I hate even to allude to that other topic, which I think should be got rid of – as some folks would say of the National Debt – with a great big spunge...' Of course, by this time Derwent and Mary had themselves suffered a similar sorrow. Sarah Fox when staying at Bolton House, Bradford, wrote to Hartley Coleridge about the death of Emily: 'To part with such a one was a bitter grief to them, and admirably borne by both.'[1]

The letter which Derwent wrote to his mother after the death of her sister, wife of Robert Southey, contains much of his philosophy on life and death.[2] He trusted his mother would be spared to them many, many years – 'in no way will the allotted period, be it longer or shorter, be so happily or so profitably spent, whether for yourself or for those around you, as by your looking on life as but lent to you day by day – and each of those days but a postponement of that happier state of existence, when this clogging body shall no more vex the liberated spirit, or put out its light, or pervert or refract it'.

---

[1] 18 December 1838. Hartley Coleridge papers. HRC, Texas.
[2] 19 November 1837. Texas.

Chapter 4
The Scriptural Character of the English Church 1839

The volume of sermons, which Derwent had promised to the publisher Parker in 1837, was eventually published in the Spring of 1839 as *The Scriptural Character of the English Church*, a book of 480 pages, in the form of 18 sermons. Derwent wrote these sermons largely at night, after his pupils were in bed, and he points out in the Preface that he wrote under difficulties – away from books, away from the opportunity to discuss with friends, and with the distractions of running the school.

This was the only full-length book which Derwent wrote. He had literary aspirations all his life but the demands of his career as a clergyman and an educator prevented him from writing any other extended works. The book reflects Derwent's personal experiences of life and death, his visiting of the homes of all classes in Helston, his problems with the Methodists and the Evangelical movement and his growing belief in the Church as 'the great organ of public education'. The book is heavily influenced by the ideas of Samuel Taylor Coleridge. Derwent says in the Preface that he is 'indebted to the same source for his intellectual and natural life'.

Derwent was impelled to write this book by the concern about the future of the Church of England which he shared with many Anglicans in the 1830s. There were glaring abuses in the Established

Church – non-resident clergy, pluralities, great inequalities of income between many of the clergy who were actually doing the work and the advowson owners who were drawing the bulk of the revenue – and the ancient parochial system, based on a largely rural social structure, did not provide for the fast-growing population of the new towns. It was an age of reform, and the Established Church was feeling threatened by the erosion of its prerogatives by Parliament. The repeal of the Test and Corporation Acts in 1828 allowed Protestant Dissenters to sit in the House of Commons. The Catholic Emancipation Act of 1829 admitted Roman Catholics to the House of Commons. The Parliamentary Reform Act of 1832 abolished a number of rotten boroughs (enlarging the boundary of the Helston constituency and reducing its parliamentary representation to one MP, when it had been returning two members for more than five hundred years) and gave votes to the middle class. Tory churchmen feared that this would open the floodgates to drastic reform of the Church – Parliament might take over the Crown's ecclesiastical patronage, might confiscate Church property and even introduce disestablishment.

The Temporalities Bill of 1833, which proposed to abolish ten Irish bishoprics and redistribute their incomes to support the poorer clergy, was seen as the thin end of the wedge of Parliamentary interference in spiritual affairs and precipitated the Oxford Movement. A small group of Oxford clergy, led by Keble and Newman, in their *Tracts for the Times*, maintained that the bishops and clergy of the Church of England owed their authority directly to Christ, through the Church of the early Christian Fathers. They claimed the divine authority had descended directly from the apostles, through the laying on of hands. In fact the Church of England was reformed and made ready for renewed activity in the mid-nineteenth century. Sir Robert Peel set up the Ecclesiastical Commission in 1835, which took in hand the worst abuses in the Church, redistributed clerical incomes and created new parishes.

Apart from the fear of Parliamentary interference, Derwent felt another threat to the Church of England in what he regarded as the irrational excesses inspired by the Evangelical movement, with its largely Calvinist theology of justification by faith and predestination of only the elect to salvation. The people of his own parish obviously preferred the full-blooded rhetoric of the nonconformists to the Coleridgean rationalism of his own sermons. His distress was sharpened by the flight to the Plymouth Brethren of Henry Borlase, Vicar of St Keyne, who had married Caroline Pridham, Mary's cousin and confidante as a girl.

'The times are critical', Derwent wrote to Southey.[1]

It seems the English Church (amid much that is hopeful – assuredly she has girded herself for battle, and seems to be renewing her strength) is tending to Popery from both ends – on the one hand by an overestimate of – antiquity, ecclesiastical precedent, and sacerdotal ceremonial, – on the other hand by resemblances, more vital perhaps, tho' far less noticed. There is a legendary love floating about among the so called Evangelical Clergy and their followers, mostly unwritten and stimulated by the ambulatory bubble blowers by which the country is at present traversed, that will match anything to be found in Romish Hagiology – as fraudulent, as foolish and as false. I belong to the Bible Society – but to attend their meetings is indeed a severe penance.

He went on to recount some of the stories told at these meetings, for instance the tale of a boy who saved up 15 shillings and spent it on a gun instead of a Bible. The gun burst and the boy was killed, which the Bible Society regarded as evidence of the working of Providence. 'That a gun bought for 15/- shd kill the man behind, rather than the bird before it, is very credible – but do fatal accidents never happen to good people?' Another story was of a woman who gave a guinea to the Bible Society instead of buying a hive of bees. On her return home from the meeting she found bees swarming on her elm-tree, so that she was able to fill three hives and sold the honey for the benefit of the Bible Society. Remarkably, the bees refused to sting a visitor from the Bible Society. 'Could any begging Friar at a market cross have gone beyond this? ... and to this a roomful of young ladies, two laymen and a platform of "Ministers" most of them "of

[1] 18 October 1837. Derwent Coleridge MSS. HRC, Texas.

150

the Establishment" – listened for three mortal hours, with the liveliest expression of admiring edification.'

The Scriptural Character of the English Church reveals the extent to which Derwent's intellectual debt was to Samuel Taylor Coleridge rather than to the Oxford Movement. STC had a passionate admiration for the English Church, as a national institution and a very pure form of Catholic religion, as he reveals in *Aids to Reflection* and *On the Constitution of Church and State*. Derwent prefaces his book by a quotation from *Aids to Reflection*: 'My fixed principle is that a Christianity without a Church exercising Spiritual Authority is vanity and dissolution.' The book contains many other quotations from STC.

Derwent says in the Preface that the real divisions in the theological press at this time are between the spirit of Protestantism, regarding Christianity as a 'subjective act', asserting private judgement and emphasising that the Gospel is to be known through Scripture, and the spirit of Catholicism, regarding Christianity as an 'objective verity', limiting private judgement and emphasising that the Gospel is to be known through the Church and the sacraments. Derwent believes these are two aspects of the same idea. His central purpose is to reconcile the actual constitution of the Church, as seen from without, with its inward and spiritual form, as cognizable in Scripture.

He maintains that the Christian church as a whole has suffered from internal corruption, from which the Reformation marks the emergence. He sees the Church of England as an integral part of the national law and life – the church of the nation. Firstly, the Church of England is rooted in our past. Secondly, the church is the great organ of public education. The clergy have always been 'the general purveyors of intellectual knowledge – among the higher orders in the universities and great public schools' and among the poor 'in the crowded alley, and in the lonely hamlet. ... Whether this state of affairs shall be allowed to continue ... is a cause still pending at the bar of public opinion.' Thirdly, he argues that the church has a pastoral task – the maintenance of social order, the support of law, the spread of civilisation, the correction of public manners. Fourthly, the church promises 'a permanence of Glory' in the future. 'We should testify our attachment to our national and ancestral Church, that hallowed structure from which violent hands are with difficulty withholden.' Above all we should give in our daily lives 'a visible demonstration that the form of Christianity is not a mere system of outward observance, but a well of living water springing up with everlasting life'.

It was with this faith in 'a permanence of Glory' that Derwent and Mary met the sadness of the death of baby Emily. Derwent urged Moultrie and his wife to show similar faith when their infant daughter died. It was this faith which Derwent recommended to his mother on the death of her sister – 'we must all look forward and upward'.

He goes on to discuss Common Prayer. He concedes that in the extemporary prayers of a sectarian ministry can be seen much piety and ability, animated by the spirit of God in some cases, but this is a personal expression. In the Book of Common Prayer 'prayers and meditations are guided in their course ... by no casual or arbitrary directions ... but follow in the track of the Gospel'. It is entirely spiritual and entirely practical and comprehensive.

Next Derwent examines the duties of the clergy. He regards the clerics as trustees of 'a great national interest' and gives a long quotation from Coleridge's *Church and State*, Chapter VIII: '... The clergyman is with his parishioners, and among them, he is neither in the cloistered cell, nor in the wilderness, but a neighbour and family man, whose education and rank admit him to the mansion of the rich landholder, while his duties make him a frequent visitor of the farm-house and cottage...' Derwent was throughout his mature life deeply influenced by his father's idea of a 'National Clerisy' whose functions were 'to preserve the stores, to guard the treasures, of past civilisation, and thus to bind the present with the past; to perfect and add to the same, and thus to connect the present with the future; but especially to diffuse through the whole community, and to every native entitled to its laws and rights, that quantity and quality of knowledge which was indispensable both for the understanding of those rights, and for the performance of the duties correspondent' (*Church and State*, Chapter 5, Everyman Ed. 1972, p. 34).

There is a plea to Dissenters to return to the fold. 'Who are we that we should attempt to form or to recreate the Church of God? Let us reform ourselves ... The Church continues holy though Churchmen be impure.'

He regards bishops, priests and deacons as the final hierarchy from the Apostolic church, as confirmed and detailed eventually by St Paul. He describes the constitution of the Apostolic church as a gift from Christ himself, solemnly conferred upon mankind after his ascension. The Scriptures show this beyond controversy. He describes the Apostolic Commission as delineated in the Scriptures, quoting John xx.21: 'Then said Jesus to them again, Peace be unto you: as my Father hath sent me, even so send I you.' He sees the bishops as the direct inheritors of this divine commission. This view, of course, vests enormous authority in the bishops. 'The Kingdom of God is amongst us; the holy, the catholic, the apostolic Church of Christ, as eternally mirrored in his own gracious and glorious person, as authoritatively represented by the apostles, their associates and successors, as effectually identified with the whole body of believers . . . has come down to us in spirit and in power.'

The book is a mixture of close argument and rhetorical claims. It is on the whole very calm, earnest, sweet-tempered and non-fanatical, as Derwent tried hard to be fair to all points of view. Sara Coleridge commented: 'I wish it could be reviewed in a just and respectful way – but when one looks round the circle of periodicals it seems hopeless to select one in which a no-party book would meet a no-party reception.'[1]

Dr Thomas Arnold of Rugby wrote to Derwent strongly criticising the doctrine of the Apostolic succession, but acknowledging 'that you have maintained your own cause earnestly without harshness or contempt towards those who differ from you'.[2] In his later career at St Mark's Derwent sought to put into practice the education of the clerisy and to make the church a real means of public education, following the ideals which he expressed in his book.

---

[1]Sara Coleridge to Miss Emily Trevenen. 13 July 1839. Sara Coleridge letters No. 1379, HRC, Texas.
[2]13 April 1840. Derwent Coleridge MSS. HRC, Texas.

Chapter 5

The Final Crisis at Helston 1839–40

In the summer of 1839 Derwent and Mary were saddened by the premature death of W. M. Praed. He died of tuberculosis on 15 July just before his thirty-seventh birthday. Derwent was with him in his last hours at his house at Chester Square in London. This gay and brilliant young man had been called to the Bar in 1829 but entered Parliament as MP for St Germans, from 1830 to 1832, and later represented Aylesbury. Although his youthful sympathies were with the Whigs, he entered Parliament as a member of the Tory party. However, he retained considerable independence. 'I believe there is no man in the House more at liberty to follow his own inclinations.'[1] His last letter to Derwent, dated 29 May 1839, thanked him for his 'volume' (presumably *The Scriptural Character of the English Church*) and for Miss Trevenen's little book.[2] 'This morning, with your letter, I duly received your four petitions, which I shall be very glad to present. Our London Meeting on the Education Question was magnificent.'[3] He continued to attend Parliament until the middle of June. With his death Derwent lost one of his oldest friends, and one of the few with any influence in high places.

Despite Derwent's undoubted talent as a schoolmaster, the

---

[1] *Poems of W. M. Praed with a Memoir by Derwent Coleridge.* Pub. Moxon, 1864. p. XLVI.
[2] MS at Cornell University.
[3] See page 168.

financial problems of the school at Helston multiplied. The coming of the railways fostered the growth of many Victorian boarding schools. Sarah Fox, writing to Hartley in 1838, referred to 'the gridiron, which it is said this rail road island is fast growing into'.[1] But the railway did not cross the Tamar until 1859, and meanwhile the remote location of Helston was emphasised. Derwent began to resign himself to the inevitable and to plan for a future elsewhere. He wanted either the headship of a school within reach of the centres of population or a secure position in the Church, preferably a living, but failing this he was even prepared to consider another curacy. Sara wrote to Emily Trevenen late in 1839 of Derwent's 'curacy project' but nothing came of it.[2] In the same letter she mentions that Mary is expecting a child in the spring, but she must have had another miscarriage.

In March 1840 Derwent presented himself as a candidate for the headship of the City of London School. He prepared an impressive batch of printed testimonials.[3] The Professors of London University had to nominate three of the candidates for the headship. They selected Derwent, Beatson and Mortimer.[4] A committee of aldermen had to make the final appointment. A friend, Thomas Hellyer, wrote to Derwent, 'If you are returned [i.e. by the Professors] your friends must be alert immediately and canvass the Electors again and again until the final decision. A personal canvass on your part wd be better . . .'[5] Attached to Derwent's testimonials is a copy of a letter he wrote to the chairman of the Committee of the City of London School,[6] making a dignified protest at the manner of the appointment and withdrawing his name from the competition. He had been before the committee 'on Friday last' to protest that 'the contest was virtually decided before my canvass commenced'. He maintained that the final election should be by the committee alone and that the competitors should be strictly prohibited from

[1] 18 December 1838. Coleridge papers. HRC, Texas.
[2] 21 November 1839. Sara Coleridge letters No. 1380.
[3] Derwent Coleridge MSS. HRC, Texas. Headed 'London. Printed by Richard Clay Bread Street Hill 1840' and inscribed in handwriting 'Printed by order of the Committee'.
[4] Sara Coleridge to J. T. Coleridge. 25 March 1840. Sara Coleridge letters. HRC, Texas.
[5] 16 March 1840. Derwent Coleridge MSS. HRC, Texas.
[6] 31 March 1840. Ibid.

canvassing the electors either by letter or by personal visits previous to the election. Sara wrote to Emily Trevenen, 'We of course regret that my dear brother should have wasted any precious time and money on those detested cheesemongers and wholesale and retail gentry who did not know how a gentleman would set about canvassing or ought to be elected; but we trust that something much better than the Mastership of the City School is in reserve for D. and M.'[1] Sam Macaulay, brother of J. H. Macaulay, was Vicar of Hodnet in Shropshire, and Derwent evidently thought of a curacy there. However J. H. Macaulay wrote to Mary on 1 October that Sam 'can no more appoint a curate of Hodnet than an Archbishop of Canterbury'. It seems that the patron of the living was an imperious lady.

In the summer of 1840 Derwent and Mary and Emily Trevenen had a holiday on the continent, at the latter's expense.[2] On Whit Monday, 8 June, Derwent wrote to Emily Trevenen, who was staying with Sara and Henry, with plans for the trip.[3] He suggested they should go to Antwerp directly on the twenty-fifth, then on to Macklin, Brussels, Louvain, Aix-la Chapelle, Cologne, Coblenz (by the Rhine, with excursions), Treves and then Metz (by the Moselle) or Treves to Luxembourg. 'If there is any direct road from Luxembourg to Rheims and so to Paris, it would be glorious. We should certainly keep a fortnight for Paris, this being your first trip and Mary embegouinée[4] de la belle ville.' (Derwent and Mary had spent a week in Paris the previous summer with Mary Powles and her sister Emma.)[5] Derwent mentioned that he was recovering from 'another of my spasmodic bilious attacks, luckily now, and with Sunday and Whit Monday to recruit; I am now convalescent and the journey will quite set me up. Mary is in her best way – but wants change'.

Meanwhile affairs in Helston were moving towards the final

---

[1] 3 April 1840. Sara Coleridge letters No. 1383. HRC, Texas.
[2] Hartley Coleridge wrote to Henry Nelson Coleridge: 'Glad to hear that Derwent and Mary are recuperating on the Continent. Miss Trevenen must be a kind friend.' *Letters of Hartley Coleridge.* Ed. Griggs. p. 243.
[3] Derwent Coleridge MSS. HRC, Texas.
[4] Bewitched.
[5] Sara Coleridge to Anne Parrot. 12 June 1839. HRC, Texas.

crisis, as revealed in a long letter which Derwent wrote to Henry Nelson Coleridge on 30 September 1840.[1]

Certain it is that my temporal success is in an inverse ratio to the pains which I bestow, to the sacrifices wh. I make, nay to the effects wh. I produce. The general scholarship of the school was never so high as during the last three years. My boys are all doing well at university – their testimonials are loud and constant in my favour – nothing is neglected which can contribute to the health or comfort of the boys – I have first rate assistance – I am lauded to the skies – yet the school rapidly declines. Fully *four* times as many new boys used to come, year after year, than come now, so that unless the tide turn at Xmas I must quit at midsummer, or in the course of next year, and get rid of this expensive establishment. But where to go, or what to do?

I have now seen my 40th Birthday. I have been working for my bread ever since my seventeenth year, the interval of my college life alone excepted. For the last 13 years I have [been] labouring constantly in this place. I have made very great exertion, in many ways, both as a Clergyman and as a Schoolmaster, and now, if I can obtain a curacy with a tolerable House, I must trust to pupils for my livelyhood, with nothing remaining from my past labours but my character and perhaps my books and furniture – certainly a heavy load of debt. Do not mistake me – I am quite ready to do this – and to beg God's blessing on my endeavours. I am nowise disturbed at the prospect, but in a worldly sense, I do not think it a bright one. I had hoped for a <u>settlement</u> of some sort or other and an independent position before this. I never shrank from labour. But I am ill-suited to a subordinate situation. I tried it twice when a much younger man, and failed quickly and signally in both instances. I am too <u>individual,</u> especially as a theological thinker, to feel myself comfortable as anyone's lieutenant – and then the precariousness! ... lastly, my years are against me as an applicant for any but situations of

[1]Derwent Coleridge MSS. HRC, Texas.

considerable eminence. All others are given by preference to much younger men...

For myself, I am ready to do anything. Will you then talk the matter over with the Judge, and Mr Powles and any other reliable friends and see what can be done. A curacy with a good House in a fit situation for pupils, wd now be accepted by me without hesitation.

Henry Coleridge wrote to Sara that he had mentioned Derwent's case to John, James and George, who would bear it in mind.[1] John had renewed his offer to pay £50 p.a. towards Derwent Moultrie's schooling. Henry thought he should go into College at Eton. He told Sara that 'the great school at Brighton, kept by Dr Evered' was for sale. 'It is called the House of Lords. This is not Derwent's line.' J. H. Macaulay, who had been Head of Repton since 1832, wrote to Mary about the school at Brighton and suggested Derwent should offer £3,000 for it.[2] He offered to lend £500 himself 'if six friends will stand security'. In a later letter to Mary he was not so keen on the Brighton purchase.[3] He referred to Mary's mention of the possibility of their emigrating to the Cape of Good Hope: 'It would break my heart if you went there.' He wrote to Derwent that he had been staying at Leeds Vicarage with Dr Hook, who had a parish of 200,000 population.[4] He had hinted to him that Derwent might accept a living there. 'He would like your preachments and influence in Leeds, but he usually tries to promote his curates.'

There was another possibility, but it was not what Derwent really wanted. Since 1838 Henry Coleridge had been involved with other young Anglican laymen (including W. M. Praed) in a plan for the Church to train teachers for the children of the labouring poor, through a network of local diocesan training schools for teachers, with a national college at the centre. This plan was to be carried out through the National Society, founded in 1811 'for promoting the education of the Poor in the principles of the Established Church'.

[1]17 October 1840. Coleridge papers. HRC, Texas.
[2]October 1840. Ibid.
[3]Undated. Ibid.
[4]Undated. Ibid.

Sara Coleridge wrote to Miss Trevenen in 1838: 'My husband is much interested about schools and concerned with young Acland and sundry others in forwarding a scheme for spreading education on a better plan than has been hitherto adopted through the country: with normal schools etc. etc. By <u>plan</u>, I do not allude to the teaching <u>system</u>, but to the scheme for extending improved schools under the care of the clergy through the land, so as to counteract the Whiggish design of spreading education not based on any form of religion.'[1]

Derwent at first regarded the whole scheme with great distrust, fearing that the National Society intended to interfere with the independence of the ancient grammar schools. He wrote to Henry Nelson Coleridge:[2]

I am in sore perplexity as to your Education scheme – and should write about it for information had I time – Is it intended to invite Grammar Schools to unite? The terms of union are such as to make <u>me</u> hesitate – annual inspection? – the use of specified books in religious teaching? – You will agree with me that government by voluntary associations, tho' incorporated, is a wretched expedient, even when necessary, and well-managed. It is too monstrous to dictate to a clerk in full orders what books he shall put into the hands of fifth form boys to assist them in getting up their St Luke. Yet the questions put to me by Canon Rogers amount to this – will 'the conductors' of the 'higher' schools ... unite on the following terms – inspection, – church formularies – specified books. Now it seems to me, that when you have ascertained that a clergyman has an efficient control over a school, you have got at your want – everything beyond is a Prussian, Broughamy,[3] reprehensible interference.

National Education can only be conducted by the State itself

[1] 18 July 1838. Sara Coleridge letters No. 1376. HRC, Texas.
[2] Unfortunately only an extract from this letter (copied in Mary's handwriting into a notebook) survives in the Derwent Coleridge MSS. HRC, Texas, and it is undated. Judging by the content, it must have been written in 1838.
[3] Henry Brougham, now Lord Chancellor, had long campaigned for grants to education and Normal Schools, both administered directly by the State on a non-denominational basis.

unchurched – or by the State through the Church as its proper antithesis: but it must be the Church, as the Church, and not merely Clergymen, directed by an unecclesiastical body. Save me from my friends, however well disposed. We have had enough of this.

As I cannot but think that Ackland would emphatically approve of these two maxims, so I conclude that when I understand your plan, I shall find that I have been fighting a shadow.—

By 1840 the National Society had bought a house, Stanley Grove, in Chelsea, for their central college for training teachers, and they were looking for a Principal. As Derwent's financial affairs reached their final crisis at Helston, and his efforts to find another job were continually frustrated by his poor degree and lack of sufficiently influential backers, he was forced to consider the possibility of applying for the post of Principal of the new college.

Sir John Taylor Coleridge wrote Derwent a long letter on 13 November, 1840, summing up the possibilities before him. He did not like the Brighton scheme. At Derwent's time of life 'habits are formed – one point of your character I rather fear is the desire to do things in a handsome way without a sufficiently watchful eye on the return to be made by your outlay. I admit you were under the disadvantage at Helleston of beginning on borrowed capital – but you have been there a good many years, and I own the fact that your incumbrances have increased rather than diminished, has rather alarmed me with a view to the much greater temptations of Brighton ... the habit of living close to or beyond your income is a clinging one – and Brighton would be a hot-bed for it to grow in.'

With regard to 'the foreign scheme', banishment from home would be a heavy drawback, with no prospect of saving enough for an early return, and would involve separation from young Derwent at a crucial time or bringing him up in a foreign land. Of Chelsea he knew little – 'I doubt whether you would like your duties – you would find that you had but a third-rate material to deal with, and would seldom meet with the stimulant rewards which masters sometimes reap in the talents and distinction of your pupils ... you would not have the means of adding very much to your income ... On the other hand it has much to recommend it in its safety – its local situation – its putting you under the eye of the Bishops – and giving you clerical opportunities. If you think of it I fancy you have no time to lose.'

He offered to help all he could. However, his own choice would be a good curacy some 20 miles from London, where Derwent could take pupils. 'I need not repeat what I said about Derwent [Moultrie]. I shall be quite ready whenever it suits you to place him at Eton or any other public school – and I would not have you delay it a moment beyond your means.'

On 14 November Derwent wrote to Sara thanking her for her long letter 'which has given us all the light on the Training School that it seems possible to obtain through letters'.[1] He thought the whole scheme was 'in a plastic state, waiting for some hand to mould it into shape'. He wondered whether they would allow enough discretion and enough power to the proper man to carry it out successfully. A personal interview with the leading person on the Committee would be needed to discuss many points.

> If I undertook it, I should undertake it in right, good earnest – but then it must be made worth my while – e.g. by allowing an addition to the salary by Sunday duty, the care of a youth to live at my own table, etc. If I am a fit man for the situation they will do wisely to cede these points; for they can never secure good service by strict rules: if I am not prepared to do far more, and other, than any outline of my duties cd. aforehand tie me down to, I am not the man in whose hands it will succeed . . . I must be on the spot to ascertain the temper and expectations of my employers, before I undertake the task.

With his future career still uncertain, Derwent made plans to leave Helston. Then, on 18 December, his old friend J. H. Macaulay, died suddenly of a stroke. He had been Headmaster of Repton School since 1832 and he built it up from local to national status. Derwent immediately set his heart on succeeding him. On 28 December he was in London, staying with Mr Powles and wrote to

[1]Derwent Coleridge MSS. HRC, Texas.

Hartley at 10.00 p.m. 'This is the 10th letter which I have endited this write-long day.'[1] Evidently he had been writing in all directions for fresh testimonials. '– One of my ten letters is addressed to William Wordsworth, Esqre Senr...' It is touching to think of Derwent, with so much on his mind, sitting by the fire, late in the evening, writing a gently bantering letter to his wayward brother – 'My very dear Brother' – before retiring to bed. The following day he was off to Rugby by train, leaving Euston Square at 5.00 p.m. and reaching John Moultrie's rectory at 9.00 p.m. at a cost of £1 2s 0d.[2]

On 30 December he called on Bonany Price, Master of the Twenty at Rugby School, and obtained a testimonial. On 31 December he went by train to Derby where he booked into the Royal Hotel. On 1 January 1841, after a sleepless night, he went to Repton, saw Kenneth Macaulay, brother of J. H. Macaulay, and found the house admirable. He was taken ill after travelling in a very cold open carriage, but next day was up at a quarter to seven, caught the eight o'clock train from Derby to Birmingham, where he changed for London, and arrived at Euston Square at 3.30 p.m. On 3 January he called on H. Seymour Tremenheere, one of the newly appointed H.M. Inspectors of Schools, who had been an examiner at Helston, and who produced a testimonial dated 10 January 1841. He also obtained a testimonial from F. D. Maurice. On 4 January he was up at 5.30 a.m. and departed by coach for the west country. It took fourteen hours (without food) to reach Bridport. This underlined the contrast with rail travel and the main reason for the decline in the fortunes of Helston School. He arrived in Exeter at 2.00 a.m. and was up again at 5.15 a.m. Proceeding by way of Okehampton and Bodmin he reached home at 9.45 p.m.

Despite his tendency to bilious attacks, and psychosomatic illness when subjected to severe anxiety with no prospect of taking any action to cope with the worrying circumstances, Derwent had remarkable physical stamina. The day after returning to Helston,

[1]Ibid.

[2]Details of Derwent's movements from 29 December 1840 to 3 February 1841 are taken from his diary – 'Harwood's Improved Paper Diary' – which John Moultrie gave him on 30 December 1840. Derwent Coleridge MSS. HRC, Texas.

following all his travels and shortage of sleep, Derwent attended the Book Club dinner and then went with Mary to Glynn Grylls's concert, followed by a ball and supper. He reached home at 2.00 a.m. and Mary came back at 3.30 a.m. – 'the first time for many, many years – and the *last*'.

On 9 January Derwent packed his books and on the next day which was a Sunday he preached his farewell sermon to a crowded congregation. His text was from Psalm XC.12 – 'So teach us to number our days, that we may apply our hearts unto wisdom'. This sermon was subsequently published, at the request of a large number of the parishioners, and was sold at one shilling a copy, under the title *A Christian Minister's Account with Time. A Farewell Sermon.*

Most people let time slip by day by day until death, he said, but the thoughtful and speculative count the footsteps of time, step by step, as they fall. Few changes in life are more impressive than change of residence. 'We are led to number our days and settle our account with time.' This had led to the reflections of 'one, who having laboured among you during so many of the best years of youth and manhood, is now about to live and labour elsewhere'. His early enthusiasm was tempered by experience. 'What if riches, honour, power be withheld? What if even a moderate independence and provision for future years be still to be earned? What if the body be less active, the health less vigorous than it once was? What if friends and relations have been removed from us sooner, perhaps, than the ordinary measure of mortality had led us to expect?' There were Christian consolations for all this. His desire was to further 'the promotion of religious peace, in union with sound doctrine'. He saw the 'visible, historical and traditional Church' as the source of all Christianity. The future was 'a sealed volume' but 'we shall remain united in the Church till the last change come – the greatest but the last – when faith will give place to sight, – when God's true saints will be made manifest, and hope be swallowed up in enjoyment'.

That Sunday afternoon Mary left Helston at 3.00 p.m., together with young Derwent and the French pupil Damain. The following day Derwent paid a round of farewell visits. On 12 January 1841 Derwent left Helston at 6.30 a.m. and arrived in Plymouth at 6 p.m.

Six days later he and Mary, together with young Derwent and Damain, sailed from Plymouth in the steamship *City of Glasgow* for London and an unknown future.

PART V
Chelsea 1841–64

Chapter 1
Origins of St Mark's College

The 1830s and 1840s were the most disturbed decades of the nineteenth century, when England probably came nearer to revolution than at any later time. The squalid new factory towns contained a growing population, poorly housed, poorly paid, working very long hours and largely uneducated. In the countryside enclosures had created a large class of landless labourers, while the Corn Laws kept up the price of bread in the interest of the landowners. It was the time of the Reform Bill riots, of the first Chartist petition for universal suffrage in 1839, of agricultural riots and rick-burning, of Owenite socialism and the Grand National Consolidated Trade Union and the deportation of the Tolpuddle Martyrs in 1834 for attempting to form an agricultural labourers' union. In 1830 revolution in France overthrew the restored Bourbons, and the revolution in Belgium broke the peace settlement of 1815. To the governing class, the fear of revolution in England was very real.

Education had long been seen as a means of social control. Joseph Lancaster in 1798 had established his school in the Borough Road, Southwark, run on the monitorial system, whereby one master taught the monitors, or older children, who then taught the younger children. It was the division of labour and the factory system applied to education. Lancaster's friends in 1810 formed what became the British and Foreign School Society, whose aim was to encourage the foundation by local efforts of schools run on the monitorial system, giving non-denominational religious teaching. The Anglican followers of Dr Bell in 1811 formed the rival National Society for Promoting the Education of the Poor in the Principles of the Established Church throughout England and Wales. They encouraged local efforts in founding schools which gave Anglican religious teaching and were also run on the monitorial system.

Despite all the building of British and National Schools, a government enquiry in 1833 showed that only about one in eleven of the total population were attending day school.[1] In 1833 the House of Commons under the Whig Reform Ministry voted £20,000 to aid school building by the National Society and the British Society: this grant was renewed annually. But this only helped areas where the Societies were already active, as they had to meet half the school building costs themselves.

In the turbulent decade of 1830–40 education was increasingly regarded as vital for social control. Dr James Kay[2] wrote in 1839 'the critical events of this very hour are full of warning, that the ignorance – nay the barbarism – of large portions of our fellow countrymen, can no longer be neglected if we are not prepared to substitute a military tyranny, or anarchy for the moral subjection which has hitherto been the only safeguard of England. At this hour military force alone retains in subjection great masses of the operative population...'[3] He saw the main function of popular education as training in the accepted truths of political economy to enable the working people to understand the true causes regulating the distribution of wealth.

A growing body of Whig opinion wanted to see the state take the initiative, instead of the voluntary religious societies, to supply the appalling need in education. The Central Society for Education was founded in 1837 to co-ordinate the efforts of those who wanted to see a Central Board of Education, publicly financed, set up by Parliament. They wanted the Central Board to administer the

---

[1] Summaries of Returns to an Address of the House of Commons on Education 1833 PP. 1835 XIIII f.400.

[2] He became Kay-Shuttleworth on his marriage in 1842.

[3] An explanation of the aims of H.M. Government entitled *Recent Measures for the Promotion of Education in England*, 1839.

annual government grants and to set up a Normal School for training properly qualified teachers. They maintained that religious education should be separated from secular instruction.

These ideas were deplored by many Anglicans who believed that national education should remain the prerogative of the Established Church. They saw education for the poor as primarily the inculcation of revealed religious truth as contained in the liturgy of the Church of England. The initiative was taken by a small group of young High Church men much influenced by the Oxford Movement, who were determined to anticipate the Whig government plans for education under state supervision. The leading spirit was Thomas Dyke Acland, heir to the Acland estates in Devon and Somerset, and in 1837, at 28, the new M.P. for West Somerset.

Gilbert Farquhar Mathison (Melter and Refiner at the Royal Mint until 1848) came to Acland in February 1838 with a plan to forestall state action in teacher training, which was obviously crucial. He wanted to set up a network of local diocesan training schools for teachers, with middle-class schools to generate a supply of students, and to cap the edifice, he favoured the creation of a national training college in London to provide the best students with a higher education which would enable at least some of them to become deacons. The deacons would help the parish clergy as well as run the parish schools. Hitherto the only training of teachers had been short courses of two to six months at the Central School of the National Society in Westminster and at the British and Foreign Society's Schools at Borough Road, Southwark, where the main emphasis was on learning the monitorial system.

Acland drew together a group of interested friends, including Henry Nelson Coleridge, W. M. Praed and S. F. Wood, who decided to use the National Society as the chosen tool to put the plan into effect. In May 1838 S. F. Wood wrote to his friend Henry Manning: 'The National Society gulped our whole plan, accepted our services, and we are formed (together with certain members of the National Society, and chapter clergy . . .) into a committee[1] to carry out our plans.'[2]

[1]This was the Committee of Enquiry and Correspondence.
[2]E. S. Purcell, *Life of Cardinal Manning.* pp. 149–50.

In 1839 a Committee of Council was set up to administer any sums voted by Parliament for education. Thus a central authority for education was created by royal prerogative without seeking the formal approval of Parliament for a measure which would certainly have been defeated in the Lords.

Dr James Kay was appointed Secretary of the new Committee of Council, which very soon declared its policy. It proposed to found a 'Normal School' for the training of teachers with non-denominational religious teaching 'under the direction of the State and not placed under the management of a Voluntary Society'. It also recommended no further grants to schools without state inspection.

The National Society was incensed by these proposals and made plans for a special public meeting on 28 May at Willis's Rooms, St James's, to be organised by the Committee of Enquiry and Correspondence. In a preliminary address[1] the Society pledged itself no longer to limit its operations to exercising adults in the art of teaching but 'to undertake the superintendence of young persons who may appear to possess the natural requisites for teaching others, and endeavour to prepare them for receiving instruction in their practical duties, by a systematic course of intellectual discipline, and religious and moral culture'. This was the objective which the Committee of Enquiry had long desired and worked for, not merely the training of adult masters in 'the system', but the education of youths as a preliminary to teacher training.

Acland described the great National Society meeting of 28 May 1839 in a letter to his sister: '– on Tuesday our explosion about education took place in the shape of an immense public meeting, the place was so full that the Archbishop had very great difficulty in getting up to his place; he was accompanied by a goodly array of Bishops to the number of 16 or 20, and they all sat in the front row ...'[2] The Archbishop of Canterbury was in the chair and the Earl of Chichester moved the resolution, seconded by Bishop Blomfield:

That it is an object of highest national importance to provide

[1] *Address from the National Society*. 23 May 1839.
[2] A. H. D. Acland, *Memoir and Letters of Sir Thomas Dyke Acland*. p. 108. Privately printed 1902, London.

that instruction in the truths and precepts of Christianity should form an essential part of every system of education intended for the people at large, and that such instruction should be under the superintendence of the clergy and in conformity with the doctrines of the church of this realm as the recognised teacher of religion.

Another resolution called for exertion to raise subscriptions 'in order to furnish the National Society with the means of establishing a Training Institution'.

The outcry among churchmen, forcibly expressed in both Houses of Parliament, persuaded the Government to withdraw its plan for a State Normal School, and Sir John Russell announced on 4 June 1839 that the grant for normal schools would now go to the training schools of the voluntary societies. In February 1840 Dr James Kay and his fellow Assistant Poor Law Commissioner E. Carleton Tufnell, disgusted at the defeat of the proposed State Normal College, rented the old St John family mansion at Battersea and set up their own training college.

A minute of the Committee of Council in June 1839 announced that all building grants in future would be tied to state inspection. There followed a dispute between Church and State over inspection which lasted for more than a year. The National Society wanted to appoint its own inspectors and meanwhile refused any further government grants. It was not until July 1840 that the dispute was resolved by a compromise. Inspectors for the National Schools were to be approved by the Archbishop and could be suggested by him and dismissed at his request. Inspectors were to report to the Archbishop and Bishop as well as to the Committee of Council. Future grants were to be in proportion to the number of children educated and to the amount of subscriptions raised for school building. This ensured that between 1839 and 1850 the National Society received 80 per cent of all government grants to education.

Once the inspection controversy was settled the National Society at last felt able to renew their application for the £5,000 state grant and to go ahead with the Training Institution. In September 1840 the contract was signed for the purchase of Stanley Grove in Chelsea for £9,000.

A Principal for the Training Institution had now to be found. On 14 September the Rev. T. W. Allies, private chaplain to Bishop Blomfield of London, accepted the appointment as Principal but he later withdrew. Possibly his new wife disliked the prospect of sharing Stanley Grove with the students – on 22 October 1840 the School Committee noted that Mr Allies wanted the Principal's domestic establishment to be distinct from that of the pupils. It is likely that he was already in disagreement with Bishop Blomfield; he was an ardent Tractarian and eventually joined the Roman Catholic Church in 1850.

The National Society was obliged to advertise again for a Principal – Derwent Coleridge, who was by now desperate for a job, decided to apply. The extent to which Derwent and Bishop Blomfield differed in their assumptions about the Principal's role is clearly to be seen in a letter from C. J. London to Henry Nelson Coleridge dated from Fulham, 16 November 1840[1]:

Mr Derwent Coleridge is well known to me by reputation, and is [sic] volume on the Church is sufficient evidence of his talent and his orthodoxy. Of his scholarship there can be no question, but we do not require any considerable amount of scholarship, as the term is commonly understood, in the Principal of our Training Institution. What we want is, a stock of general information, with a taste for, and a knowledge of, the process of instructing those who are to be themselves instructors. It is important that the person who is appointed, should be acquainted with the elementary parts of mathematics – with astronomy, the use of the globes: and the principles of Natural Philosophy. How stands Mr D. C. in these respects?

I have made known his name to the Committee of the National Society, but I am not sure whether they have not gone too far with another candidate to be able easily to reject him.

On 17 December the School Committee read a testimonial from the Bishop of Lichfield in favour of the Reverend C. Lawson as

---

[1]Derwent Coleridge MSS. HRC, Texas.

Principal and from Sir Charles Lemon in favour of the Reverend D. Coleridge as Principal. But as we have seen, on 18 December J. H. Macaulay, Headmaster of Repton, died suddenly and Derwent threw all his efforts into succeeding him. On 21 January 1841 Derwent wrote from Mr Powles's house in London applying for the Headship of Repton with 13 completely new testimonials, dated late December 1840 or January 1841.[1] But it was not to be. On 3 February Derwent wrote in his diary, 'My appointment to the Principalship dates from this day. Repton decided in favour of Pill.' Thus, with equal reluctance on both sides, Derwent was appointed to the post which he was to occupy for the next twenty-three years.

Derwent's appointment as Principal of St Mark's came by one of the quirks of fortune which determined his career, but it was a turning-point in his life and in the history of education.

Derwent was now aged 40 and sobered by his experience as a clergyman and a schoolmaster in Helston. He had proved his ability as a teacher but the school had run into financial difficulties owing to its remote location. Although he had been teaching the sons of the middle class and the gentry he had learned a great deal about the problems of the working class as a conscientious clergyman paying regular visits to his parishioners, especially to those in difficulty. He had visited the sick and dying, baptised their babies and joined their Friendly Societies. He had started a National School for the children of the poor and run a Sunday school. He had made himself popular with all classes of society.

Derwent retained his *grandeur d'âme* and his enthusiasm for all he undertook. He now moved from the small society of Helston onto a much wider national stage. At St Mark's he was faced by a much bigger challenge. The new college was the first really national college for the education of teachers of the poor, as distinct from merely training them in the monitorial system. Derwent had to deal with the narrowly sectarian views of the Committee of the National Society and with the government, represented by the Committee of Council. He spent the next twenty-three years trying to use these bodies for the realisation of his ideals.

[1] Ibid.

Chapter 2

Teachers of the People (1841–61)

Derwent Coleridge's ideas on education were essentially based on his father's philosophy. STC taught in *The Constitution of Church and State* that the ultimate aim of the State should be to balance the opposite interests of permanence (represented by the landed interest) and progression (represented by the mercantile and manufacturing classes). 'Progress' had merely produced a 'wealth-machine' accompanied by pauperism, and the general well-being and happiness of the people had not advanced. The balance was to be effected by the National Church, concerned with spiritual and cultural advancement. The National Church was not merely the clergy, but the clerisy, which included all learned men, not only in universities, but schoolmasters as well as parsons who must be so distributed as to leave no corner of the country 'without a resident guide, guardian and instructor'. The State must set aside adequate funds, the Nationalty, for the maintenance of the clerisy.

The task of the clerisy was 'to diffuse through the whole community, and to every native entitled to its laws and rights, that quantity and quality of knowledge which was indispensable both for the understanding of those rights, and for the performance of the duties correspondent'. He pointed out: '. . . civilisation in itself is but a mixed good . . . where this civilisation is not grounded in *cultivation*, in the harmonious development of those qualities and faculties that characterize our *humanity*. We must be men in order to be citizens.' The Nationalty is consecrated to 'the potential divinity in every man, which is the ground and condition of his civil existence, that without which a man can be neither free nor obliged, and by which alone, therefore, he is capable of being a free subject – a citizen'.

STC wished 'to convey not instruction merely, but fundamental instruction, not so much to shew my Reader this or that fact, as to kindle his own torch for him, and leave it to himself to chuse the particular objects, which he might wish to examine by its light'.[1] He wished to establish 'Education of the Intellect, by awakening the Method of self-development...'[2]

At the new college Derwent sought to put Coleridgean principles of education into practice, and there was a conflict from the start with the ideas of the founders of the college. The Acland/Mathison group wanted a Principal who would see the new college primarily as a High Church Tractarian bastion against state encroachment on the prerogatives of the Church. Mathison's real views on popular education are shown in a manuscript letter[3] found in the British Museum copy of his book *How can the Church educate the People?* (1844).[4]

I confess that elementary day schools for little children who go to plough at 8, and always earn their bread in some way at 12, have never appeared to me as great a panacea, as to many others for national wants.

Still, as aids to the clergy, and in order to rescue a most destructive implement from other hands, I have done my best to advance and promote them.

By doing so, through the good will of the upper classes, we keep up a moral bond of union, in times when the spirit of democracy would dissociate one class from the other.

I cannot help thinking, however, that Colleges, where

[1] *The Friend.* I. p. 16.
[2] From the *Treatise on Method*: quoted in K. Coburn, *Inquiring Spirit*, p. 71.
[3] Dated 31 May. Royal Mint.
[4] The cover is stamped 'Rt. Hon. Thos. Greville' and the book inscribed 'From the Author'.

select youths may be trained, and loyalized, are now a real desideratum.

Mathison's underlying motives clearly emerge as the support of the Church against the State, and the use of education as a means of social control.

Derwent did not see the new College as primarily a means of supporting the power of the Church against the State. High Church Tory though he said he was, Derwent was a Coleridgean High Church Tory, and he deplored fanaticism of any kind. As he wrote to Dr Arnold of Rugby in 1833: 'I am a Conservative of the school of Burke but I trust not a Bigot.' He welcomed State aid. He praised and defended the Committee of Council set up in 1839, the destruction of which had been the underlying purpose of the Acland/Mathison group. He had invited to preside over his last Helston speech day H. Seymour Tremenheere who had given him a testimonial for Repton, and who was one of the newly appointed state inspectors of schools.

The Committee of the National Society expected in the Principal a man who would see the new College primarily as a supplier of teachers, equipped to inculcate in the children of the poor 'the Principles of the Established Church' but not much else. Secular education – 'the knowledge that puffeth up' as Mathison described it[1] – was suspect unless firmly tied to religion. Thus the sums in the National Society's handbook on 'Elementary Arithmetic' were based not on real life situations but on the Scriptures, e.g. 'The children of Israel were sadly given to idolatry, notwithstanding all they knew of God. Moses was obliged to have three thousand men put to death for this grievous sin. What digits must you use to express this number?'[2] The Society's Central Model School taught reading, writing and arithmetic and rote learning of the creed, the catechism, the collects, and parts of scripture history.[3]

Derwent Coleridge loathed such methods. To use the Bible as a sum book was equally bad education and bad religion, and a

[1] *How can the Church educate the People?* p. 34.
[2] *Central Society of Education. Second Publication of 1838.* The Woburn Press, 1968. p. 358.
[3] *Central Society of Education. Second Publication of 1838.* The Woburn Press, 1968. p. 371.

perversion of the ideal of harmonising spiritual and secular education. Rote learning of words which meant nothing to the learner was an affront to a man with a profound belief in the value of language as a means of communication. It could not produce the educated man. Although he accepted without question the stratified society of his time, he wanted to develop 'the potential divinity in every man' through education. All who had the capacity should have the opportunity to grapple with the classics, which seemed at the time to be the best means of education, and to read English literature.

The National Society believed it important that the education and training of the students should teach them humility and not give them ideas above their station. 'The Principal will exercise a paternal but strict discipline, – keeping always in remembrance the humble sphere of life to which they belong, and for which they are designed.'[1] But Derwent Coleridge wanted to raise the status of teachers – to enable them to climb the social and professional ladder, even into the Church. He believed it was important to build up the teacher's self respect, not to humiliate him. He saw the College as the modern counterpart of the medieval Oxford and Cambridge colleges,[2] educating not only clerics but teachers, fit to take their place in his father's clerisy, with whom lay the duty and the only real possibility of advancing civilisation and social progress.

In 1841 Chelsea was on the edge of London. West of World's End on the King's Road, where the built-up area ended, lay nursery gardens and beyond these was Stanley Grove, a large house standing in 11 acres of ground between the King's Road and Fulham Road. The house was built in 1691 on the site of a house belonging to a member of the Stanley family. It was bought in the early nineteenth century by Mr William Hamilton, who, as private secretary to Lord Elgin when he was British Ambassador at Constantinople, had

[1]National Society Annual Report 1841. p. 20.
[2]'. . . if the elder religious foundations, which have hitherto presided over the education of this country, be regarded as affording a model, to which, with a due allowance for change of circumstances, the present efforts of the Church in the same cause should be more or less accommodated'. *Account of the Training College for Schoolmasters* by Rev. Derwent Coleridge. National Society Annual Report 1842. Appendix V p. 93.

played a large part in bringing the Elgin marbles from Greece. He had added to the house the present Hamilton Room, embellished with plaster casts of sculptures from the Parthenon.

When Derwent was appointed Principal of the new Training Institution at Stanley Grove on 3 February 1841 he not only became responsible for the practical problems of setting up and staffing the new College and recruiting the students, but also took on overall responsibility for the National Society's established training institutions, that is the Men's Boarding House at Cannon Row, Westminster, and the Women's Boarding House at Smith Square, Westminster, where adults pursued a short course of study and training in teaching method at the Central School. His first task was to examine the masters and mistresses for admission to the adult institutions.

Within a week Derwent had appointed as his assistant at Stanley Grove Mr Crank, who had been on his staff at Helston Grammar School. A week later he appointed Rev. C. A. Johns, his first assistant at Helston, to be in charge of the masters in training at Cannon Row.

After a month spent preparing the new college, it is recorded that Mr Coleridge advertised in the newspapers about the admission of youths to Stanley Grove. The National Society School Committee had decided the first ten pupils were to be educated free after passing an examination and after a three months' probationary period. On 23 April Mr Coleridge submitted a report to the General Committee on the rules and regulations of the Training Institution at Stanley Grove. The entry age should be 14 to 17 years. After three months' probation the future teachers should be apprenticed to the National Society until the age of 21 and they should be charged £25 p.a., paid half-yearly in advance. The establishments for training youths and masters should stay separate for the time being.

On 24 June 1841 the General Committee of the National Society decided that a Training Institution for school mistresses should be provided by purchasing Whitelands, a house adjoining Chelsea Hospital. The Head of this institution should be 'a lady in mind and manners', to be aided by a clergyman and masters 'under the general direction of Mr Coleridge'. Thus Derwent's responsibilities were further enlarged, but there is no record of his having any close involvement with Whitelands.

The first students at Stanley Grove slept in the attics of the original house but on 30 March 1841 the School Committee requested the architect Edward Blore to draw up plans for three new wings built in the Italian style round a quadrangle, to accommodate 50 to 60 pupils. Blore[1] had done work at Lambeth Palace and Buckingham Palace and was a fashionable architect. The National Society regarded the building of a chapel at Stanley Grove as a matter of first importance and employed Blore as architect, but it is clear from Derwent's correspondence that he drafted the original plan for the Chapel, built in the Byzantine style between 1841 and 1843.

In a letter to the Rev. John Sinclair, Secretary of the National Society, 14 October 1842, Derwent said: 'The part I have played in the design and arrangement of St Mark's Chapel has induced other church builders to compare notes with me.'[2] A draft letter from Derwent to the Bishop of London contains a crossed out paragraph: 'I furnished Mr Blore with a plan for the building which with a few modifications he was kind enough to adopt and which he has worked out with so much taste and ability.'[3] Probably Derwent decided to omit this as he was anxious not to appear boastful, an interesting contrast with his pretensions as an architect at Helston. He certainly succeeded in concealing from posterity that he drew up the original plans for the chapel, which has always been attributed to Blore.[4]

The chapel is a dignified building of unusual design, with a round chancel arch, an apsidal end and an ambulatory behind the chancel. Among Derwent's papers[5] is a draft on the chapel windows 'with painted glass by William Waites of Newcastle to an agreed general design'. Subscriptions were to be opened so that any individual might give a window or part of one. Derwent noted that it was most

[1] 1787–1879.
[2] Derwent Coleridge MSS. HRC, Texas.
[3] 11 November 1842. Derwent Coleridge MSS. HRC, Texas (in a bound book inscribed 'N.S.T.C. Copies of letters').
[4] In the archives of the College of St Mark and St John there is one of Derwent's original plans for the Chapel and Practising School, annotated in his handwriting with 'Suggested Aug. 26, 1841, D.C.' written in the bottom left-hand corner.
[5] Derwent Coleridge MSS. HRC, Texas.

St Mark's College, Chelsea: The Chapel and Practising School.
(From the Minutes of the Committee of Council on Education 1842–3)

important that all five ambulatory windows be painted, though they were not all seen at the same time from any point in the nave. He was concerned with the enrichment of the chancel and the effect produced by the reflected light and progressive appearance of different windows as the spectator advances up the chapel which would make 'a much stronger impression on the mind than any mere *coup d'œuil*'. He drew up a scheme for the subjects of all the windows in the chapel. Later he wrote to William Waites giving a critique of the specimen he had sent. Derwent certainly also drafted the plan for the octagonal Practising School. The General Committee minutes for 26 August 1841 record that the plan proposed by Mr Coleridge and approved by Mr Blore for the Practising School was approved.

In this first year, as well as launching the unprecedented experiment in teacher education at Stanley Grove, deciding on the rules for admission of students and examining them, deciding on the curriculum, appointing staff and teaching the students himself, designing some of the new buildings and having overall responsibility for the other teacher training institutions of the National Society, Derwent had a host of minor duties laid upon him. These included reporting on the National Society's Experimental Infant School in Tufton Street and making recommendations about building a new boundary wall to Stanley Grove after a combination of high tide and north-easterly gales on 18 October had caused the canal to flood, damaging the boundary wall, the lodge and garden.

He was still in personal financial difficulties. In October 1841 Henry Nelson Coleridge made arrangements for Derwent to borrow £200 from his cousin Edward.[1] Henry wrote to Sara:

This will put him out of his pressure from stranger debts, as far as I know them. One question is – will he not under the ease of delicate creditors, sleep upon his new debts? I hope the best of him and for him, tho' I think that personal gratification up to a certain point is your brother's weak part ... but the mischief is, that Derwent has for so much of his life lived upon the

---

[1]Henry Nelson Coleridge to Derwent Coleridge. 9 October 1841. Coleridge papers. HRC, Texas.

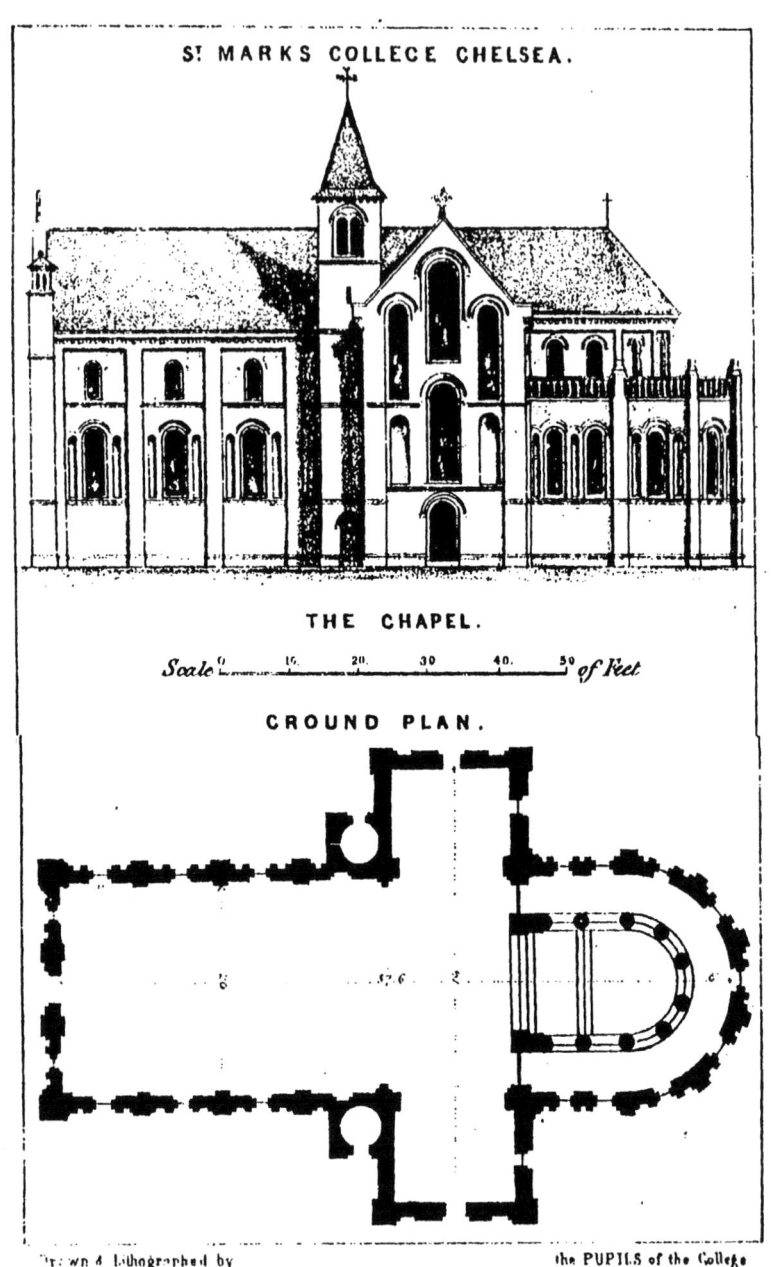

St Mark's College, Chelsea: The Chapel
(From the National Society Annual Report 1844 Appendix III)

supplemental help of friends, that he scarcely feels money borrowed from them to be any debts at all, and certainly does not abridge a single luxury or comfort for the purpose of discharging or diminishing them.[1]

Derwent throve upon his new responsibilities which gave scope to his intellect and imagination. His sister Sara wrote to their cousin, Sir John Taylor Coleridge:

Derwent's sensitive, transparent face, which always shows what is passing within his mind very clearly, assures me, when I see it now, that he is in good heart and hope. A certain amount, not merely of the comforts, but of the elegancies of life, is rather too much a condition of his cheerfulness and useful activity: but this is not incompatible in him with much solid Christian goodness, and never did I know anyone who made friends without an effort, merely by giving full scope to his natural tastes and dispositions, more readily than he does.[2]

Mary's responsibilities are glimpsed through Sara's letter of 18 October to her husband:

There are now 20 boys in the Institution – and it is intended to increase to 56. Mary's management of the housekeeping department seems judicious and even clever. She has introduced Cornish dishes, and continues to make a little money go far by variety in the dressing of the food. The table of the Stanley Grove boys is a cut above that of the boys at Dr Kay's, they being of better families and condition. The former however do not have meat every day but one day soup with no meat in it and another soup with but a little, but made very good and relishing.[3]

Ten days later Sara reported to Miss Trevenen Mary's optimistic

[1]10 October 1841. Coleridge papers. HRC, Texas.
[2]25 March 1841. Sara Coleridge letters, HRC, Texas.
[3]Sara Coleridge letters, HRC, Texas.

view 'that taking all things together it was the best sort of situation that D. could possibly have, his habits and turn of mind considered'.

On 14 June 1842 Derwent addressed a long letter to the Rev. John Sinclair, entitled An Account of the Training College for Schoolmasters at Stanley Grove, Chelsea.[1] He began with a manifesto, criticising the efforts so far made towards popular instruction and outlining what he saw as the aims of the new College. He went on to give a detailed account of the working of the College.

Derwent declared:

the means at present available for popular instruction are not merely inadequate in extent, but unsuitable, or at least imperfect, in kind...

The majority of the people cannot so much as read to any purpose. They cannot *so* read as to attain the objects of reading. Evil has grown, not because of education, nor in spite of education, but simply for want of it. There is need, not so much to extend the means of instruction – though this be most needful – as to improve its quality...

The truth is, that the education given in our schools ... is too often little more than nominal, imparting, it may be, a little knowledge, – sometimes hardly this, – but leaving the mental powers wholly undeveloped, and the heart even less affected than the mind.

To what end do we seek to educate the poor man's child? Is it not to give him just views of his moral and religious obligations – his true interests for time and eternity, while at the same time we prepare him for the successful discharge of his civil duties? – Is it not merely to instil knowledge, but to elicit and to exercise the powers of thinking?

But is this an easy task? Can we hope that it will be duly performed for less than labourer's wages, without present estimation or hope of preferment, by the first rustic, broken-down tradesman, or artisan out of employment, whom necessity, or perhaps indolence, brings to the office? ... But

---

[1]Published as Appendix V, N.S. Annual Report 1842.

will not a little preparation suffice? May he not be taught a system? He may indeed be taught a system; but surely it will not suffice. He wants the first conditions of a teacher. He cannot teach what he does not know. He cannot explain what he does not understand ... He must first himself be *educated* before he can educate others ... Here then, I think we have the root of the evil. The object on which so much zeal and ingenuity have been bestowed has been – not to procure proper masters, but to do without them. The attempt has been to educate by systems, not by men ...

Even an educated teacher who trusts to mechanical arrangements, must expect a mechanical result ... Every child is an individual, thinking and feeling for himself. He must be dealt with accordingly. The influence of the master must, as far as possible, be personal...

In plain terms, then, and in old-fashioned language, my conclusion is that the schoolmaster must be *an educated man*. I do not speak of birth, or social position, or habits of life, or manners, or appearance, but of a certain condition of the mental faculties, as well moral as intellectual; of that which *constitutes* education ... And this necessity is not at all affected by the class of children which he has to train. The amount of acquirement may differ; but this is the least thing to be considered...

Derwent continued his report with a detailed description of the college at Stanley Grove. To 'the excellent mansion-house' had been added 'an extensive range of dormitories, attached to the building, and, at a small distance, a school for the children of the neighbourhood, and a chapel of considerable dimensions serving as a place of worship for the adjoining district, as well as for the inmates of the Institution'.

The chapel was not yet finished. In the mansion-house the Hamilton Room (with the Parthenon frieze) was known as the lecture-room and with the adjoining class-room gave accommodation for 60 students. The Principal's residence was on the first floor. 'The garrets ... supply sleeping-rooms for the servants, and for a certain number of the students.' The dormitories provided accommodation for 50 students and two masters, with a separate sleeping apartment for each. In a separate building were a laundry, an infirmary and storerooms for garden and farm produce. There was a small farm-yard, two kitchen gardens and three small meadows as dairy-land.

The college is intended to consist of sixty students, under the superintendence of a Principal, assisted by a Vice-Principal (not yet appointed), who will divide with him the duties of the chapel, and two resident Teachers. All the students, after they have remained on probation for a period of three months, will be apprenticed to the National Society for a term of years, commencing with the date of the indenture, and expiring when the apprentice shall have completed his twenty-first year...

Of the Teachers, one only, with the Vice-Principal, will be employed in the school-room, the other being fully occupied in directing the labours of the apprentices out of doors. The latter is also the Steward of the establishment, and has the general oversight and management of the farm and garden. A master has also been appointed for the practising school. [This was Bennet Johns, brother of C. A. Johns, who was appointed in March 1842]. Vocal music and drawing are taught by occasional masters; and a drill-sergeant attends who gives lessons in gymnastics. One out-door servant, who acts as gardener and hind, a matron, and a cook, with two other female servants and an errand-boy, complete the establishment. The washing is performed by a laundress, who, with her assistants, resides on the premises...

The matron, who is also the housekeeper, has the general regulation of the household, but in a subordinate capacity. She does not supply the food by contract, such an arrangement being unfavourable both to economy and to discipline. The important article of diet could with difficulty have been put on a satisfactory footing, if the youths were not made to feel that their simple and uncostly fare was ordered with an exclusive view to their own benefit. The same remark applies to clothing. Everything, to the minutest detail, is managed by the

184

Principal, in the name of the National Society, between whom and the pupils no interest is interposed.

Derwent does not mention the important part played by Mary in the housekeeping arrangements.

He went on to describe the College life. 'The object being to provide schoolmasters for the poor, the endeavour must be, on the one hand to raise the students morally and intellectually to a certain standard, – while, on the other hand, we train them in lowly service, not merely to teach them hardihood and inure them to the duties of a humble and laborious office, but to make them practically acquainted with the condition of that class of the community among whom they will have to labour.'

He had concluded that the sons of farmers, shopkeepers and artisans were best suited to the training obtained at the College, since boys from such homes were less ignorant than those of 'the lowest rank'; and the sons of 'the more liberal employments' were often left with 'an inheritance of penury' which made the prospect of 'an honourable, though humble, livelihood' as a teacher an attractive one. However, youths of this class were generally expected to be supporting themselves by their fifteenth year, severely limiting the number of candidates who could be expected to be 'sent to Stanley Grove, or to any other Training-college ... at a considerable expense to their friends'. He hoped that further free apprenticeships could be endowed.

Boys should be serious, but lively, and need only be able to read with comprehension and write from dictation, though a majority of entrants had not even those qualifications. 'A slight provincial accent ... connects a man with his birthplace and the homestead of his fathers' and was no hindrance; but 'the schoolmasters of the people must ... be well able to teach their own language', and it was for this reason that he favoured the teaching of Latin, to help the uneducated mind to grasp the idea of the rules of language in the abstract, so that he might then understand them in his own tongue. He did not seek to provide a grammar-school classical education. However, English grammar and composition and the best English classics were an important part of the curriculum. The Bible and the Articles and History of the Church were also studied, as were

185

elements of Euclid, algebra and trigonometry, while botany was given prominence among the sciences. He added:

> The drawing of plans and elevations, both geometrical and perspective, has been taught with considerable success... Two lessons a week are given in vocal music under the superintendence of Mr Hullah. Half an hour is also set aside for daily practice. The daily service of the chapel will, it is trusted, set forth the paramount object for which this acquirement is studied...

The timetable (on page 187) gives an overall view of College activities.

Coleridge continued:

> The food is of the plainest description, but is of the best of its kind, and carefully prepared. It is not given out in rations; if any youth were to eat habitually in excess, he would be reproved for it, as for any other fault, but with this exception (if exception it may be called), there is no stint... The dietary varies with the seasons; but a general notion may be gathered from the following table:–

Sunday	Cold boiled beef and plum pudding.
Monday.............	Soup, during winter.
Tuesday............	Roast legs of mutton.
Wednesday.......	Mutton-and-potatoe pies.
Thursday	Boiled pork, with suet dumplings; occasionally roast beef.
Friday................	Irish stew and rice pudding.
Saturday	Broth and boiled mutton.

N.B. One cup of small beer is allowed to each youth at dinner.

The boys wore uniform.

> The clothing comprises a Sunday and working suit: the former is made of black or very dark cloth, with shoes and

General Timetable

Summer

A.M.	5.30	Rise. Half an hour allowed for washing and dressing, etc.
	6.00	Housework, particularly cleaning the shoes and knives, working the drainage and forcing pumps; also, farm business, feeding the animals etc.: three quarters of an hour.
	6.45	Assemble in the lecture room. Morning studies:– Repetitions; Collect; Portions of Scripture; Articles of the Church of England, with Scripture references, etc.: three quarters of an hour.
	7.30	Morning prayers, after which a short lecture: forty minutes. At eight o'clock the waiters leave the room to prepare for breakfast.
	8.10	Breakfast – bread and butter with milk and water: twenty minutes.
	8.30	Out-doors work; farm, gardens, lawns, shrubberies etc.: an hour and a half. Bell rings at ten.
	10.00	Put by tools etc.; wash hands and change shoes, etc.: ten minutes.
	10.10	Forenoon studies: two hours and twenty minutes. On Friday a lecture on Botany, at half-past eleven.
P.M.	12.30	Voluntary study or recreation: half an hour. Bell rings ten minutes before one.
	1.00	Dinner; see dietary: half an hour.
	1.30	Voluntary study or recreation: half an hour.
	2.00	Afternoon studies – occasional lessons. On Monday and Thursday, singing in two classes: one hour each. On Wednesday and Saturday, drawing: two hours.
	4.00	Outdoor work as above: two hours. From five to six a lesson in gymnastics, twice a week during the summer months. Bell rings at six.
	6.00	Put by tools, etc. as above: ten minutes.
	6.10	Tea, the same as breakfast: twenty minutes.
	6.30	Practice singing: half an hour.
	7.00	Evening studies: one hour.
	8.00	Evening prayers and lecture: three quarters of an hour.
	8.45	Voluntary study: three quarters of an hour.
	9.30	Put up books and go to bed.
	10.00	Extinguish the gas lights. N.B. These are all in the corridors, and light the rooms through two small circular panes of glass in each door.

gaiters, and consists of a single breasted frockcoat (or round jacket, according to the size and age of the youth), waistcoat and trowsers, a black silk hat, and a white cravat; the latter, a round velveteen jacket and waistcoat, with fustian trowsers, and heavy shoes, a brown holland blouse to wear over, or instead of the jacket, according to the weather, and a straw hat. The linen consists of six day and three night-shirts, six pair of cotton socks, three pair of drawers, two coloured and two white cravats, and six pocket handkerchiefs. Each boy has also a cotton umbrella and a pair of strong leather slippers, which are always worn in the house. All these articles are furnished by the College of an uniform quality, seven guineas being charged towards the first outfit. The probationers wear their own clothes, except in peculiar cases.

Derwent argued that the uniform promoted self-respect and prevented foppery.

The practising school had been in operation for five weeks, and although intended for 120 scholars, had been made to accommodate 130 and there was a waiting list. The school fee was fourpence a week 'but a certain number of free scholars (exclusively from the poorest classes) are received on the recommendation of the parochial clergy, and in particular of the Rev. Charles Kingsley, the rector of the parish, to whose countenance and support the school is much indebted. Six pupils from the College are constantly engaged in teaching the children, under the superintendence of the master Mr Bennet Johns, who has recently been appointed to this office, having been for a short time one of the Society's organising-masters.'

Derwent regarded the service of the chapel as 'the keystone of the arch . . . from which are derived the consistence and stability of the whole'.

Finally, he sought to answer some objections 'not uncommonly made to this Institution, and which have appeared plausible, I believe, to many of its friends and well-wishers'. It had been suggested that youths living such a sheltered life would be unprepared for the hardships and temptations of the real world. Derwent maintained they would be 'in some degree fortified against the allurements of the world by the education which they have received'. He also envisaged that the elder youths during their training would be given 'a larger measure of liberty', for instance, teaching in the schools of the neighbourhood or of their own parish, and that when students first left the College they would work as assistant teachers under supervision.

The second objection was the expense of the Institution. Derwent maintained the original outlay of £20,000, raised by subscription, was not extravagant. He envisaged the annual outlay as £3,000, of which a third would be paid by the pupils. This meant that the education of each schoolmaster, for the whole three year period of his training, would cost from £150 to £200. He maintained that time was an indispensable element in successful training and the cost not large compared with the cost of preparation for other callings.

A further objection was that the young men might not become 'National' schoolmasters after training. Derwent hoped that 'in the eyes of a serious and high-minded youth . . . the office of a National schoolmaster, from its immediate connexion with the Church . . . will be invested with more real dignity, than any for which it could be exchanged'.

During the first five years Derwent reported constantly to the committees of the National Society on the difficulty he had in filling the new Training Institution with eligible pupils. In March 1842 the General Committee of the Society resolved to make a further grant of £300 to establish ten exhibitions of £10 each for three years.[1]

The first college register, extending from April 1841 to November 1849, shows that 207 students were admitted.[2] The age of entry varied from 12 to 24 years, but there were very few adults and the average age was about 15. Some students' premiums were funded from exhibitions given by the National Society and the remainder were paid either by their parents, by benefactors (frequently local clergy; Acland paid for one and Mathison for two and a half), or by local Boards of Education (under the aegis of the National Society).

[1]Minutes of General Commitee. National Society 2 March 1842.
[2]Archives: College of St Mark and St John.

The recorded occupations of the students' fathers were:

artisans	60
tradesmen	20
farmers	16
schoolmasters	12
clerks	8
professional businessmen	8
soldiers, sailors, coastguards	5
labourers	4
domestic servants	3

Thirty-nine students were either orphans or the sons of widows. Most of the students had received their previous education at National Schools. Their previous education could be broken down as follows:

National Schools	61
private schools or academies	30
Grammar schools	15
commercial schools	15
boarding schools	14
charity schools	13
National Society Training Schools for teachers at Wells and Exeter	6
St Mark's Practising School	4
parochial schools	4
choristers schools	2
British School	1
workhouse school	1

The students from St Mark's Practising School gained exhibitions given by the National Society. Under the heading 'State of acquirement on admission', Derwent constantly refers to entrants not knowing the meaning of words and not understanding what they read. An entry for January 1847 is typical – 'reads and spells very badly, slight knowledge of Scripture, history and geography'.

The National Society was anxious to keep down the expense

of the new institution. On 9 March 1842 the General Committee appointed a special sub-committee to consider how to reduce the expense of producing masters at Stanley Grove. This sub-committee reported on 6 April that no reduction was possible in the cost of maintenance of the pupils but the three-year training rule could be revised; many pupils could be proficient in less time, and this would increase the usefulness of the Institution without increasing expenditure. Again, on 5 January 1846, we find the St Mark's Sub-committee recommending for consideration which youths should be found employment as assistant teachers at the end of one or two years rather than three. On 22 January 1846 they received a letter from Mr Coleridge saying that he deemed any curtailment of the period of training utterly inadvisable.

In April 1842 Derwent applied to the National Society for a Vice-Principal to be appointed to help him in his undertaking. Despite the opposition of the Bishop of London on the grounds that it would be expensive and unnecessary, the Rev. Thomas Helmore was appointed in July at a salary of £120 p.a. plus board and lodging. Sara Coleridge wrote to Hartley:

> About D. I did not tell you that he has gained all his points with the committee – the principal of which was a resident Chaplain – to help him both in the School and the Chapel. He will thus be enabled to have 3 weeks holiday in the year. I hope he will now make no more requests – if possible for the present. Acland told Edward that D's mind teemed with schemes – and that he was just the man for them – only that his schemes were a little in excess – practicability and pecuniary matters considered. He hoped he would now rest quiet for a while – and go on more jog-trottishly.[1]

On 14 July 1842 the School Committee agreed that the Chapel at Stanley Grove should be S. Mark's, 'an allusion to the passage of Scripture where it is stated that Paul and Barnabas in their first

[1] 13 July 1842. Sara Coleridge letters. HRC, Texas.

191

Apostolical journey had John whose surname was Mark for their minister.' On 24 November 1842 the first use of the term 'S. Mark's College' is recorded in the minutes. On 21 November 1844 it was decided that there should be a sub-committee for S. Mark's College, to meet there not less than once a month and report to the School Committee.

Throughout the early years Derwent Coleridge conducted a running fight to retain the daily choral services in the Chapel. These were responsible for the growth of the Choral Revival throughout the whole country.[1]

At the beginning of the nineteenth century the surpliced choir facing each other in stalls on either side of the chancel was unknown in England outside the cathedrals and a few college chapels.[2] In most Anglican churches at this time the chancel and the altar were neglected and the church was dominated by the pulpit. In some churches the altar was used as a dumping ground for hats and coats or as a desk for signing the parish register. The Oxford Movement and the Choral Revival which grew out of it were protests against apathy and neglect in the Anglican Church and an attempt to increase reverence and devotion in the church service. For more than a century the versicles and responses and the psalms had been read in most parish churches. If there was a choir they monopolised the singing, and the congregation did not take part. Derwent was determined to make the services in S. Mark's Chapel as beautiful as possible, the service of the chapel being 'the keystone of the arch'. From the beginning, with that in mind, vocal music played an important part in the education of the future teachers.

On 13 May 1841 the School Committee minuted that Mr Coleridge was to agree with Mr Hullah for singing instruction. John Hullah was at that time a young man of nearly twenty-nine, who on

[1]'By means of systematic musical training and daily participation in those choral services, teachers trained at S. Mark's were deliberately equipped to take with them into the towns and villages of the land the musical competence and the specialised knowledge of music previously lacking in most parishes.' Bernarr Rainbow. *The Choral Revival in the Anglican Church 1839–1872*. Barrie and Jenkins, 1970. p. 48.
[2]At Oxford, New College, Magdalen and Christ Church; at Cambridge, King's, Trinity and St John's had choirs. Bernarr Rainbow. Op. Cit.

a visit to Paris in 1839 had been deeply impressed by the massed singing classes of artisans. They were learning to sing from notes, according to Wilhem's method of teaching singing by the monitorial system. It was to John Hullah and one of his most able pupils, Edward May, that the basic musical training of the students at Stanley Grove was entrusted.

The Rev. Thomas Helmore was appointed Vice-Principal of S. Mark's on 14 July 1842 and he was the man who trained the entire student body of the college and the children of the Practising School to perform the daily choral service, originally in the Practising School and later in the Chapel after it was opened for services. He used to say: 'Hullah grinds them; I strop them.'[1] The achievement of Helmore, Hullah and May in training the raw youths at St Mark's in musical proficiency was truly remarkable. All the services in the Chapel were performed without musical accompaniment – there was no organ in the building until 1861. Each day at Morning Prayer the responses were sung in Tallis's setting and the psalms were chanted to Anglican or Gregorian chants. The Canticles were sung to settings, with an anthem for every service.

In December 1844 Derwent addressed a Second Letter on the National Society's Training Institution for Schoolmasters, St Mark's College, Chelsea, to Archdeacon Sinclair (now Treasurer of the Society).[2]

He included the Precentor's Table for the services in the College Chapel for the week beginning 15 September and went on to point out: 'Singing cannot, any more than reading, be taught soon, or easily, or for nothing. It must be sufficiently valued *to be made a point of*, both at school and in the church – not occasionally, or by fits and starts, but day by day, and week by week, and month by month; in which case each year will produce a richer harvest than the last.'[3] By 1844 the students were devoting a good deal more time to singing and less to 'industrial occupations'. Every morning there was sung Morning Prayer in Chapel from 9 to 10. On Wednesdays from 12 noon to 12.50 p.m. there was a singing lesson with the children of

[1]F. Helmore. *Memoir of the Rev. Thomas Helmore*. Masters, 1891. p. 34.
[2]National Society Annual Report, 1844. Appendix III.
[3]Ibid. p. 89.

the Practising School. Each day there were music classes from 5.40 p.m. to 6.45 p.m. Evening prayers from 9.00 to 9.35 involved more singing. By January 1847 Helmore was able to write that the choir was prepared to sing in the Chapel ten entire cathedral services by Tallis, Farrant, Byrd, Gibbons, Bevin, Batten, Chreyghton, Rogers, Aldrich and Boyce, with two other morning services by Bancroft and Travers, a communion service adapted from Vittoria and another from Palestrina. They had 70 anthems in continual use, and sang 70 metrical Psalm tunes and some of the choruses from Handel's *Messiah*.[1]

The St Mark's Chapel services were open to the general public on Sundays and were so remarkable that they soon attracted a growing congregation, including celebrities and visitors from a distance. But the reactions were not all favourable. These were the years of bitter evangelical opposition to Tractarian High Church views and practices. Militant protestants would demonstrate outside St Mark's Chapel against the Popish practices they believed to go on there. In 1845 the evangelical paper *The Record* produced a pamphlet on 'The National School Society – the Popish Character of the Religious Instruction provided for the pupils and children of the Training Institutions at Westminster, and at St Mark's College, Stanley Grove, Chelsea'.

More serious for Derwent Coleridge was the fact that Archdeacon Sinclair, Secretary and, later, Treasurer of the National Society, was very critical of the Chapel services.[2] In writing his *Second Letter*, Derwent found it necessary to devote 13 pages to justifying the chapel service, 'which has from the first excited considerable attention'. He maintained that 'the education of the young cannot be attended by too much dignity, or set off with too much grace'. The choral service helped to keep up attention in a congregation of young persons, and would teach students skill in the art of singing which they would pass on to their pupils and which would improve church-singing in the whole country. In fact many of the teachers

---

[1]*Memorials of S. Mark's College.* Ed. G. W. Gent. White, 1891. pp. 111–112.
[2]'St Mark's was from the first marked as in sympathy with the High Church party. Mr Sinclair, the secretary of the National Society, so Sir Thomas Acland told me, was hostile to the College for that reason.' *The Letters of Peter Lombard* (Canon Benham). Ed. E. D. Baxter, Macmillan, 1912.

trained at St Mark's were able not only to teach music in their schools but to form a choir in the parish church. A leading article in the monthly journal *The Parish Choir* said in 1848: 'There is perhaps no institution of modern times which has done so much for the choral music of the Church of England as St Mark's Training College'.[1]

The rest of Derwent's Second Letter gives a survey of the College in December 1844. 67 youths were then in residence. During the past year 46 had been admitted, all paying the full premium. Derwent observed that of those now on probation, or recently apprenticed, a fair proportion were intelligent lads, of suitable temper and disposition, but comparatively few were *properly prepared* for the institution. 'Not many of those recommended possess even that modicum of acquirement which might fairly be expected from a promising boy of twelve, not to say fifteen, years old ... in a majority of cases it is necessary to ground the probationers afresh in the simplest rudiments of learning – to go over again the work of an elementary school...' Most of the youths were 15 years old on admission.

The staff now consisted of the Principal; the Vice-Principal, who shared in the general as well as the musical teaching; Mr Thomas Stanley, BA of Queens' College, Cambridge, who had taken the place of Mr Crank as Tutor and Mathematical Lecturer; Mr H. C. Stubbs, an old pupil of the college, Assistant-Master; Mr Bennet Johns, Normal Master, in charge of the Practising School; Mr Henry Strickland, Industrial Master and Steward; and Mr Henry Ingram, another former student of the college, Master of the Chelsea Parochial School, which was now being used as a second practising school. In addition part-time tuition was given in music by Mr Hullah, now Professor of Music at King's College, assisted by Mr May; in drawing by Mr Rawlings and in gymnastics by Mr Cousins.

In addition to the industrial occupations mentioned in the previous report, (in the farm and garden), bookbinding and lithography had been introduced for some of the students and 'a little carpentry, glazing and house-painting'.

[1] *The Parish Choir* Vol. I p. 99. Quoted in Bernarr Rainbow, Op. Cit.

Derwent went on to examine some of the objections which had been raised to the course of study at the College. 'An impression has, I believe, been received by some of those who take a sincere interest in the institution, that the youths are too highly qualified for the office which they will have to discharge.' This might mean that they were too well qualified and would be led to aspire to a higher walk in life. Derwent pointed out that none of the youths who had left the college had 'shewn any signs of instability', and if the office of schoolmaster continued to rise in public estimation, which he anticipated, he did not think they would seek other careers. Some objectors thought the students should simply be taught the art of teaching, which would cost less; others would not teach Latin or history but would devote more time to mensuration and algebra, chemistry and mechanics on the grounds that these subjects would be more useful to the children of the labouring classes. Derwent declared that he had not lost sight of the need for the teachers he was training 'to teach a little, and that effectually, where no more can be attempted, and superadd, wherever it may be practicable, the sort of information required in each district for the uses of life'.

He argued that a fuller, a better and a higher education was required for every class of the community in order to raise the existing standard of civil and religious allegiance. He maintained that the teachers who were to perform this work could not be too highly educated in moral or intellectual discipline. 'Must he not be trained in much the same way, though of course with a special adaptation, as if he were intended for a yet higher ministry?'

His fear was 'lest a few only of the young men should be found to reach the standard of public expectation', particularly in view of the lack of proper preparation of the students at school. Derwent recognised that it could be argued that as the majority of the youths were so little advanced 'a plain English education would be preferable'. But he stoutly defended the teaching of Latin on the grounds firstly, that to drop it would impede the progress of the more promising youths, and secondly, because it helped the others by strengthening the memory, teaching the meaning of words, and enlarging the vocabulary.

'When it is proposed to substitute calculation for grammar, that is for reading or literature, in the education of youth, I cannot but remember that the former thus left to itself supplies no examples of conduct, kindles no generous ardour, awakens no kindly sympathy; above all, that it leaves undeveloped the sense of beauty, shutting out a source of innocent enjoyment, open in rich abundance to the poorest man . . .' Lastly he argued that, if the youths were to study the liturgy and articles, the history and constitution of the Anglican Church, a competent knowledge of Latin was highly desirable.

The students were divided into three years, and each year was sub-divided into two sections, consisting of the more and less advanced. The two sets of third year students were engaged as class-teachers in the practising schools every alternate week for twelve months. Derwent went on to describe the octagonal practising school in the grounds of the college (which, it will be remembered, he had designed). There was a central octagonal shaft, in alternate sides of which were small fireplaces. The shaft served as a common chimney, as well as a support to the roof. Internally the school took the form of a Greek cross, so that there were four distinct rooms, the triangular spaces in between being used as vestibules, coal-houses and book-stores, There were black-boards on the central shaft. One of the rooms was a gallery (i.e. with rows of benches) and the other three rooms were subdivided by curtains, making six class rooms, with about 20 boys in each. The writing desks were at the back of the classes. Because of the need to accommodate more children, two additional classrooms had been created in a cottage on the Fulham Road. There were 152 children in the school.

The children of the first class selected from the most forward boys received extra instruction in music and were employed as choristers. They were given a suitable dress for Sundays and festivals and had an evening meal prepared for them by the lodge-keeper's wife. Derwent noted that it would be *most desirable* that the best of these children should be taken into the college as free exhibitioners. They would be found properly prepared for the college. The majority of the children paid fourpence a week and were, for the most part, children of respectable working people, market gardeners, mechanics and the like. The children on the free list belonged to the very poor. Many of them walked two or three miles to school, bringing their dinners with them. The children all came at five to nine and attended the chapel service for an hour. Then they had lessons from

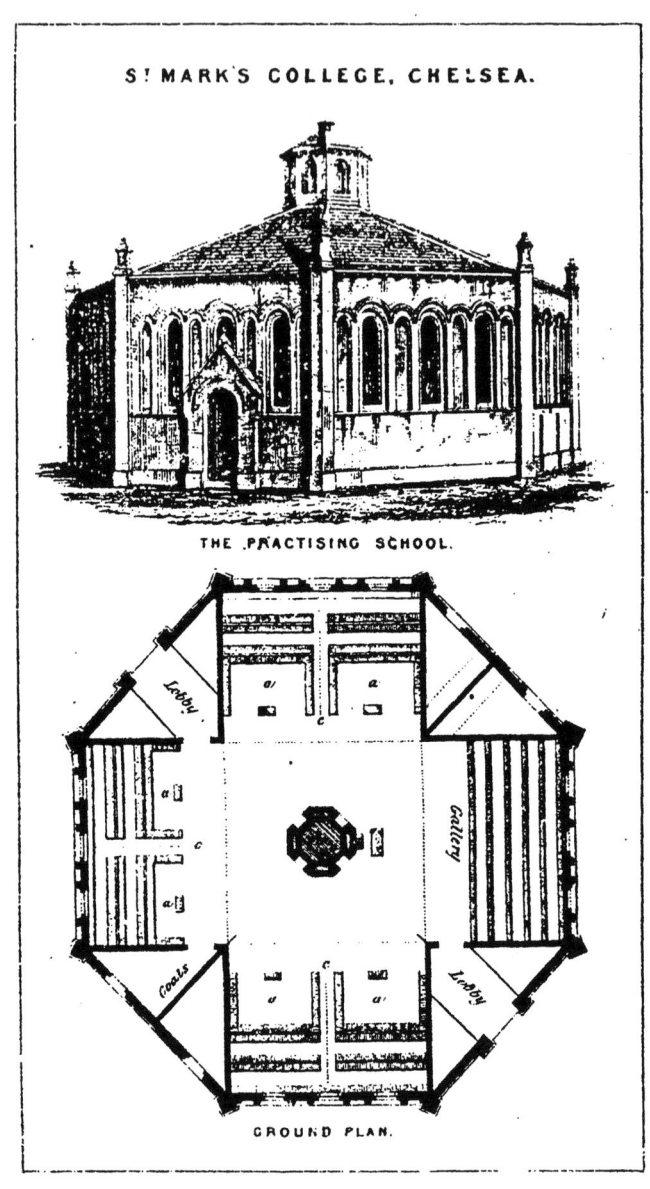

St Mark's College, Chelsea: The Practising School.
(From the National Society Annual Report 1844 Appendix III)

ten to twelve, and from two to five, Wednesday and Saturday being half holidays.

One of the old students of the college, Henry Ingram, had been appointed master of the Chelsea parochial school and this school also was used as a practising school. The children here came from poorer families (some of them paid twopence a week) but the majority were taught free and a large number were also provided with clothing by the Parochial Committee.

Next, Derwent made some suggestions as to the mode of examining school children. He deplored rote-learning and the kind of examination which merely tested this. '... is it after all, the knowledge itself, however useful and fitting, which is most valuable to a child, and not rather the awakening of the faculties, the ability to learn, to understand, to feel – in a word, the culture of the mind?' He insisted that the best way to test a child's mental capacity was to hear him read a few sentences and to question him on the content. He regarded intelligent reading as the gateway to knowledge. He regarded geography and history as next in importance.

As to arithmetic, he considered that it should be carefully taught in every school, but refused to regard it as the prime test of efficiency. He maintained that arithmetic would flourish almost anyhow, 'We are surrounded by ignorance, dark, misleading, degrading ignorance of every kind – except that of figures. It will perhaps be said that I overlook the difference between a mechanical and a liberal education. Looking to essentials ... I should reply that Christianity has abolished this distinction ...'

Derwent was led on to make some stringent social criticism:

When I remember the long period of progress and immaturity through which every child is *naturally* destined to pass, and the analogy – not fanciful, but as I think, most real – that subsists between education and growth, I am led to anticipate that the process of sound instruction must be necessarily slow ... It may, indeed, be replied that the provisions of Society make it impossible to follow nature in this point – that the necessities of the labouring poor leave but a very short time for the instruction of their children – and that education must be taxed to make the most of it. The children of the poor, it is urged, are

199

called away from books to labour. Society, in this advanced state of civilisation, does not allow them time for learning, – no, nor in many cases to take their natural rest. But nature will not, and education cannot, consent to such perversion, nor is it, I think, the part of true benevolence to make any compromise with the 'course of this world', when it is so manifestly evil and wicked. One of the best results of national education would be, to supplant the deadly mischief of infant labour; and if so, is it not the present duty of the educationist to protest against, to interfere with, and to encroach upon it.

It is apparent from the first inspection of the college that, in spite of all the difficulties with semi-literate entrants, Derwent was largely successful in his attempt to provide the future teachers with a liberal education, but the low priority he gave to mathematics was also revealed. The Rev. John Allen, one of the new inspectors appointed by the Committee of Council, inspected the college in May and June 1843. He first attended a public oral examination in the large Lecture Room, and then set written examinations lasting for six days. Besides marking all the papers himself, in the case of the more important papers of the Senior Class, he had his marking checked by the professors at King's College, and others.

He concluded that Mr Coleridge's pupils 'will leave the college educated men; their papers show ... a remarkable power of apprehension, habits of reflection, skill in discrimination and judgement'. He remarked that 'there appears to be a deficiency in mathematical skill, but the *viva voce* examinations with which my inspection commenced did not lead me to anticipate great attainments in that respect; and in all ways the promise of excellence held out by what was then witnessed, (the precision and fullness of the answers given to the questions in history, language, grammar, and especially in scriptural knowledge, and in the doctrines and articles of our Church), proved in my subsequent examination to be amply fulfilled'.[1] The external examiners found the Latin examination papers to be 'on the whole very creditable performances'.

The Rev. H. Moseley inspected the College again in 1846 and

---

[1]Minutes of Committee of Council on Education, 1842–3. p. 335.

reported to the Committee of Council that there were 51 students at St Mark's and their average age was 17. He observed:

> From its commencement, this Institution has affixed a high standard to the education of the elementary schoolmaster, and prescribed an elaborate course for it. It receives its students at an earlier age than any other, and keeps them a longer time: it has thus placed itself in advance of the existing educational movement. In respect to its course of secular instruction, there appears to me, however, to be little to distinguish it from other schools of the upper and middle classes, or as a place for the education of teachers rather than of any other class of persons.

Derwent wanted his future teachers to be as well educated as 'the upper and middle classes' and he did not regard them as members of an inferior class. So he presumably welcomed these comments of the Rev. Moseley in some respects. The Inspector, however, does not seem to have appreciated the extensive teaching practice in the final year, nor the intensive musical training.

Like other colleges St Mark's had its successes and its failures. Between 1841 and 1849 207 students were registered there.[1] 45 of these failed to complete their training; many left because the probationary period showed them to be unsuitable (e.g. 'sent home after 3 months for dullness and deficient education'); some withdrew for financial reasons; several left because of ill-health and four died while students, one dying in college and another 'went home and died of consumption'. Several died of consumption as young teachers. Derwent noted that there was a tendency among parents to put in for teaching those of their offspring who were 'too weakly' to do anything else.

Despite the inadequate preparation of most of the entrants, by providing his future teachers with a liberal education Derwent Coleridge assisted their social mobility. All the 162 students who qualified in these first eight years went first into elementary schools, mostly National Schools and some charity schools, in both industrial

[1]Archives: College of St Mark and St John. First register of students.

and country towns and villages all over England, and a few in Wales and Scotland. At the end of their careers 58 were still elementary teachers. But no less than 38 were ordained, and by the end of their careers 33 were parochial or missionary clergy and two were cathedral clergy. One was Master of the choristers and a Lay Clerk of Chester Cathedral. Two were Training College Principals (one in Madras), and one a Vice-Principal, and two were tutors in Training Colleges. Three were Inspectors of Schools, in New Zealand, Guernsey and the Madras Presidency. Five were teaching overseas; one in charge of the Native College for the Instruction of Native Teachers at Otago, New Zealand, and one the Principal of Doveton College, Madras. Six were teaching in Grammar Schools, and 16 were running private middle-class schools. 14 finished their careers in professional or public service occupations, including the Librarian at the Middle Temple and the Accountant with the London City Mission, while 14 more finished in trade and business, including two booksellers and two bank managers.

The learning of Latin was of course the key to entry to university or theological college, but many of the old students were ordained on the strength of their having been at St Mark's. The Bishop of Exeter, Dr Henry Philpotts, wrote to Derwent in 1847:

I am ready to admit to Deacon's orders, such young men, from time to time, as you shall recommend to me – being appointed simultaneously Schoolmasters in some important Town or District in this diocese.

I shall be strict in my requisition of Qualification in Theology (to a sufficient extent) and in knowledge of the Latin language . . .

They will not be promoted to the Priesthood as a matter of course; not till they have given full proof of their being fit in all respects. In truth I think it is better they should not look beyond the Diaconate at first. It may be, and I hope will be, that sometimes they may prove themselves likely to perform well the office of Priest in some of our mining Parishes.[1]

[1] *Memorials of S. Mark's College.* Ed. G. W. Gent. White, 1891.

Canon Benham wrote in 1891:

> Some of the men who have been ordained went in due course
> to one of the Universities after leaving S. Mark's, and others,
> like myself, have gone through a Theological College. That a
> University Education is a priceless boon I need not stay to
> demonstrate. But, perhaps, I may venture to say, without
> egotism, that the training under Coleridge and Clark supplied
> so much that would otherwise be lacking, that S. Mark's
> students, who have taken Holy Orders, have many a time seen
> reason to bless the memories of their old masters, and to thank
> God. They were learned, refined, thoughtful . . . I have rapidly
> glanced down the list of the ordained men, and will undertake
> to say that those that I have known are as proud of their early
> teachers as any Bishop or Priest who reverently cherishes his
> Alma Mater, let him be who he may.[1]

Derwent dearly wanted to see his future teachers educated to the
top of their abilities and see them enjoy the social fruits of their
education whatever their social origins. A survey of the path taken
by six individual students shows how St Mark's was for them the
gateway to a distinguished and useful career in education and the
church.

Charles Daymond, the son of a widow, was among the first ten
students who entered the college in 1841. He was then 16. In 1844
he became head of the Central National School, Brighton. In 1850
he became Normal Master at St Mark's College. While there he was
ordained deacon and priest and in 1858 he became Principal of the
Training College at Peterborough.

Storer Lakin, son of a farmer near Loughborough, educated at
Sheepshead National School, entered in 1841, aged 15. His first post
was as Master of the National School, Bickerstaffe, Lancashire, with
a salary of £30 p.a. and free board and lodging with the clergyman.
He went on to the National School at Torquay and in 1850 became
Assistant Tutor at St Mark's College. He was ordained deacon in
1851 and priest in 1852. In 1854 he entered Sidney Sussex College,

[1]Ibid.

Cambridge. In 1858 he became a minor canon of Salisbury Cathedral, in 1875 Librarian of the Cathedral, in 1879 Succentor and eventually Precentor.

Charles Morgan, son of a draper of Olney, Bucks., educated at a National and then a commercial school, entered in 1843, aged 15. By 1853 he was Normal Master at Carmarthen Training College. In 1855 he went out to British Guiana, where he was ordained deacon in 1856 and was Training Master of the Bishop's college, Georgetown, and Diocesan Inspector of Schools in British Guiana. He finished his career as Rector of Rhoscrowther, Pembrokeshire.

William Benham, son of a blacksmith at West Meon, Hampshire, was educated at the village National School, and by the Rector, who taught him Latin and Greek. He entered St Mark's on the last day of 1844, aged 14. He taught first at the National School at Wantage, then at the Blewcoat School, Westminster. In 1853 he became private tutor in the family of Sir John Sebright. Two years later he became a student at King's College, London and in 1857 he returned to St Mark's as a tutor. The same year he was ordained deacon and in 1858 priest by the Bishop of London. He lectured at St Mark's in Divinity and English Literature and taught also at Queen's College, Harley Street where in 1866 he became Professor of Modern History. He continued the latter appointment when in 1867 he became Vicar of Addington. While there he did much writing and edited the works of Cowper. He later became Vicar of Margate, where he was Chairman of the School Board and lectured in the Church Institute, and then Vicar of Marden. In 1882 he became Rector of St Edmund's, Lombard Street, where his church was famous for his sermons and lectures, for thirty years. He was eventually made an honorary Canon of Canterbury Cathedral.

John Bamforth, son of the parish clerk at Hunslet, educated at the National School, and teaching there as an assistant, entered St Mark's in 1847, aged 16. He went out to the National School at Wells, then he became Tutor to St Thomas's College, Colombo, Ceylon, where he was ordained. Afterwards he became Chaplain to the Bishop of Colombo, then Principal of Doveton College, Madras.

One of the stranger careers was that of Thomas Rossiter, son of a farmer from Croscombe near Wells, who entered St Mark's in 1848. He went out to a National School at Gosport, but in 1859 sailed for Norfolk Island in the Pacific to act as storekeeper and schoolmaster to the former inhabitants of Pitcairn Island, descendants of the mutineers of the Bounty. He was still in Norfolk Island in 1891.[1]

Derwent had done a great deal to create members of the 'clerisy' to which his father had been committed and to educate his students for self-development. Greater help from the state towards education between 1846 and 1861 made possible a period of great improvement and expansion at St Mark's College. Derwent's greatest problem in the early years at St Mark's had been the lack of any adequate system of secondary education for the sons of artisans and tradesmen who were the majority of entrants to the college, and the consequent low standard of literacy of the new students.

The Committee of Council had been set up in 1839 to administer parliamentary grants to education. Kay-Shuttleworth, Secretary of the Committee of Council, in 1846 introduced Minutes which created the pupil-teacher system. This gradually provided much better-educated entrants, and provided financial assistance to the College.

The 1846 regulations provided that children of 13 and over could be apprenticed to the teacher for five years as pupil-teachers. They helped in the school and were taught by the master for 1½ hours a day. If his work was satisfactory, the pupil-teacher received a stipend which enabled him to continue his education, and the master was paid for teaching him. At the end of his course the pupil-teacher could compete for a Queen's Scholarship worth £25 towards the expense of his first year.

All training college students were to be examined annually and if they obtained certificates they earned an annual grant to the college. The certificated teacher obtained an augmented grant to his salary of £20, £25 or £30 a year depending on the

[1]The information about these students is taken from the first College Register, 1841–49. Archives: College of St Mark and St John.

class of his certificate (one, two, or three years) on condition that the school managers provided him with a rent-free house and an adequate salary, and provided that the Inspector's annual report was satisfactory. Teachers who served for a minimum of 15 years were also entitled to pensions.

The immediate result of the Minutes of 1846 was to provide the college with an assured source of income from the State, provided the students passed their certificate examinations. The first Teacher's Certificate examination was held in December 1847, and old students returned to St Mark's to take the examination in the hope of earning augmentation grants to their salaries. Of the 51 students examined, 32 obtained certificates of proficiency.

In 1849 the National Society decided that St Mark's should have its own governing Council, elected by subscribers and donors to the College, which was to report annually to the National Society. This gave Derwent a much greater degree of independence, although the National Society kept a tight hold on the reins. The College Council was not to make new arrangements with the Committee of Council without the agreement of the National Society. The Bishop of London was to be ex-officio President of the Council and the National Society was to send its Inspector and Surveyor to the college at least once a year.

For the National Society this was a way of saving money. The regular income of the College would be £3,000 p.a. (including £1,000 from the Committee of Council) plus the income for certificates earned by the pupils, plus voluntary contributions raised by the College Council.[1] The National Society Annual Report of 1850 remarked that by the system of separate management for St Mark's and Whitelands 'expenditure has been considerably reduced'. The financial arrangement was 'most satisfactory to the Society', whereby a grant of £2,100 was the whole annual payment from the Society.

The years from 1847 to 1861 were a period of expansion and development at St Mark's. With the prospect of a better income, including augmentation grants and payment for pupil-

---

[1]National Society Annual Report, 1849.

teachers, teaching became a more attractive occupation. The first ten Queen's scholars entered the college in 1851 and this was the beginning of a period when the standard of entrants was much better, especially after the Committee of Council Minute of August 1853, which allowed the training colleges to take Queen's Scholars up to their full numbers, instead of the previous limit of 25 per cent.

A Committee was set up by the National Society in 1847 'For the collection and disposal of a Special Fund which it is proposed to raise by Public Subscription for the Enlargement of St Mark's College, Chelsea'. They printed an Address by Derwent Coleridge, dated August 1847[1]. The address gives a summary of the achievements of the College up to that date, mentions the need for a preparatory school, and continues: 'Under all these circumstances, considering the success which appears to attend this method of training, the pressing demand which exists for masters so trained, and the inconvenience and insufficiency of the present accommodation, an opinion has for some time been entertained that the College ought, at the first favourable opportunity, to be very considerably enlarged.'

Derwent went on to say that it was proposed to provide accommodation for 150 pupils in training. A proportion of these would be Queen's Scholars. The remainder would pay a premium, in addition to their annual grants for passing examinations. He said that experience had shown that these youths would in general be too young to 'commence residence with a view to leaving the college after three years' and it was for this reason that it was proposed to add a junior department.

> It will be necessary to erect a large dining hall, with a kitchen and other domestic offices; a spacious lecture-room ... with a number of smaller class-rooms, a chemical laboratory, etc.; an extensive range of sleeping-rooms for the pupils in training, and a dormitory, differently arranged, for the junior department; and lastly, suitable chambers for the masters and officers of the College. It will be further necessary to erect a second

[1]Archives: College of St Mark and St John.

St Mark's College Staff, about 1858.

A. C. Daymond   William Benham   Jerome Mercier

Alfred Chas. King   Derwent Coleridge   Thos Williams   C. F. Eastburn

(Courtesy College of St Mark and St John, Plymouth)

model school, on a larger scale, to supply the students in training with the fullest opportunity of observing and practising the art of teaching. It is calculated that a sum of not less than 25,000l. will be required to complete the whole.

In fact by 1858 all these plans had been carried out, with the exception of the 'junior department' which the pupil-teacher system rendered unnecessary. The resultant buildings were known as the Coleridge Building. By 1856 accommodation had been provided for 100 students and there were 84 in residence. The previous December, 65 students were examined and 57 obtained certificates. Nine students took the third year, highest grade exam, three in Latin, four in higher mathematics and two in physical sciences. By 1858 there were 105 students and a large hall had been added.

Chapter 3
Private Life 1841–62

The life of the Coleridge family at Chelsea was deeply involved with the life of the College, not only mentally and spiritually but socially and in a material way. The Principal's family occupied the first floor at Stanley Grove, where Derwent's study was situated, and they used as their dining-room the Committee Room on the ground floor, which also did duty as a class-room. The first students slept in the attics at Stanley Grove which later became the sick bay. In a memorandum to the Committee of the National Society in 1844, Derwent asked that the carpets of the stairs and sitting-rooms in the Principal's House should be considered the fixed property of the National Society, as they were in constant public use.[1]

Derwent and Mary were *in loco parentis* to the young students, who were mostly away from home for the first time in their lives. John Hutchinson, the son of a farmer from Herefordshire, came to the college in January 1842 at the age of 13. In 1913 he wrote his reminiscences for the college Year Book.[2] His father drove him to Cheltenham, whence he travelled by coach to White Horse Cellars in Piccadilly.

[1]Derwent Coleridge MSS. HRC, Texas.
[2]*Old Days at St Mark's. By One of the First Students.* Reprinted from the Year Book of 1914. Archives: College of St Mark and St John.

At the White Horse Cellars I was met by the then Steward of the College, Mr Henry Strickland, and conducted in a carriage to my destination, down the Brompton and Fulham Roads, past the Consumption Hospital, then hardly finished, the remainder of the large open field being, I noticed, filled with rows upon rows of ... Cos lettuces, past many other open spaces, now filled up, till I found myself entering upon the grounds of what was then still known as Stanley House ... I was led by my kindly conductor to the parlour of the housekeeper, whose name I think was the Cornish one of Purdue. There I was supplied with some refreshments, consisting of bread and cheese and a glass of very mild beer, very comforting after my long journey. After this meal I was informed the students were assembling for Prayers in the Lecture Room, so to that apartment I was shown by the manservant or butler who was, I think, also from Cornwall ... On entering the room ... I was shown to a seat near the door to take my part in the religious ceremony, which, I well remember, was conducted by the Principal himself, his wife, Mrs Coleridge, being present, with the female domestics of her household. Till then I had never seen either the Principal or Principaless, but at the end of the prayers I was sent for to be introduced to them. They received me kindly and asked after my parents at home, which made me feel more 'at home' than ever − so much so that, overhearing some talk about 'having baths' by the students ... I innocently asked of Mrs Coleridge if I was to have one too. This those who heard it, I discovered afterwards, considered a *liberty* ... but 'her Ladyship' (as they deemed her, and rightly) only smiled at my *naiveté* and said, 'Of course I was to, and no doubt I should be told all about it'.

William Benham, who came up at the age of 14, wrote in 1891:

It was on the last day of December, 1844, that my kind old friend, Archdeacon Jennings, took me down to S. Mark's College. There, in what was then 'the Committee Room' ... I first saw Mr Coleridge. His handsome face beamed with

211

genuine loving-kindness, as it did as long as I, or any other man, knew him. It was holiday time, and he was wrapped in that red dressing gown with which we were all so familiar in after years.[1]

Although the college employed a Matron, Mary had overall responsibility for the housekeeping and the domestic staff. Sara wrote to Sir John Taylor Coleridge about Mary, 'she has undertaken to superintend the general establishment at Stanley Grove, and will have all the cupboard responsibility which seldom proves in the long run a very light weight upon her shoulders'.[2] In October 1845 the Matron, Mrs Jennings, left. Her successor robbed the College considerably and on discovery tried to kill herself by cutting her throat. Mary had to look after her for a harrowing week before she was removed. On 24 October St Mark's Sub-Committee minuted that they 'especially wish to return their cordial thanks to Mrs Coleridge, who in this instance has added to the many benefits which her able and judicious management has conferred on the Institution'.[3]

From 15 October until after Christmas, Mary acted as Matron. She wrote to her friend Arabella Brooke that she had arranged all the linen, cut out sets of shirts, comforted very sick boys, laughed at sham invalids – 'I assure you I have been in my opinion the very best Matron I ever had!'[4] There is a story in the Coleridge family that Mary suspected the milkman of watering the milk, so one day she opened the door to him herself.[5] Holding two jugs, she told the milkman: 'I'll have the milk in this one and the water in the other – I prefer to mix them myself.'

Apart from her domestic responsibilities in the college, it is clear from Derwent's daily letters to Mary when he was away, that she had a rôle in the college administration and was thoroughly familiar with his professional preoccupations. He wrote to her from Ludlow

[1]*Memorials of S. Mark's College*. Ed. G. W. Gent. White, 1891.
[2]24 March 1841. Sara Coleridge letters. HRC, Texas.
[3]Minutes of St Mark's Sub-Committee. Archives: College of St Mark and St John.
[4]9 December 1845. Coleridge papers. HRC, Texas.
[5]Recounted by Mr A. H. B. Coleridge in a letter to G. H. Hainton.

asking her to send 'a few of the printed advertisements' and, if not already done, to send one to Deighton and one to Parker, the Cambridge and Oxford booksellers.[1] A few days later he wrote 'Have you a questions paper? Strickland should have left some with you.' At the same time Strickland, the college Steward and Industrial Master, was writing to Mary from Okehampton asking her to send him some prospectuses. In 1850 Derwent wrote to her from Helston in detail about his plans for asking Daymond to replace Staley, who had resigned as head of the Practising School. 'Staley should be reminded to send in his resignation to the Council as well as me and his abrupt and immediate departure should not be taken as a matter of course. The opening of the school at Wandsworth can surely be postponed for a week or a fortnight if necessary. What does Clark [the Vice-Principal] say to this?'[2]

As well as being wife and mother, having responsibility for the domestic life of the college and an administrative rôle, and always being available for Derwent to talk over his professional worries, Mary was hostess to their many friends and visitors, both in a private and a public capacity. Every June the National Society held a public examination 'at which the bettermost students were trotted out'.[3] Sara Coleridge wrote to Sir John, 'On that day there is to be breakfast for 20 − cakes, sandwiches and wine for about 150, at the cost of the Nat. Society, but as my sister says, at her trouble.'[4] Archbishop Howley, Bishop Blomfield, F. D. Maurice, and Dr Christopher Wordsworth were some of those who presided in different years. It was an occasion rather like the School Meeting at Helston. After the early years the other gala day in the college year was St Mark's Day, 25 April, when old students were invited to return for the festivities and the college was decorated with daffodils; perhaps there were memories of Flora Day. Christabel Coleridge, recollecting in middle age her childhood at the college, says: 'St Mark's Day stands out as the great event of the year, and from nine o'clock when the public breakfast began, until eleven at night when

[1]23 June 1844. Derwent Coleridge MSS. HRC, Texas.
[2]8 January 1850. Ibid.
[3]William Benham. *Memorials of S. Mark's College*. Ed. G. W. Gent. White, 1891.
[4]June 1843. Sara Coleridge letters. HRC, Texas.

the oratorio was over, it seemed perfectly delightful.'[1]

Apart from these big public occasions there were many visitors to the college, and Derwent's finances, never his strong point, were strained. As usual, he turned to relatives and friends. Sir John Taylor Coleridge contributed £50 a year to young Derwent's school fees[2] and Miss Trevenen also helped to pay for young Derwent's education. In a draft memorandum to the Committee of the National Society Derwent stated that his last three years' experience showed that the income attached to his appointment did not enable him to meet the necessary expenses of the situation.[3] He found it impossible to separate his private domestic expenditure from his public capacity. He suggested that, as a 'temporary and practical accommodation' which 'may enable him to retain his appointment', the carpets of the stairs and sitting-rooms in his home should be taken over by the National Society, the Principal's family washing should be included in that of the establishment, a small sum be given from the Chapel funds to the officiating minister for the expense of vestments, and an annual stipend be paid to the Medical Attendant for attending on all the inmates of the College. Though 'fully aware of the difficulties encountered by the Committee of the National Society in questions of a pecuniary nature', he was impelled to write by 'motives of extreme urgency'.

By the autumn of 1841 Mary's mother and sisters had come to live in Chelsea. Mr Pridham had died in 1838 and no doubt Mrs Pridham wanted to be near her eldest daughter. She and her other daughters were frequent visitors to St Mark's. In June 1843 Mary's sister Kate was helping with the preparations for the Examination Day.[4] The following month she became engaged to Thomas Helmore, the Vice-Principal, and the National Society agreed to rent a house for Helmore at 18 Devonshire Terrace, near the College, where he had previously been living.[5] His

[1] *Memorials of S. Mark's College.* Ed. G. W. Gent. White, 1891

[2] Sir J. T. Coleridge to Derwent Coleridge 13 June 1841. 'So long as I am able, and you need it, while his education is going on I mean to contribute £50 p.a. to it.' D. Coleridge MSS. HRC, Texas.

[3] Presumably written in 1844. Derwent Coleridge MSS. HRC, Texas.

[4] Sara Coleridge to Sir J. T. Coleridge. June 1843. Coleridge papers. HRC, Texas.

[5] 14 September 1843. Minutes of School Committee, National Society.

marriage to Kate Pridham took place the following year.

It was no doubt through Derwent's influence that Mary's young brother John Pridham obtained a post in October 1841 as organising master with the National Society, travelling about the country advising on the running of Schools. It is clear from Mary's earlier letters that John's behaviour as a boy had been difficult. Sara wrote to Miss Trevenen: '... what a very happy thing it is that young Pridham has now obtained a creditable employment, and seems likely to perform it well, and be steadier than hitherto. What a comfort for his mother if even thus late he begins, and perseveres in, a useful career!'[1]

At Christmas time 1842 Sara's son Herbert, aged 12, spent part of his holiday from Eton at St Mark's, while his father, Henry Nelson Coleridge, was in the last stages of the progressive spinal paralysis which had been overtaking him throughout the year. His death was a tragic blow to Sara, for theirs had been a marriage of true minds and they were deeply devoted. Sara bore her loss with Christian fortitude and henceforth devoted a great deal of her time to editing her father's works. She visited Derwent and Mary more frequently, when she could borrow a carriage from Sir John Taylor Coleridge or Joanna Patteson, and turned increasingly to Derwent for comfort.

On 25 May 1843 Mary gave birth to Christabel Rose Coleridge. She was to be their second surviving child and proved a great joy to them. When she was six months old Derwent wrote to Miss Trevenen. 'Christabel Rose (Blowsalee Rosy would not have been a bad appellative) is very well, very bonny, and very merry, but is still wholly independent of the dentist. Molars, incisors and canines are all alike to her; she falls under none of the Linnæan orders, poor little nondescript!' He went on to say that Derwent was flourishing at Charterhouse 'adorning the inside of his head with Greek and gossip, and the outside with bear's grease and curling-tongs, – as often as he has opportunity. I think you will find the tout ensemble improved, tho' you may not quite approve of the toupeé.'[2]

---

[1] 27 October 1841. Sara Coleridge letters No. 1388. HRC, Texas.
[2] 6 December 1843. Derwent Coleridge MSS. HRC, Texas.

In June 1843, at Sara's request, Derwent wrote to Mrs Gillman, saying that STC's children would like his coffin to be transferred from the common vault, where it lay, to a family vault 'where the spot itself could in future ages be pointed out'. Sara wanted her husband's remains to lie next to those of her father, to whose ideas he had been so devoted. On 3 July Derwent went with Sara to Highgate churchyard, where they made arrangements with the sextons for the enlargement of Henry's vault and the transfer thither of STC's coffin. Derwent undertook to pay for the new oak outer coffin for STC's remains and to consult Blore on the subject of the monumental slab.[1]

At the end of the month Derwent achieved his long-cherished desire of returning to the Lake District, for the first time since his departure in 1820. He stayed at the Knabbe, on the shores of Rydal Water, with his brother Hartley, whom he had not seen since 1822. The reunion caused some tension on both sides. Derwent wrote to Miss Trevenen about Hartley: 'he is <u>much, very much</u> aged – tho' little altered in other respects – I cannot but look upon [him] with considerable pain and I fear this is a mutual feeling. I mean that my company gives him by no means unmixed pleasure.'[2] To Mary, 'my dearest wife', Derwent wrote 'Hartley is everywhere and by everyone <u>beloved</u> and <u>excused</u> – his propensity as a sort of bodily infirmity, like palsy, for which he is hardly accountable'.[3] He described Hartley as 'fat, short, white, bald, with a very broad nose like old Mr Pridham's'. A few days later he told Mary 'every man, woman and child in the vale appears to have a smile and a bow for him when they meet. In his unfortunate wanderings go where he will the cottage door is open to him, and the best entertainment that the house affords. They seem to look upon him as a sort of superior being left perfectly helpless, in a world unsuited to him, to be cared for by everyone; the object at once of their respect, their compassion and their amusement.'[4] Finally he wrote to Mary 'I fear there is nothing to be done for Hartley but to add to his comforts and keep

[1]Sara Coleridge to Sir J. T. Coleridge. 3 July 1843. Sara Coleridge letters. HRC, Texas.
[2]24 July 1843. Derwent Coleridge MSS. HRC, Texas.
[3]22 July 1843. Ibid.
[4]28 July 1843. Ibid.

up his spirits by letters of encouragement ... a very, very painful thought to me ... I have some essays of his for Moxon.'[1]

Hartley wrote to their mother:

> By the way, I think Derwent is a wee bit proud of his wife's beauty, which, I doubt not, is still a beautiful autumn[2] ... Derwent himself is as little altered, as could be expected in the time; yet I am not sure, I should immediately have recognised him, had I met him unawares. I see little likeness to Papa, except in the metaphysical turn of his mind, which is differenced by, a professional, or at least practical purpose ever present. The quantity of French phrases wherewith he tambours his conversation would have made Papa blaspheme outright without reverence to the cloth. He is the happiest mixture of Divine, Philosopher, Poet, Man of Business, and fine Gentleman (I had almost said <u>Courtier</u>) that I ever saw, and would be an ornament to the Bench. But I fear he is too definite and uncomplying in his opinions to reach a Mitre – as he might have a fair chance of doing, if he went the right way about it. His reading in the desk and at the Communion Table are the best I ever heard ... Derwent was exorbitantly admired by high and low ... I wish he could have stayed longer. He was so much sought after, that we had very little quiet time together, and beside, the meeting after so long an interval, in which so much to regret, and on my part, so much to blame, had taken place, produced a degree of nervous feverishness, which was only just subsiding, when his leave of absence expired. I own, the irritability was, chiefly, on my side – he has great command of temper, and if he be moved to wrath, anger makes him eloquent, while it renders me a pitiful stammerer.[3]

Later Hartley wrote to Mrs STC about Derwent:

> he is most exemplary in all relations, and has no fault but a

[1] 10 August 1843. Ibid.
[2] Mary was 36!
[3] 25 October 1843. *Letters of Hartley Coleridge.* Ed. G. E. and E. L. Griggs. OUP 1936.

certain measure of, I will not call it presumption but assumption, probably owing in part to his habits of command and a little to the worship universally paid him – which is greater than either his father, or W. or S. obtained at his age . . . Of course, you have read Moultrie's address to him. I confess I should not like to be so praised in print, but alas! I know that I deserve it not . . . Derwent, however, can bear it, for he has few faults for any to discover. If he had, his freedom of rebuke and fearless assertion of his opinions, which are not those, not precisely those, of any sect, party, or denomination in Church or State would provoke some people to expose them with little mercy.[1]

Derwent emerges at the age of 43 as self-confident, authoritative and having very definite opinions which he did not hesitate to express, but at the same time making himself universally popular.

Derwent's time in the Lake District was taken up by visiting old friends and new acquaintances and walking in the hills. He saw his old teacher Mr Dawes, and his schoolfellows, Allen Harden and Herbert White, called on the Wordsworths, had tea with Mrs Arnold at Fox How, where he met the Archbishop of Dublin and dined with Mr and Mrs Charles Fox. He travelled on top of the mail to Keswick, where he met Cuthbert and Kate Southey and Aunt Lovell. He wrote daily to Mary, 'my dearest love'.[2] He was 'pining to have you here. Keswick far more than realises my fondest, fairest recollections – and has so rekindled all my old love of natural beauty that I shall not be able without an effort to bring myself to think with pleasure of seeing York or Lincoln. Before I came here it was the other way. I thought more of the glories of architecture than of woods and lakes, for so it was in my continental tours, but here it is otherwise.'

He was invited by Captain Henry Peachey to stay a day or two on Derwent Island, 'not, alas, Derwent's Island'. He told Mary: 'To my taste and feelings it would be the most delightful residence in the

---

[1] 7 February 1844. *Letters of Hartley Coleridge.* Ed. G. E. and E. L. Griggs. OUP 1936.
[2] Derwent Coleridge MSS. HRC, Texas.

whole world.' While staying there he took a boat to the shore, walked to Borrowdale and climbed Castle Crag, alone, and was 'in a more complete <u>sweat</u>, through to my braces, than for years'. He walked back via Portinscale. Next day he climbed Saddleback. On another day he walked with Hartley from Rydal to Sourmilk Gill in Easedale. One Sunday he preached both at Ambleside and Rydal, involving nine miles' walking. 'Half the Ambleside congregation sallied forth to hear the Archbishop preach at Rydal Chapel – who came to Ambleside to hear <u>me</u>! The <u>stayers</u> twitted the <u>gadders</u> famously on their return.'

On his last Sunday he preached at Crosthwaite, where Southey, who had died earlier that year, took him to church as a boy. On 9 August he breakfasted with William Wordsworth, who gave him the last edition of his *Guide to the Lakes*, which he autographed, and walked back with Derwent, in his dressing-gown and cap, to the Nab. There Derwent bade farewell to Hartley, with a 'heavy heart', and set forth in Mr Richardson's market cart for Pennybridge, where he visited his old friend, Mrs Machell, 'as shy as ever'. Next day he went in Mr Machell's phaeton to Ulverstone, where he took a carriage to Bardsea, went by steamer to Fleetwood and then by rail to Manchester, Leeds, York and home.

In June 1844 Derwent went to Cheltenham to meet John Moultrie. He stayed at 2 Imperial Square and visited Mary's brother John Pridham. In one of his frequent letters to Mary, Derwent told her that he had been to Seven Springs, the source of the Thames – 'my thoughts found it navigable all the way to Chelsea, up the Kensington Canal, and so in through the back garden and farmyard to where Nurse was sitting with Baby on her little stool under the viranda'. He cured one of his recurring stomach upsets with pills and 'a deluge of Cheltenham water' at Montpelier Spa[1], before proceeding with Moultrie to the potteries at Worcester, to Great Malvern and to Ludlow. Here they decided to abandon their projected Welsh tour and went to stay with the Rev. George Moultrie, Moultrie's father, at Cleobury Mortimer in Shropshire. Mary wrote to her friend Arabella Brooke that Derwent was not to

---

[1] 17 June 1844. Derwent Coleridge MSS. HRC, Texas.

go to North Wales, as travelling *en seigneur* was expensive and he could not rough it.[1]

> Moultrie thrives well on clouted shoon with a knapsack on his back and a dry crust in his pocket but Derwent has no power for this – he cannot turn into a wayside Public, sup heartily upon cheese and ale and sleep soundly afterwards upon a heather bed – his nerves would scream every one of them at such pain and insult.

Mary and Derwent's second son was born on 9 April 1845. Hartley declined the honour of having the baby named after him 'having a Shandean Superstition respecting Christian names, and never having known that of Hartley (which as a prefix is by no means confined to myself) attended by fortune or the virtues that adorn prosperity, I would advise you to pause before you make your youngest hope in aught to resemble his heterodox Uncle'.[2] The baby was therefore christened Henry Nelson Praed Coleridge. Alas! he fell ill and died in July.

In early August Derwent accompanied Sara and her daughter Edith, and maid Martha, to Herne Bay. Sara wrote to Sir John Taylor Coleridge about Derwent:

> I must say that the dear man's conversation, in one way and another, is highly instructive and amusing ... Last Wednesday we went to Canterbury to see the Cathedral and St Augustine's. The former I admired more than ever, and Derwent's architectural lore and anti-protestant opinions made our excursion all round the outside and through the inside, of this more beautiful than sublime structure, all the more rememberable and interesting.[3]

Derwent decided it was a suitable place for Mary, Christabel and young Derwent to join them. He wrote enthusiastically to Mary that he thought the place was 'of real service to health ... but I

[1]Coleridge papers. HRC, Texas.
[2]*Letters of Hartley Coleridge.* Ed. G. E. and E. L. Griggs. OUP 1936.
[3]10 August 1845. Coleridge papers. HRC, Texas.

would not have you do anything against your better judgement or any strong feeling ... We have sustained a loss and disappointment – a trial to us both, but in different degrees and in a different way. To me it is a blessing and a comfort withdrawn – a pleasure and a delight the less. To you it is all this, and something more, but you will see through it, look beyond it. May God bless and comfort you, my sweet wife'.[1]

On 24 September 1845 Derwent's mother died suddenly of a heart attack. Derwent had to hurry to Eton to break the news to Sara, who was staying there for a week, although she had spent nearly her whole life with her mother. Mary wrote from Chester Place to tell Hartley – 'could we have ventured to form a wish of how it would please God to take her we could not have chosen a calmer end – no pain – not bed-ridden – a thing she so much dreaded – and her faculties clear to the very last! – She is a great loss to us all, her presence was a comfort to Derwent and to me whenever we came to this house – and her little nervous attack once over – her conversation was most cheerful and agreeable – but her nervousness – and all her anxiety is over – she is with her Saviour ... I must write many letters today – so Farewell my dear brother – God comfort you. I trust that Sara and I shall be able in <u>some measure</u> to supply her place to you.'[2] Writing later to Hartley, Derwent described their mother as 'a spirit <u>just</u> and <u>true</u> far beyond any ordinary standard even among the admirable and good – above all – a spirit evermore passing out of itself in love first for her nearest and dearest, yet counting many near and dear, and not <u>limiting</u> her affections here or anywhere'.[3] Mrs STC had visited St Mark's on at least one occasion, in August 1842, when Derwent wrote to Hartley 'Our mother has just been <u>here</u> – her first visit. We took her by surprise and got her into the carriage in spite of herself.[4]

It is a pity that Mrs STC did not live to see Derwent created Prebend of Islington in St Paul's Cathedral by the Bishop of London in January 1846. As Bishop Blomfield wrote, it was 'a

[1] 5 August 1845. Derwent Coleridge MSS. HRC, Texas.
[2] 24 September 1845. Coleridge papers. HRC, Texas.
[3] 10 October 1845. Derwent Coleridge MSS. HRC, Texas.
[4] 22 August 1842. Ibid.

profitless dignity as a mark of my good opinion'.[1]

In March 1846 Helmore was appointed Master of the Choristers at the Chapels Royal and resigned as Vice-Principal of St Mark's, although he remained Precentor, in charge of the Chapel services and the practices for them. Samuel Clark was appointed Vice-Principal. He was largely self-educated in his limited spare time, having been employed in his father's business in Southampton from the age of 13, until he was helped by F. D. Maurice, who encouraged him to go up to Oxford in 1840 at the age of 30. There he continued to work part-time to meet his college expenses and did not graduate until 1846. He was appointed Vice-Principal and ordained on St Mark's Day 1846. The Rev. H. Moseley, who inspected the college in December 1846, remarked in his report: 'With extensive attainments in literature, the Vice-Principal unites an intimate acquaintance with some important departments of experimental science: and an opportunity is thus afforded of adding to the course of instruction here, an element in which it is essentially wanting.'[2]

Derwent and Mary's last child was born on 8 December 1846 and christened Ernest Hartley. Mary wrote to Hartley on 16 February:

I have been full of good intentions towards you for some time past, but I am such a busy woman that many a pleasant duty goes unfulfilled for lack of time. I would not let Derwent write to tell you of our new little Baby – our precious 'Ernest Hartley' – because I wished to do so myself. He is in truth a very pretty fellow, and seems very bright and intelligent. Christabel is growing extremely fond of him ... She is a most striking child, full of intellect with much personal courage, and the tenderest heart in the world – a strange mixture of boldness and timidity. Her large blue eyes, which resemble her Grandfather's, are sometimes wild as an ocelot, sometimes soft and tender as a dove. The baby boy is like his father. Dervy is said to be very much like you. He has just matriculated at

[1]16 January 1846. Ibid.
[2]Committee of Council Minutes, 1846. I.

Exeter Coll. Oxford. He will read with his father until he goes up to reside ... We all send kindest love to you dearest Hartley — and ever think of me as your affect. sister — Mary Coleridge.

The Coleridge children were very much part of the college. Christabel remembered in later life:

Great garden parties were also given on my birthday in May, when the students used to dress splendid. May poles for me and my little friends to dance around. Everyone was kind to the Principal's children, and I have the most affectionate remembrance of some of the old college servants, Mrs Lane the cook, and many others.

Once they all clubbed together, and had the portrait of the old dog Carlo, painted in oils, as a present to my mother on her return from the summer holidays.[1]

Christabel remembered one or two of the students being chosen to give arithmetic and geography lessons to her and some of her friends.

It was part of the tragedy of Hartley Coleridge's life, that his addiction to drink prevented him from ever seeing any of his nieces and nephews. He was devoted to children, wrote a sonnet to Christabel and in his letters frequently wished he could see his brother's and sister's children, but he accepted that he had to stay at Rydal, where his irregular habits would not embarrass his family. Sara was much distressed when Hartley showed signs of wishing to come to their mother's funeral, but he was persuaded not to do so. Derwent wrote him a long letter in 1845, begging him to give up alcohol.

Oh my Brother, need I remind you what this cruel enchantment has cost you? that it cuts you off from those who yearn to have you with them, to love and cherish you — My circumstances have ever been such that the bare possibility of

[1] *Recollections of St Mark's College, Chelsea*. C. R. Coleridge. *Memorials of S. Mark's College*. Ed. G. W. Gent. White, 1891.

your losing your self-respect – has put it out of my power to see you – a long privation both to Mary and myself. Not to say that my health would immediately give way under the misery which it wd occasion me. This may also be said of your widowed sister. There is, so far as I know, but one course open to you – to turn water-drinker, with Fell's[1] advice – *et dedoluisse semel.*[2]

Think not that I have written with any assumption or feeling of superiority – I deeply sympathise with all your weakness. God has preserved me from some outward ill effects of the disease within – but I am, (as you I trust are,) only struggling for more complete emancipation.

Mary continued to send Hartley shirts (cut out by herself and sewn by girls in the Chelsea parochial school) and wrote affectionate letters with detailed descriptions of the children to this brother-in-law she had never seen. Sara wrote loving letters to him and paid his bills out of his small income from the estate.

On 17 December 1848 Hartley was taken ill and developed pneumonia. His hostess, Mrs Richardson, sent for Derwent, who arrived at Nab Cottage, on the shores of Rydal Water, on 27 December. On 30 December Derwent wrote to Mary that Hartley was decidedly better and the next day he took communion with Derwent and Angus Flecker from Easedale. Derwent had been up Loughrigg and Nab Scar and felt ten years younger. 'If I could pitch my tent in one of these vales before I lose my physical powers I should be well pleased, but I do not disturb myself by a wish so little likely to be accomplished.'

On 1 January Hartley's condition began to deteriorate. Two days later Derwent wrote: 'He is constant in religious exercises but evidently suffers much in mind.' There was a hard frost and the lake had frozen overnight. Dr Green attended daily but on 6 January at 2.30 a.m. Derwent wrote:

My very dear wife, I write by the bed-side of a dying brother.

[1]Hartley's doctor.
[2]Give over grieving once and for all.

He is growing weaker and weaker and I am expecting, – I may say hoping to hear his last breath, – and see his protracted struggle exchanged for <u>rest</u>. After dispatching my letters yesterday I took a walk across the frozen lake, and up the brow of the opposite hill. On my return I found him worse, – and made up my mind to leave him no more ... Such a death-bed, – such a struggle, physical and mental, – I have never witnessed. In the course of the afternoon, I had some remarkable conversation with the sufferer, of which I have taken notes. It related to religious belief...

At half past six o'clock I sent for Dr Green, or Fell. They both arrived before eight ... He was then, as he is now, labouring for breath and we did not know that he was sensible when suddenly he asked Mr Fell if he would take the sacrament with him. I instantly made up my mind to offer it – and judge of the collectedness of his mind, as I went on. He joined in the service throughout most fervently, – The two medical men, and his two house friends communicating with him. – Again, after the lapse of some hours, after he had lost the power of articulation, I at length divined his meaning, and on my kneeling down in prayer his hands closed, and he even joined in some of the responses audibly – his lips moving evidently with meaning throughout...

Eight o'clock – and no relief. Dr Green told me he never witnessed so severe a death. I have passed a fearful night, – I watched poor Praed through his last hours, – but his sufferings were as nothing compared to these. I have a hope, bordering on assurance, a deep satisfaction in believing that my dear Brother's end will be a <u>conquest</u> ... 12 o'clock. Hartley is still alive, but oh! how changed ... All the love I ever bore him seems to rush into my heart at once – and what with my night of watching ... I am now unfit to be in the room. But I am not wanted now – It is marvellous that he goes on from hour to hour – but he cannot last long.

... The first of the horizon shining on the ice this morning was most beautiful...

If no further change takes place I shall send this letter as it is. I shall drop a line to Sara.

Your loving Husband,

Derwent Coleridge.

Tell Christabel I shall have much to tell her about her Papa's lakes and mountains, and how the little minnows may be seen by thousands, flinking about under the ice – and about a beautiful great Newfoundland dog, half as big again as Carlos, ten months old, who has a white kitten for his friend and playmate, out on the lawn of his Master's House –

The struggle is ended – His breath left him gradually as a child going to sleep – Half past two.

On 9 January Derwent wrote to Professor Wilson (an old friend of Hartley's) that the burial would be on 11 January in Grasmere churchyard – 'in the south-east corner by the river, close to the spot which his old friends Mr and Mrs Wordsworth have chosen for their resting place. Mr Wordsworth went with me yesterday to mark out the grave. His sister, daughter, nephew and two young children lie together in the same cluster. "When I turned from my daughter's grave," said the old man, "the first face that met me was Hartley's standing there."'[1] Writing to Mary and Sara on 7 January, Derwent told them Wordsworth said: 'It is a sad thing for me who have known him so long. He will be a sad loss to us. Let him lie as near to us as possible, leaving room for Mrs Wordsworth and myself. It would have been his wish.'[2] In the same letter Derwent reflected: 'So he is gone – and I did not think to shed so many tears over the thought of anyone going or gone for me – out of my own household – tears not of sorrow, not altogether of regret – but of tenderness and affection. – I did not shed so many for my dear Mother...'

Derwent spent the days before Hartley's funeral packing his

[1]Derwent Coleridge MSS. HRC, Texas.
[2]Ibid.

books and papers in five large packing cases, to be sent by goods train to St Mark's. He sent various books to local friends in gratitude and memory of Hartley and visited eight of Hartley's friends in Grasmere and another eight in Ambleside. He made up his mind to publish a collection of Hartley's works, both unpublished and those scattered in various periodicals; something which Hartley had never been able to summon up the will-power to do.

On the evening of 11 January Derwent wrote a description of the funeral to 'My very dear wife, and sister . . .'

The weather has been cold, but fine, with a few skuds of slight sleet, – and gleams of sunshine. One of these greeted us, as we entered Grasmere, and another smiled brightly through the church windows. No words can describe the beauty of the vale. The mountains capped, and mantled with snow, leaving the vallies below with barely a sprinkling . . .

The hearse, a very plain one, was drawn by Mr Richardson's own horse, and driven by his eldest boy, Hartley's godson, to whom I have given his Bible. The body was carried by Mr Richardson, James and two other young men – friends of the family – no hired men . . .

After the funeral I took a walk in Rydal grounds – and stood for some time before the beautiful waterfall. I have no wish in the way of simple gratification, so strong, as to introduce you, Mary and our sweet Christabel, to this scenery. Edith too – Hartley was so fond, and so proud of the drawing which she sent him.

The following day Derwent made more visits to old friends of Hartley and himself. Sleet and frost turned to sleet and rain, followed by hard rain. 'I have made up my mind that there is no bad weather in these vallies, none in which a well clad pedestrian, in good health, cannot enjoy himself – tho' some may be preferable to others.' He went to bed past midnight, 'tired enough'. On the Saturday he breakfasted with Wordsworth, took affectionate leave of him (for the last time, for he died in April 1850), and by ten was on the road to Keswick, travelling on the outside of the coach, on a misty, drizzly day, and 'was richly rewarded. The foaming beck, as we mounted Dunmail Rise, the sweet *piano* of its summer music exchanged for an impetuous *strepitoso* – and the white rills and infant glaciers (doomed to speedy dissolution) that streak the mountain sides – gleaming through the mist had a grand, mysterious effect – and as we descended upon Leatheswater the weather cleared.'

Having arrived in Keswick he visited Kate Southey for half an hour, then took up his quarters with Mr James Stanger of Lairthwaite. Passing by the old carding mill, he 'listened to the rumble of the wheels and water, which with the darkness of its nether region used to strike me with awe, since 40 years ago', and proceeded to Greta Bank, which:

> I found a very picture of desolation and desertion – my hospitable friends the Dentons having been driven away from it, by the vile curmudgeon who has got possession of Greta Hall ... turning my back on the old haunts, now desecrated, I plodded away to Lowdore – holding up Deddale's umbrella first in one hand and then in the other for it rained all the way, there and back. All the cascades and waterfalls were in full force ... But Lowdore! You hear the roar for several miles – losing it from time to time as we come near the lesser cataracts – reminding one of a great man's fame, seemingly overpowered by the prattling of some ephemeral reputation, but in reality keeping on in deeper note and swelling out again finely in the distance. Think of me, standing alone, beneath and among those great rocks, with the great waterfall before me. I got up close to it, grappled with it – it has many arms! – lay at its feet, looked up at it – heard it declaim its grand epic *ore profundissimo*, – great primæval monster – bard of the mountains that it is – sitting in its winter house, bare of its laurels.

During the next two years, in the intervals of a busy professional life and despite much family worry and distress, Derwent collected from Hartley's manuscripts and letters those poems and other writings which he thought worthy of permanent preservation. He was urged on by Sara, who, though busy editing their father's writings, found some sources of Hartley's work, and Mary transcribed in her beautifully regular hand many of the poems, for Hartley's writing was often barely legible. Derwent wrote to many of Hartley's friends for their recollections of him, and, in October 1850, again visited Nab Cottage, Ambleside, Keswick and Grasmere. In October 1851 he had published by Moxon two volumes of Hartley's poems: the first a reissue of poems published in 1833 and long out of print, the second poems hitherto unpublished. The first volume also contains a long memoir of Hartley, running to 169 pages, written by Derwent with remarkable frankness and insight into his brother's character and showing a tender understanding and a total lack of self-righteousness. Two months later Derwent brought out two volumes of Hartley's essays, again published by Moxon: the first volume a collection of miscellaneous essays, reprinted from various periodicals, some now defunct; the second volume consisting of notes mostly transcribed from the margins of Hartley's books, for he had inherited STC's habit of writing extensive marginalia. Derwent followed up the *Essays* by bringing out a new edition of Hartley's *Northern Worthies* with additional notes and corrections. Thus Derwent carried out the resolution he had made in Nab Cottage a few days after his brother's death, to present to the world the best of Hartley's writings and to explain to the world the weaknesses and goodness of his brother's character.

It will be remembered that Derwent had befriended Mary's only brother, John, who was five years younger than herself. In 1849 Kay-Shuttleworth asked Derwent for a Normal School master for Mauritius, to train schoolmasters for the island. John by this time was married and his wife was expecting a baby. Derwent recommended him to the post by virtue of his experience as an Organising Master under the National Society and 'his residence for so long in or close by St Mark's College'.[1] When John and his wife, Bessie, reached Mauritius, they discovered that no such post as Normal School master existed. John was appointed to teach at the Royal College, but soon found that the Creole Committee which controlled the College wished to disallow

[1]23 August 1849. Derwent Coleridge to unidentified recipient. Derwent Coleridge MSS. HRC, Texas.

the house-rent allowance with which he had been appointed in England. In June 1849 John wrote asking Derwent to obtain testimonials of his appointment from the British Government.[1] In December 1849 John wrote to Derwent that 'among the minutes of the budget for 1850 my name was found as follows! "Mr Pridham – £96 for rent to be disallowed and a free passage offered home to England."'

John wrote to appeal to Earl Grey, through the Governor of the island, and sent a copy of his letter to Derwent, asking him to take it to the Privy Council office. The story had a tragic sequel, for in 1850 John had to return to England in broken health. In November Derwent wrote to Kay-Shuttleworth pleading for help for John Pridham, who had now been living with his mother for some months in a hopeless state of health – 'his brain is apparently softening, his memory and speech are seriously affected, and his whole frame is extremely enfeebled. We can look, humanly speaking, but for one result!' Derwent pointed out that John, his wife and infant were now dependent on his widowed mother, whose means were very limited, and asked if the Colonial Office would consider paying an annuity or compensation.[2] John Drake Pridham died on 2 January 1853 at 8, St Mark's Terrace at the age of 40. The cause of death was certified as general paralysis for three years.

After Christmas 1849 Derwent set off on a three-week tour in the west country, revisiting old friends. As he always did when away from Mary, he sent her a daily journal of his adventures, addressed to 'My dear love'. On 29 December he was staying with Sir J. T. Coleridge at Heath's Court, Ottery St Mary. He went on to visit Edwin Coleridge at Buckerell, then proceeded by coach to Exeter where he walked through the Cathedral. By 4 January he was in Plymouth, where he lunched with George Pridham and dined with George Wightwick, the architect. He spent three hours visiting people he had not seen for nine years and surprised the old artist Ambrose Johns at his gate: 'God bless my soul – Coleridge! – Come in, I can't speak – I can't tell you

[1] Ibid.
[2] 1 November 1850. Derwent Coleridge MSS. HRC, Texas.

what I feel – we were all talking of you at the Artists' meeting last Friday.'

Next day he had an eight-hour ride on the outside of the Telegraph coach to Truro, in rain, wind, sleet, snow and hail. As there was no public conveyance to 'poor forlorn Helston' he was 'fain to take a fly and pay my guinea like a gentleman'. In Helston he stayed with Miss Trevenen for eight days, and had a 'most gratifying' reception from everyone, rich and poor. Miss Trevenen gave him £20 and he bought some clothes in Helston.

There was no outside place on the coach to Bodmin, 'But with two pairs of drawers and two pair stockings I bore the cold perfectly well ... I have lost all my pains, aches, bruises and weaknesses and bore up gaily against a strong nor'easter at freezing point over Bodmin moors.' Thus Derwent wrote to Mary at 10.30 p.m. the same night from Mr Grylls' house at Luxulian. His enthusiastic temperament always responded to a change of scene and renewal of old friendships. He was up early next morning, writing six letters before breakfast. Returning to Plymouth, on 17 January he walked on the Hoe before breakfast and visited more old friends. 'I am very anxious on many counts to be at St Mark's, but my long walks, change of scene and air are doing me so much good – in fact I am thoro'ly well, strong and active from morning till night.' He took the train from Plymouth to Ashburton on 18 January, Friday, and decided to get the most out of his holiday and not return to London until the Monday. 'I hope to see the Dart tomorrow in its wintry grandeur swollen with the rain and melted snow.'

Derwent Moultrie Coleridge, Derwent's and Mary's firstborn, did not share the family talents. At Helston he had 'taken the run of the school' with boys older than himself; Derwent could not afford to send him away to school or to engage a tutor for him. When the family moved to London, after a year at King's College, he was sent to Shrewsbury at the age of 13 for two terms. This was not successful, and after a term as a private pupil with Mary's brother-in-law, he was sent to Charterhouse in January 1843. When he was 14 his mother wrote to Hartley 'He is a sweet fellow but not as gifted as a Coleridge ought to be.'[1]

[1] 7 October 1842. Coleridge papers. HRC, Texas.

Derwent wrote to him in July 1843, from the Lake District, that he wished he could have had him 'in this beautiful land, amid the scenes and with the companions of my own boyhood. There is much that would have interested you and amused you ... mountain sides to clamber up, boats to row and to sail in, jolly picknicks etc.' He must come one day. 'Meanwhile you have to use diligence and take care that you reflect credit on the name you bear, particularly in these vales, where it is associated with so much that is high and intellectual. Work, work, work – and then I have no objection to all your play, play, play.' That autumn, when his son was 15, Derwent wrote to Moultrie:

> Derwent Moultrie is doing nicely – not brilliantly; but we are all apt to expect too much of our children, and to trust too little to Providence – to compare them with what we think we remember ourselves to have been; forgetting that boys and men are both better and worse than they were – better as well as worse – that even in the case of our own children, we know not what is in them, and that our duty is to do all we can, and to hope. Derwent appears very amiable and domestic and dotes upon his sister, – and if he does not make a scholar, he may make something else. He is bright, lively and observant, but he has not the philological organ. He has malaprop'd from his infancy.[1]

In January 1845 we find Derwent writing to Mary from Cheltenham: 'Derwent must do at least ten verses every day or his task will not be ready.[2]

Meanwhile Derwent Moultrie was growing into a handsome young man concerned with his appearance. At 15 he was 'much interested in the cut of his jacket and very anxious that his pumps and silk stockings should make a proper impression', his mother wrote to her friend Arabella Brooke.[3] In July 1844 Sara told Mary that she

[1] 24 October 1843. Derwent Coleridge MSS. HRC, Texas.
[2] 4 January 1845. Ibid.
[3] 8 December 1843. Coleridge papers. HRC, Texas.

and Mrs John Taylor Coleridge rejoiced over Dervy's 'extreme good looks'.

In 1847 young Derwent went up to Exeter College, Oxford. He seems to have got into bad company and his Coleridge cousins circulated in the family rumours about his behaviour. Unlike Derwent, they had all been at Eton and do not appear to have befriended him. Sara's son, Herbert, who was still at Eton, had spent a good deal of time with Derwent during his holidays and was fond of him, but Sara wrote to Mary that Herbert had heard of Derwent's 'goings on'. What these consisted of is not explained, but in one of her letters to Mary Sara says: 'I do not believe D. has any craving for drink like H.' Samuel Clark, the Vice-Principal, was sent to Oxford to enquire into Derwent's behaviour and returned with a reassuring report. But in December 1847 Derwent Moultrie was rusticated from Exeter College for ten terms, which amounted to expulsion.

The reasons for this are not clear. Sara wrote sympathetically to Mary: 'I feel with you a strong assurance that he is not – cannot be – false as a general characteristic . . . I suppose there is no doubt that he has in some instances departed from truth.' Of Herbert she said 'I wished him to feel that it is the sin which is infinitely of most importance – not the imprudence from excess or contrariety to the world's law.'

In 1848 young Derwent lived at home and an unsuccessful attempt was made to get him a secretaryship in the Privy Council. In the autumn of 1849 he was sent to King's College, with a view to preparing him for possible entry to Cambridge. In June 1850 his father stayed for two days with Lord Charles Harvey at his rectory at Chesterford, near Saffron Walden, and went over to Cambridge to undertake delicate negotiations to get Derwent Moultrie admitted to the university. Derwent saw, at Jesus College, Mr Skinner, an old friend of STC, and had a long interview with Mr Birkett, the Tutor, who agreed to admit Derwent Moultrie. 'I have suffered, I need not say, very much in mind –' wrote Derwent to Mary, 'but I think I have conducted the affair thus far as well as possible – and if no unexpected obstacle start up, matters look brightly enough as far as Derwent's position is concerned, but if he commits the least indiscretion it is impossible to say what may happen. He must be made aware of this.'[1]

Derwent Moultrie went up to Jesus College in the autumn of 1850 at the age of twenty-two and appears to have embarked at once on a career of reckless dissipation. By 20 November his father was in Cambridge, trying to sort out his affairs. Derwent wrote to Mary:

He has taken up two bills for £20 each of a bill-lender named Tarrant, and I wait to hear the result of a communication with him, but the more I enquire the more hopeless the matters appear to me. Reckless, extravagant, and idleness always, without an effort to the contrary. No cessation in evil – not apparently for the last three months, for the letters from girls crowd upon him. Friday he was dead drunk, and on Saturday affected with liquor. The girl Mordecai he picked up in the street last Wednesday. He attempted to marry her at St Ives on Monday. <u>Nothing can exceed the kindness of Birkett and Drake.</u> I am staying at Deighton's but am writing now from Ingram's ... Ingram will see the old Mordecais, and tell them what a bad bargain they have got. I have got Derwent's spoons and letters and seen his things packed.

This is an unsatisfactory letter but I have done all I could. What my mind is in the matter, I will tell you when I see you.

God bless and uphold you
    Your ever loving husband
        Derwent Coleridge
Do not expect me till late.[2]

It was a bitter ending to Derwent and Mary's hopes for their son. Derwent Moultrie was already thinking of emigration and his parents rapidly decided that the only thing to do was to send him to Australia, where he would have to work for his living. The story is told in a letter of Mary's.[3] She says that Derwent went to Cambridge

[1] 3 June 1850. Derwent Coleridge MSS. HRC, Texas.
[2] 20 November 1850. Derwent Coleridge MSS. HRC, Texas.
[3] Undated. Addressed to 'My dearest Friend' – probably Arabella Brooke. Coleridge papers. HRC, Texas.

and gave his son £14 to pay a debt, but Derwent Moultrie got tipsy and was robbed of the money:

> ... the next morning he took from a doctor strong stimulants to enable him to appear in Coll: this made him worse ... he again went out with some girl to a place and dined – woke at last from his intoxication – was frightened to death – thought it was all up at Camb: and with his friends remembered other debts behind – the friends of the girl promised him, if he would marry her, to give him money enough to live till the time of notice was expired at the Registry Office – I daresay he never' thought of Church in such a case – and then he was to solicit his friends to give him money enough to emigrate as a common man – the girl was good-looking and clever – some years older than himself – tho' he thought her 18 – seemed thrifty – and would do he thought – poor victim to his delusions – for an emigrant's wife. Thank God! we saved him from that. I think his eyes were opened to his escape before he sailed but he was in despair – and well he might be after such a career. As they traced him the country people told them that the 'young gentleman' could not eat and was agitated – but that the 'woman' was quite at her ease. He was taken at last by the Inspector of Police – and brought back by Graves without an attempt at resistance.
>
> You see there was no choice for the future. Mr Batten kindly took him in – and proposed that he should go at once to his friend Captain Sturt the discoverer, and now Colonial Secy. at Port Adelaide, where if he will he may get employment and perhaps do very well – but he is left to find employment, a few pounds only to be given to him on landing and Capt. Sturt will have orders to allow him what is absolutely necessary until he can obtain employment. He has sailed in the 'Thomas Chadwick' – a regular trader ... I need not say to you what all this labour and expense has cost us in the way of anxiety – independently of our misery for the cause of it all.
>
> [In the same letter Mary says:] Sometimes I was sustained by the sad but imperative need of the step – at other times a

gust of unutterable tenderness towards my poor erring child almost drove me to declare that I could not sanction the step, and this is partly why it was determined that his father and I should not take leave of him but chiefly I yielded to this because it would have been wrong to have hidden from him our just displeasure – and to part with him on any but loving terms we felt would be impossible – so we bade him farewell by letters ... Neither did he desire to see us – he said he could not bear it...

Young Derwent wrote to his mother on the eve of departure:

My dearest Mother,
I cannot set forth upon my perhaps lifelong pilgrimage, without leaving behind me a few farewell words. I say a few because as regards the past, the less said the better, and for the future, I or anyone can as yet say nothing. All I speak of now is the present. As you read this I shall be on my way to a new world, to find new friends, to lead, I hope in all ways, a new life. What I shall do wherewith to gain my bread I know not... I once more bid you hope, I myself do though in fear. I may even now at the eleventh hour become by degrees as great a comfort, as I have till now been a burden and distress – and already look forward to a time when I may be worthy once again to look you and all my friends fairly in the face. In a word that I may become an honest upright man. Teach the dear children still to love their exiled Brother. He will often, often think of them ... and may [you] one day find joy from your dearly attached son.
I sail tomorrow morning early – kind good Graves and Batten will see me off. Never from this time doubt Batten's good heart. He has indeed been a good kind friend to me ... glad to hear that you are going to Withyam – may it lend some of its peace to you.

Young Derwent sailed in late November 1850, and Mary took the children to stay at Withyam in Kent, near Tunbridge Wells. She wrote to her friend: 'I felt that nothing but rest and quiet would still the throbbings of my aching heart.' Derwent stayed with them for a few days, but then had to return to St Mark's, to deal with his son's debts, to lecture in college and take the Chapel services in spite of a bad cold, and to cope with the annual government inspection. He also deposited with Moxon, the publisher, his manuscript of Hartley's life. On Monday, 23 December he was writing to Mary that he longed to be at Withyam with all of them but it would probably be Saturday before he could come, he was 'so torn with business'. It must have been a sad Christmas for them all.

Derwent Moultrie had inherited that weakness of will which was the besetting sin of STC and of Hartley, but he had none of the genius of his grandfather or the intellectual brilliance of his uncle. Perhaps his failure to match up to his parents' expectations in academic achievement drove him into revolt against their moral standards.

On 14 August 1852 Derwent wrote to his mother from Mosquito Plains, New Country, South Australia. 'It is nearly two years since I left England and I cannot withhold any longer from writing to you ... I have been waiting for some good news to send you.' He had been leading 'a life ever struggling against difficulties to one brought up as I have been almost insurmountable ... from very first landing I have had to depend on the work of my own hands for my daily bread and my shelter at night. How often have I been without either! Sturt tried in vain to get me a situation — after 3 weeks, hunger forced me into a Government road gang at 3/6 a day — nothing found. The money you sent from home took 2 months to arrive.' He had taken a job as tutor to a publican's family but found it 'a dead take in' — he was expected to work as Boots, barman and ostler and after five weeks gave his master a horsewhipping. He had worked as a barman, in a mine which failed and as an engine stoker. 'People here change places — birth and education are nothing — the man who can do the hardest day's work and earn most money is the best gentleman out here.' On his way to the gold diggings he had met a Helston man and a Chelsea man, with two sons at the Practising School. But it was 600 miles to the gold diggings and after three weeks' walking and sleeping out, wearing out his shoes and living on biscuits and water, he had taken a job on a sheep station, first as a cook at 10s a week and then as a shepherd at 16s a week. He was hoping to save up to get to the gold diggings and make a fortune.

There is an abject letter of apology to his father dated 7 August [1853] begging his pardon and forgiveness for 'wrong done to you as a father, as a friend, as a gentleman'. In its self-abnegation it is unhappily reminiscent of Hartley's letters to his parents. His father wrote to express his forgiveness in November 1853.

My very dear Derwent,
– for very dear you have ever been to me, seldom absent from my thoughts and ever present with me in my prayers. I accept your letter, not merely in hope but in trust, making request for you to the good spirit of God who worketh in us both to will and to do, to strengthen you in the right way upon which, so far as your feelings and intentions are concerned, I cannot doubt that you have entered ... You are older and I doubt not wiser than you were. The stern realities of life have been your teachers, and your better nature has lived thro' all your errors. Your past follies may indeed be thrown aside like an old cloak ... But there are some propensities, and in particular that fatal yearning for the stimulus and support of fiery liquors which was the lifelong misery of your dear Uncle Hartley, I say there are some propensities and this in particular, for which time offers no cure, and for which the best feelings and the strongest intellects are sometimes unable to contend. A man may have given way to excess in gay company without having this propensity and such I trust has been the case with you ... You will, I am sure, see the necessity, of the most guarded prudence in this particular, and then I trust and believe that all will be well.

...I prefer your choosing some way of business, some clerkship or office of trust for which your education may have fitted you, if the opportunity should present itself, rather than hear that you were connected with the police force, but of this you are a much better judge than I can be. Perhaps you may have no choice, and if you have you know what sort of duties you are likely to fulfil with credit and without risk of failure. Wherever you may be and in however humble a post as long as your conduct is good ... be assured you will enjoy not only the fullest share of my affection, but of my respect and friendship.

You were probably not suited for a studious life, but your education has been of a high order and your talent, if accompanied by self-control, sufficient to have earned for you a place in society everyway suitable to the name you bear ... none knows better than you do that you cannot be helped except in proportion as you help yourself.

A letter from young Derwent to his Aunt Sarah [Dusautoy] says that he had received seven letters from home the day before. '... I am one of you again – no longer an outcast – and this thought does indeed bring joy to my heart.' In a letter from Invergerarty to Captain Sturt, dated 7 August 1853, Derwent says that he left Adelaide in January 1852 and had been in the bush ever since, chiefly in the New Country and Glenelg districts, mostly as a shepherd. His present station owner had promised to help him to get into the Melbourne Cadets and had written to the Chief Police Magistrate about it. He did in fact join the police and wrote from their barracks at Casterton and at Hamilton, Victoria. Later he taught in Sydney, then in 1859 at Geelong Grammar School and in 1861 at Brighton Park School, Melbourne. But in 1861 he was to be found working in a Survey Office in McQuaire Street, which he found 'less irksome in many ways than teaching'.

In June 1863 Derwent Moultrie returned to England at the age of 34 and stayed until the following April. His father took him to Keswick for a week in June and they sailed from Cockermouth to the Isle of Man to visit Aunt Eliza Fricker (Mrs STC's sister). In July and August Derwent Moultrie accompanied his parents, Christabel, Erney and the Massons on a seven-week tour of Switzerland and Germany. His parents would have liked him to stay in England but he determined to return to Australia and in April 1864 went back to become Head Classical Tutor at a large school near Sydney. By 1865 he was working in the Surveyor General's office. In 1866 his father wrote to John Moultrie: 'It is the old story with Derwent'. His clothes had been seized for rent, he had been 24 hours without food, and his father was obliged to supply him with the means of sustenance. 'He knows that he has only himself to blame – but when I think of his Uncle – it <u>seems</u> like a fate, or, a necessity.'[1]

In 1869 his father, writing to John Moultrie, mentioned 'what I send out to Derwent'. On 29 December 1869 Derwent Moultrie wrote a miserable self-pitying letter to his mother: 'Ragged! well nigh shoeless in a horrid low public lodging. I laid in bed because I was ashamed to be seen in the public streets. Why do you talk about clothes and not <u>send</u> them?' He had lost every pupil and his clothes were detained by the laundry. 'Stop your 200 blankets and send clothes to your first-born son.' Derwent and Mary continued to send him a monthly allowance, which they could ill afford. In 1874 his father wrote to Moultrie: 'We have heard from Derwent. With no situation to lose and but little money to spend, he is going on apparently well – I mean respectably, earning a small part of his bread and all his comforts, by his pen as a writer for the provincial papers: for sorry pay but depending on me for clothes and lodging ... He is an odd mixture, with some talents, no judgement, much kindliness, little principle – a cheerful, buoyant, half-manly nature – with no temperance – as if some part of his brain were wanting. God preserve and save him.'[2] It is uncannily reminiscent of STC writing about Hartley suffering from 'a kind of moral IDIOCY'. Derwent Moultrie married in Australia, but remained dependent to the last upon his father's allowance, until he died late in 1880. In February 1881 Mary wrote to his wife, Emma, that the monthly allowance was to be paid to her until 1 March 1881, and in September 1882 Derwent instructed the English, Scottish and Australia Bank in Sydney 'to pay over the balance in the name of Derwent Coleridge (late) Rector of Hanwell, Middlesex in your hands to Mrs Emma Coleridge, widow of Mr Derwent Moultrie Coleridge, late of Sydney, New South Wales'.[3]

Dervy must have been a tragic disappointment to his parents.

[1]Derwent Coleridge to John Moultrie. 29 April 1866. Derwent Coleridge MSS. HRC, Texas.
[2]Derwent Coleridge to John Moultrie. 27 August 1874. Ibid.
[3]26 September 1882. Derwent Coleridge MSS. HRC, Texas.

Derwent showed great tolerance in continuing to send him an allowance out of his own small income and his letters to Moultrie about Dervy are remarkably free from bitterness.

Despite all their family worries, at St Mark's Derwent and Mary entertained a wide circle of literary and other friends. Emily Trevenen and John Moultrie stayed frequently at the College. Caroline Fox has given us an account of an evening at Stanley Grove in her journal for 2 July 1849 (when she was 30): 'Dined at St Mark's College. Derwent Coleridge talked on the duty of dignifying the office of a schoolmaster and giving him the hope of rising to preferment in the Church.' Mary Coleridge spoke

of S.T. Coleridge and her earliest intercourse with him: when in the midst of the highest talk he would turn to her, smooth her hair, look into her face, and say – "God bless you, my pretty child, my pretty Mary!" He was most tender and affectionate, and always treated her as if she were six years old. They tried hard to bring him to Cornwall, but the Gillmans would not suffer it, though the old man wished it much; and all his family felt so grateful to the Gillmans for having befriended him and devoted themselves to him when he was most lonely, that they had not the heart to insist on any change ...

We explored the Chapel by twilight: it is Byzantine and very striking; the coloured glass, the ambulatory separated from the church by pillars, and the architectural feeling throughout very impressive. They are criticised by High and Low Church, because they choose rather to take their own position than unite with either party. The ecclesiastical feeling of the whole colony, combined with so much of Poetry and Art, would have exceedingly met the tendencies of that religious epicurean, S.T. Coleridge.

A frequent guest at the Coleridges' dinner table was F. D. Maurice, who dedicated the second edition of his *Kingdom of Christ* to Derwent Coleridge in 1842, and in his dedication acknowledged his deep indebtedness to the thought of S.T. Coleridge. Maurice was chaplain at Guy's Hospital, Professor of English Literature and History at King's College, London, and later Professor of Theology there. He founded Queen's College, Harley Street, for the higher education of women. In 1866 he became Professor of Moral Philosophy at Cambridge. He declared himself to be a Christian Socialist. Derwent and Mary read his many writings with admiration. Another guest was T. B. Macaulay, Derwent's contemporary at Cambridge, who was now deeply involved in politics and literature. In 1856 Macaulay, who was Liberal M.P. for Edinburgh, wrote to Lord Granville on Derwent's behalf, putting forward his name for a vacant canonry at St Paul's, an application which was as ill-fated as all Derwent's pleas for preferment.

The Coleridges' guests also included Thomas Carlyle, R. C. Trench (poet, author of works on history, literature, divinity and philology, and originator of the Oxford English Dictionary), James Spedding (editor of Bacon's Works) and the veteran diarist Henry Crabb Robinson, who found Mrs Coleridge 'a charming woman – one of the most charming I know'.[1]

In the summer of 1851 Derwent took Mary and the children on their first visit to the Lakes. Erny, at four and a half, was now old enough to make the railway journey to Windermere. Both Derwent and Mary were weary and sad at the collapse of their hopes for their first-born, and in need of bodily and spiritual refreshment. Mary wrote to Arabella Brooke that she 'came with indifferent spirits and no great hopes of feeling equal to meeting Derwent's old and dear friends'.[2] However, they stayed two weeks at the Nab, and one week at Keswick, which Mary found 'the most perfect vale'. Mary found Mrs Wordsworth 'a charming picture of calm, dignified patience, so cheerful, so forgetful of self, though she must feel every moment that the glory of her house hath departed, and Miss Wordsworth is a wearisome burden to have to bear alone.' At last Derwent was able to introduce Mary and his family to the beloved scenes of his youth, and a visit to the Lakes became an annual pilgrimage for them all.

It was in September 1850 that Sara Coleridge learned that the tumour in her breast might become cancerous. From this time her

[1]Diary, 24 April 1855. Typescript, Dr William's Library, London.
[2]29 July 1851. Coleridge papers. HRC, Texas.

health steadily deteriorated, until her death on 3 May, 1852, at the sadly early age of 49. Pickering, publisher of STC's works, was very behind in his payments to the family, and Sara was convinced that he was overcharging for printing and taking too large a share of the profits. She became too ill to continue the battle, so Derwent undertook the negotiations with Pickering and eventually arranged with Moxon to purchase the entire stock of STC's works in 1851 for £831. As Sara's final illness progressed she redoubled her efforts at editing her father's works. She was in constant correspondence with Derwent, who was assisting her and whom she expected to take on this work after her death. On 4 December 1851 Derwent administered Holy Communion to her at her home in Chester Place, as she was too ill to get to church. In January 1852 Sara wrote almost daily to Derwent on editorial matters. On 6 January she gave him her final view on the organisation of the new edition of STC's work in 20 volumes.

The Poems were published in 1852, a few weeks after Sara's death. Derwent added an Advertisement, dated May 1852, stating 'This volume was prepared for the press by my lamented sister, Mrs H. N. Coleridge, and will have an additional interest to many readers as the last monument of her highly-gifted mind. At her earnest request, my name appears with hers on the title page, but the assistance rendered by me has been, in fact, little more than mechanical...'

Derwent's editions of *Lay Sermons* and *Church and State* were published as separate volumes (on Sara's advice) in 1852.

Derwent's editorial work on STC included:

The Dramatic Works of Samuel Taylor Coleridge. A New Edition (1852)
Notes on English Divines (1853)
Notes – Theological, Political and Miscellaneous (1853)
Aids to Reflection (1854)
A new revised edition of The Friend (1863)

In 1870 he added a new and enlarged edition of the *Poems*, with a brief life of the author, to this catalogue.

He wrote to Blomfield, the Bishop of London, on 13 May,

1852, that the death of his sister had left him 'alone in my generation – the only surviving representative of STC.' He had thus become editor of his works 'which for various causes are not yet before the world . . . I have not sought this office – rather avoided it.' On the death of STC, the task of editing his works devolved upon Henry Nelson Coleridge, and then on Sara, 'whose habits of study, powers of mind and ample leisure, fitted her in a remarkable degree – in a very remarkable manner and degree considering her sex – for the undertaking'. Derwent continued:

from my seventeenth year to the present time I have always had too much to do – too much of active duty incumbent upon me – for speculative pursuits, except as a relief from necessary labours, for which in their severer forms they were hardly fitted. My sermons – or rather Essays (for they were never preached) on the Scriptural Character of the English Church, were written at night, when I had a large school, five and twenty boarders and five private pupils to attend to – from early morning to late evening.

The peculiar sensibility and sensitiveness of public opinion in this country – its singular quickness of misapprehension, and its intolerance, have also[?] to make it advisable that I should be known rather by my work than by my words, being assured that my imperfect sympathy with any of the theological parties which divide the Church and distract Christianhood, would make me no very popular advocate for what I believe to be the truth.

In the summer of 1852 Derwent, Mary and family spent six weeks in the Lake District. Derwent wrote to Emily Trevenen:

Our affections, as far as they can be moved by place, or scene, tend thitherward ever more and more. I could wish, if it should please God, that I might lie down at last by my brother's side – at 52 one begins to look towards that rest – and meanwhile, I should be glad to look forward to some period of retirement – partly for its own sake, partly for the work which I have cut out before me – and which my present occupations leave me little time or strength to execute – but all this is little more than a dream, and if it is always to continue so, I shall still be content...

Mary must have told you all about everybody and every place. How Moultrie and I trudged over the hills together – an excellent young friend Mr Wheatley with us – how we went to Wastwater and slept at John Ritson's and rowed down the Lake, and saw a glorious sunset, and Scawfell in glory – we got up at four next morning – I lay down in the mountain beck – before 6 we began clambering – to the top of Scawfell, down to Styhead Tarn by Sprinkling Tarn, and then over the Green Gable, – an enchanting view from thence, Buttermere and Crummock, and Ennerdale – and the Great Gable and Pillar and the other giants around us. We met Mary and the children at Gatesgarth – the milk we drank and the dinner we ate...[1]

The dream of semi-retirement in the Lake district, in a country living where he could follow his literary pursuits, remained in Derwent's mind. In March 1853 he wrote to his friend Dr David Leitch of Derwent Bank, Keswick: 'for some time... I have indulged a faint hope that I might ere very long set up my earthly rest among my native hills – and that... I might succeed Mr Lynn in the vicarage at Crosthwaite.'[2] He wanted to know 'without letting my name appear' the exact value of the living and condition of the house.

In 1853 Derwent embarked on a scheme to have an engraving made of Allston's 1814 portrait of STC – Sara had deplored the fact that her edition of the *Poems* had as its frontispiece an engraving of the 1798 portrait of STC, painted by Shuter and formerly in the possession of Thomas Poole. It is not a very good engraving. Derwent tracked down the Allston portrait at Ashton Hall, near Bristol.[3] He wrote to Mary that it was 'a striking likeness – much the most satisfactory record of his face that remains when those are gone who saw the original'.[4] The owner agreed to lend the portrait for

---

[1] 14 September 1852. Derwent Coleridge MSS. HRC, Texas.
[2] 14 March 1853 Ibid.
[3] Now owned by the National Portrait Gallery, on long-term loan to Dove Cottage, Grasmere.
[4] 5 May 1853. Derwent Coleridge MSS. HRC, Texas.

engraving and Derwent collected subscriptions for the project, but he lost £40 over the undertaking.

Derwent wrote to de Quincey in July 1853, saying that he wanted to renew their old contact.[1] He described himself as 'the last of my Father's house – almost the last of your early friends and lovers, and I am ever more and more anxious to gather together what still remains to me of human kindness ... from that happy spring time. I am endeavouring to tie up again broken links of remembrance – and in this mood, which has become permanent, I draw, once in each year, actually and by bodily movement, with my wife and children, and all the years thro' in yearning and affection, to Grasmere – to Grasmere – and to Grasmere Churchyard, where my Brother lies, close to Wordsworth – as to some Hartleap Well.' This was not meant to suggest 'that life has been to me a hurt and a heartbreak'.

He went on to describe some of his early recollections of de Quincey. There was, he said, a plot of ground, close to Town End, part of the hanging wood that looks upon the lake, on the left hand of the old wood, which he would buy if he could and build a cottage there. He hoped one day to 'do something for my Father's memory', like his brother's; perhaps a collection of his letters with a biographical interconnection. He asked de Quincey if he could supply any documents or communications. 'That you could render much assistance in such a work there can be no doubt.'

For their summer holiday that year they rented High Close, 'the farmhouse that looks down upon Loughrigg Tarn and into Langdale'. It stands high on the road between Grasmere and Elterwater. Mary wrote to Arabella Brooke: 'We never enjoyed it so much as this year ... We walked daily through beauties of hill and vale, rock and streams, sweet air and wildflowers that hardly seemed of this world – how far greater the enjoyment than from anything else the world has to offer.'

On 15 March 1854, Derwent wrote a long letter to Blomfield, Bishop of London[2] stating his aspirations.

My relations, and indeed some young friends in the Committee

[1] 9 July 1853. Ibid.
[2] Derwent Coleridge MSS. HRC, Texas.

of the National Society certainly led me to suppose that if my work were well done I should be in a fair way for preferment ... Other interest had I none, for though many of my early friends have attained high places in the state, yet with the exception of Praed, who was cut off prematurely in his career by death, they were and are all attached to what has proved to be the winning side in politics but from which the associations of my family excluded me. Macaulay, with whom I was very intimate, once said 'It is impossible to do anything for Coleridge.' I have therefore only to look to the Church itself.

His salary had never been sufficient, with whatever economy, to enable him to meet the necessary expenses of his position, having children to educate. It had not increased since he took up his responsibilities at the College. He had no wish to quit his situation 'deeply interested as I am in the eventual success of this undertaking ... if I could either look forward to any retirement, or if in any way my income could be rendered more adequate'.

There had crossed his mind 'a country living which might leave me some time for literary pursuits'. He expressed strong interest in 'the living of Keswick, my native vale' but it was not worth more than £400 a year 'and indeed unless I should be considered to have earned a retirement from the National Society, I fear the net income would not afford me the means of subsistence'.

Meanwhile, affairs at St Mark's brought additional strain. There had been a series of attacks on Derwent in the *Record*, an evangelical periodical, including an account of the choral service at St Mark's and his supposed leanings towards Puseyism and towards Rome. In May 1855 matters reached a head when the College Council instructed Derwent that the intoning of the prayers should be discontinued, 'without seeking a personal conference or giving opportunity for explanation', as Derwent wrote to Dr James Hessey.[1] Derwent was particularly annoyed that the Committee of the National Society had interfered in this matter, thus over-riding the autonomy of the College Council.

[1] 29 May 1855. Derwent Coleridge MSS. HRC, Texas.

These annoyances, together with his longing for a quiet country parish where he could pursue his work on STC, strongly inclined Derwent to accept when on 1 August 1855 the Bishop of London offered him the living of Northolt in Middlesex. The value of the living was said to be £600 p.a., of which £100 p.a. was the value of the house and garden. Derwent was staying up in Grasmere with someone called Bix, to whom he was showing the Lake District; Mary and the children were away from home. Derwent wrote to Mary on Wednesday, 1 August that the Bishop was leaving for Germany on Tuesday, and 'must have an early answer'. Derwent hurried back to St Mark's where the house was upside down. He mentioned to Mary in a P.S. 'The front stairs are in the full odour of becattitude – whether this have anything to do with the ill savour of Pus(s)eism from which we have suffered so long I cannot say.' On Saturday 4 August Derwent walked over to Fulham immediately after breakfast, saw the Bishop and finding that the population of Northolt was small (and would therefore presumably afford him some leisure for writing) he accepted the living. He later discovered that the available income would be 'little more than half what I now enjoy' and had to withdraw his acceptance of the living.

The Northolt fiasco was a bitter disappointment to Derwent. He battled on at St Mark's for another nine years, without complaining or repining, but for the next four years he had recurrent bouts of ill-health, which seem to have been at least partly psychosomatic. He described his typical symptoms in a letter to his friend Dr David Leitch at Keswick.[1] These included skin trouble or psoriasis on his elbows, knees, back, even on the back of his hands 'and elsewhere, as you predicted, and for 6 months I maintained a pretty strict regime, taking the liquor palafice[?] and trying to take Fowlers Solution [which contains arsenic], abstaining from wine etc. For the last six weeks or more I have suffered much from cold, influenza, intermittent catarrh, hay fever or however this polymorphous and polyonymous malady may be designated ... The irritation of the skin I think has a vicarious character, for it has taken the place of a worse inconvenience – apthous mouth.' The latter condition, an

[1] 18 June 1856. Ibid.

ulcerated mouth, was one Derwent used to develop under nervous stress and anxiety.

In the same letter Derwent had some interesting reflections on ageing:

> I feel no encrustation – no ossification. My communication with the outside world is as free – the chord of inward sympathy vibrates as readily to the touch – as ever. I am weaker – feebler – not duller than formerly. My active faculties, not my passive sensibilities, are the worse for wear. On the contrary, I think I am more responsive than in my youth, certainly than in my earlier manhood, to every true appeal, whether of beauty, or of love – beautiful scenery, beautiful poetry, noble sentiments – the sorrow and the sins of human kind – affect me more deeply, more tenderly . . . I value friends more not less highly than when I had more of them . . . I am still a sad truant from my desk, always greatly preferring reading, or it may be thinking and dreaming – to fixing my thoughts on paper – not so much from want of time . . . but from defects of energy and animal spirits.

Derwent and Mary kept their friendship green with Miss Emily Trevenen. She visited St Mark's once or twice a year and Mary wrote to her frequently, Derwent less frequently, for, as he said to her, 'my pen moves so much more nimbly in Mary's fingers'. In the summer of 1855, when Miss Trevenen was ill, Derwent and Mary and the children visited her at Helston. At the beginning of May 1856 Miss Trevenen was ill again and sent for Derwent. He went down to Helston, though suffering from 'one of the worst colds I've had in my life', and wrote to Mary on 3 May that Miss Trevenen was suffering from exhaustion and feeling difficulty in hitting upon words and names – 'her mind otherwise unimpaired'. She wanted to talk to Derwent about her ' "things" – an interview I rather dread . . . That she loves you and me better than any other persons in the world, by many times over, there can be no doubt – but I do not think, as I have often told you, that she will be influenced by this, to any extent, in the disposition of her worldly property. What she wants, I fancy, is to be guided in the selection of some memorial presents.' In fact the discussion did not take place, as two days later Derwent wrote that she was weak and exhausted and he could not make out her meaning – 'she is just glad to have me here'. He stayed for six days before returning to Chelsea.

Emily Trevenen died on 19 July 1856, aged 71. She left a letter that Derwent was to be sent for at her death. He was staying at Keswick with Mary and the children when the news reached him on 21 July. He left Keswick that day, by coach to Windermere, and then by train to Birmingham. After a few hours in the station hotel there, he was roused at 1.45 a.m. and went on by train to Bristol and Dawlish. He stopped off there and went on the next day by train to Plymouth, coach to Truro, and gig to Helston, arriving at 11.00 p.m.

The funeral was on 25 July, after which the will was read. Miss Trevenen left £4,000 in trust to her cousin Tom Trevenen and his children. To Derwent she left £3,000, all her books (some thousand volumes) and her silver cream jug (which no doubt had happy associations for him), to Mary £1,000 and her high-backed chair, to Christabel £200 and her tortoise cabinet and its contents, to Ernest Hartley her cabinet full of minerals. They were also to choose a piece of furniture – they chose the drawing-room chiffonier.

To Charles Grylls, James Penrose and Mrs Mawle she left £1,000 each, and to the five daughters of Tom Grylls £2,000 to be divided between them. £300 was left to Arabella Brooke. There were small legacies to the servants. She also left £500 to Helston National School (which she had founded) and £500 to Helston Grammar School for the purpose of founding a scholarship to Oxford or Cambridge.[1] Glynn Grylls (her cousin, married to another cousin on the Trevenen side) was one of the executors.

The Coleridge family legacy, after deduction of 10 per cent duty, amounted to £3,780. Derwent wrote to Mary that the legacy was to be paid in six months if possible, but the estate had to be cleared of debt first. It was in fact at least ten years before the legacy was paid. There were endless delays on the part of Emily Trevenen's debtors and by the lawyers, and no doubt

[1]This Exhibition still exists. It was held by Henry Spencer Toy, author of *The History of Helston*, OUP 1936, and former headmaster of Launceston Grammar School.

there was a good deal of resentment that she had left a large sum to people outside the family and outside Helston. In December 1865 Derwent placed all the facts before Lee and Bolton, Solicitors. In January 1866 Mary was writing to Arabella Brooke about the legacy – 'What iniquity has William Trevenen perpetuated?' But in a later fragment to Arabella, Mary writes 'Hip Hip Hip Hurrah!!! – get the enclosed properly signed and send it off to Lee and Bolton ... In the infernal regions lawyers should always be waiting for the settling of legacies which never do get settled – I'm afraid Dante didn't think of that.'

In January 1857, six months after Miss Trevenen's death, her old servant, Mrs Withers, joined the Coleridge household at St Mark's. Mary wrote to Arabella Brooke that it was 'a pleasure to see her about the house'.[1] Withers had been a great invalid with rheumatism for two months, but Mary said it was a job where no exertion was required and she could work when she liked. She found her 'a great help and comfort'. Withers was 'a true mourner of her beloved mistress' – she even parted her hair and wore her cap bows in imitation of Miss Trevenen.

In March 1857 Mary's mother came to live at St Mark's, as she was 'too infirm to receive visitors and too lonely', as Mary wrote to her friend Arabella. And in July Edith Coleridge, Sara's daughter, joined Derwent's household and lived with Derwent and Mary for the rest of their lives. Edith was now twenty-five. Her brother, Herbert, had married and she felt it no longer appropriate to live with him.

In 1856 Derwent paid two visits to Brighton in the attempt to get rid of his constant colds, or hay-fever. He stayed there for a few days in June and again in October, for ten days, when he was struggling to write a memoir of Praed as a preface to his poems. Mrs Praed apparently wished him to include all the political material supplied by Hildyard. Derwent objected to this plan and felt too unwell to do much work on the biography. He eventually published an edition of Praed's poems in two volumes, with a 54-page memoir, in 1864, the year after Mrs Praed's death.

In June 1859 Derwent went to Malvern for three weeks for the

[1] 6 June 1857. Coleridge papers. HRC, Texas.

cure, as recommended by his Keswick friend, Dr David Leitch. He was under the care of Dr Wilson, who pronounced that his psoriasis and catarrh were due to nervous dyspepsia. He recommended strict diet and care, with no wine and a rest from headwork; as Derwent wrote to Dr Leitch: 'He recommends a certain system of living – which would be all very well – only for many persons it would be *"propter vitam, vivendi perdere causas"*.' The spa treatment included sitz baths, fomentations, taking the water, rubbings and compresses. Derwent found 'the mode of life is tedious to me beyond description'. He wrote to Mary on 17 June from 'The Aquarium, Malvern ... Having been two days in this well-watered establishment, I am beginning to feel a little less like a fish out of water and very completely like a man in it.' Next day 'The Life here is in the extremest degree opposed to my habits – inaction without repose, company without society, no retirement, no excitement – but the very tedium amuses me.'

On 19 June he wrote to Erny, aged twelve and a half, who was now boarding at Highgate School:

My very dear boy –
Thank you for your nice letter. You will of course take care that your visiting and novel-reading do not interfere with your work, – and in particular with the time necessary to do your verses and composition really well. I shall be glad to see any of your school exercises – which you do in regular course...

Having dispatched the business part of my letter, I may proceed to give you a little account of our doings here ... As for the mode of life it is an endless succession of sousing and dowsing, rubbing and scrubbing, bathing and swathing, soaking and croaking. –

Scene – a bedroom. Time, a quarter before six A.M. An elderly gentleman is discovered lying in bed. Enter a Merman – who packs him in wet towels and blankets – tight and round – like a large salmon ready to be sent off by the coach.

Interlude – Scene a dining room, 50 feet long – gentlemen and ladies are seen sitting dispersedly on each side of a very long table – Time 8 A.M. Breakfast going on. Tea and Cocoa –

White Bread and Brown – Milk and Butter – Dry toast –
N'eggs, A few carnivorae are seen prowling about the side
table.

Scene II. Time 10 o'clock – Elderly gentleman is seen
secretly arming himself with a magic girdle – ten inches wide –
supposed to be the belly-band of one of Neptune's Horses. The
process of investiture furnishes an effective tableau – worthy of
the pencil of Giorgione.

Scene III. Time – noon. Elderly gentleman discovered
being boiled over a spirit-lamp – like a cup of coffee on the top
of Helvellyn.

Interlude. Scene – Dining Room as before.

Dinner on the table. Elderly gentleman sings –

'Water, water everywhere,

And – nothing else – to drink'.

Scene IV. Time 5 P.M. Elderly gentleman discovered sitting
in a tub, like a half-Diogenes – and quite cynical enough for a
whole one. The attitude recommended as a study to young
gentlemen of heroic and sentimental aspirations.

Interlude – Time 7 P.M. A repetition of the first. Nothing
for the Carnivorae.

Last scene of all – that ends this strange eventful history – is a
Rubber of Whist – Elderly gentleman loses half a crown. So
much for that popular Drama – The Water Cure.

You ask about the walks. Well, there is a hill sticking
up in the middle of a fine plain – as if the Catbells had
gone to Malvern to be water-cured. It is called the Beacon. I
have been to the top of it, – and did not forget you, or your
favourite pursuits. There found a fossil from the pleistocene
formation, *Cancer Cockneiopicnicus*, which you can put in your
cabinet. Also a fragment of a valuable crystal-vitrium snobbo-
boosicum . . .

Despite his scepticism about the water cure Derwent told Mary
(who was staying at Blake Hall, Mirfield, in Yorkshire) that on his
return to St Mark's he was 'much better than when I left it'. He
stayed at Malvern for the three weeks, partly because Mary's sister
Sarah was there with her husband William Dusautoy, who was now

an invalid, said to be suffering from 'softening of the brain'. The doctors considered that it was impossible for him to resume his duties as chaplain of the Royal Military Asylum in the King's Road, Chelsea (a school for the children of soldiers' widows) and the chances were he would get worse and become quite helpless. Derwent had to break this news to Sarah – 'it is well that I am here to support her' – and it fell to him to tell Dusautoy the situation and to encourage him to resign his post.

After the Northolt fiasco in 1855, Derwent made several other attempts to get preferment. He longed to escape financial difficulties and to have time to write about STC. 'Had I been differently circumstanced', he wrote in 1853, an account might have been written of his father's 'life, character and opinions – a history of his influence – but as it is I must not dream, or only dream, of such an undertaking'.[1] But a comfortable retirement, following upon his considerable achievements at St Mark's, was not to be Derwent's fate.

---

[1]Derwent Coleridge to unidentified recipient. 17 January 1853. Derwent Coleridge MSS. HRC, Texas.

Chapter 4

The Campaign against the Revised Code
1861–64

St Mark's had benefited greatly from the liberal financial assistance by government to pupil-teachers, to students and to the College under the regime of Kay-Shuttleworth at the Committee of Council. In 1856 the Whig government under Palmerston was becoming concerned about the increasing Parliamentary vote for expenditure on education and appointed a Vice-President of the Council, who was to be a member of the Government and directly accountable to Parliament for the doings of the Committee of Council on Education. In 1859 Robert Lowe was appointed Vice-President of the Council; he disliked democracy and was determined to economise on education. In these views he was ably supported by Lingen, who had succeeded Kay-Shuttleworth in 1849 as Secretary to the Committee of Council.

The Newcastle Commission was set up in 1859 'to enquire into the present state of popular education in England, and to consider and report what measures, if any, are required for the extension of sound and cheap elementary education to all classes of the people.' It reported in 1861.

Among other matters they stated that 'the junior classes in the schools, comprehending the great majority of the children, do not learn, or learn imperfectly, the most necessary part of what they come to learn – reading, writing and arithmetic'. They recommended that every child in every grant-earning school should be subject to 'searching examination' and that the prospects of the teacher should depend on the results of the examination.

The Revised Code of regulations contained in the Minute of the Committee of Council dated 29 July 1861, was drawn up by Lowe and Lingen. They ignored the Newcastle Commission's recommendations for County Boards of Education and for a contribution out of the rates; they ignored also the relatively generous financial proposals and the suggested capitation grants, not dependent on examination. They merely seized on the idea of payment by results of examination and decreed that the only grant for schools was to be based on this.

The Code laid down that the managers of schools might claim ld per scholar for every attendance after the first 100, at the morning or afternoon meetings. One third of the sum was to be forfeited if the scholar failed to satisfy the inspector in reading, one third if in writing and one third if in arithmetic. The children were to be examined in age groups – 3 to 7, 7 to 9, 9 to 11, and 11 and over. There were to be no other grants for schools.

The augmentation grants to teachers' salaries for their certificates were abolished. All moneys were to be paid direct to the managers of schools, and teachers had to make their own bargains with the managers, i.e. the teacher's salary was largely determined by his success in cramming pupils for examinations.

Grants to pupil teachers were abolished and managers were left to make their own local agreements with pupil-teachers. The old indenture, binding the pupil-teacher to the teacher was abolished. At the end of his time in school, if the pupil-teacher wanted to teach he could become an assistant in a school, become a Queen's Scholar in a training college or become provisionally certificated to teach in a small rural school, when he had until he was 25 to pass the certificate examination.

Lowe said triumphantly in 1865: 'The Revised Code swept away the vested interests of some 10,000 teachers, who had begun to consider themselves as government employees, having a claim on augmentation grants for the rest of their lives ... We got rid of the enormous incubus of some 15,000 pupil teachers who were receiving grants.'[1]

Thus, by a simple Code of regulations, Lowe and Lingen destroyed Kay-Shuttleworth's carefully built-up system of well-taught pupil-teachers, who went on to earn by their certificates permanent augmentations to their salaries as teachers. Their motives were economy and the saving of taxation, hostility to the Church, and hostility to the new profession of teachers who were thought to be getting above themselves.

With regard to the Training Colleges, there were to be no more State grants for building or fitting up premises. The only State grants were to be annual: for certificated teachers on the staff, to lecturers qualified for special grant by examination, and to Queen's Scholars. The certificate examination was to be open to Training College students of one year's standing, thus removing the necessity to stay longer, and was also open to acting teachers of over 22 years who had either been pupil-teachers or had been favourably reported on twice by the Inspector, so that it was possible to become certificated without going to a Training College.

Derwent Coleridge naturally saw the proposals of the Revised Code as a threat to all his aspirations for the higher education of schoolmasters and the improvement of elementary schools. As he wrote to Sir John Coleridge, 'half of my life has been devoted to carrying out an idea, which I am loth to see choked and asphyxied if I can help to keep it out of the smother'.[2]

In November 1861 Derwent published under the title *The Education of the People* a letter addressed to Sir John Coleridge, dated 30 September 1861. Sir John had urged him to print it and offered to indemnify him against any loss.[3]

Derwent began by saying that the various grants to St Mark's College would probably be diminished by more than £800 and the funds of the National Society would apparently be lessened by the annual grant of £1,000, hitherto appropriated to the support of its Training Colleges. The standard of instruction in the College would

---

[1]Hansard. CLXXVII, 869.
[2]25 October 1861. Derwent Coleridge MSS. HRC, Texas.
[3]Sir J. T. Coleridge to Derwent Coleridge. 20 October 1861. Derwent Coleridge MSS. HRC, Texas.

be lowered and the ordinary period of training might be lowered to a single year.

With regard to the Elementary Schools, Derwent foresaw that the money grants to each school would be generally, if not universally, diminished and that the greater the difficulty of the school, the less help would be on offer. The Revised Code 'ministers aid not in accordance with total, but with partial results, which it measures by a barely practicable, and most delusive test. It separates secular from religious studies...' The present system, Derwent maintained, had brought up the supply of school buildings almost to a level with the need. It had provided those schools with 'a living machinery of instruction and supervision altogether without a parallel, both in extent and in efficiency'. It had encouraged the improvement of school apparatus. It had helped to bring up the attendance of school children to the highest percentage ever attained without compulsion in Europe.

Derwent pointed out that pupil-teachers and Training College students had had definite prospects of salaries, augmentation grants and pensions held out to them which amounted to a virtual contract and to withdraw these advantages without compensation would be most inequitable.

He argued that public opinion had been misled as to the extent and the cause of the defects in popular elementary education. He pointed out that the Reports of the Inspectors showed a vast improvement in the attainments of school children compared with the period before the present system had been introduced. He freely conceded that a large number of the children who passed through the schools could not read, write and cipher well – 'but to expect that a condition of semi-barbarism should be removed in half a generation, is absurd. Indeed, there are circumstances connected with the social condition of the country, which must make such success, as can be achieved by school-teaching alone, very limited; and yet what is done may be unappreciable in value.'

Finally Derwent maintained:

It is NOT true, it is the reverse of true, that first class men make

258

inferior Schoolmasters . . . The Education given at the Training School has raised the whole body of Schoolmasters, *not* above their work, but with incalculable benefit both to their respective schools, and to the class of society in which they move . . . The great majority are most efficient Schoolmasters, in charge of the best and largest schools. It is undoubtedly true that of these first class men, a certain percentage rise to a higher range of work. They become Organizing Masters, Normal Masters, or Tutors of Training Colleges, or even Chaplains and Principals, it is believed with the best results. In the colonies they rise to the higher posts of missionary and colonial education. Middle school education has also been assisted in the same way.

St Mark's College is supposed to lie particularly open to this objection, such as it is. Now the fact is that these men have risen to the higher, because they have first done pre-eminently well in the lower sphere. Any how the community is benefited when useful work, of whatever kind, is done efficiently at less than the average cost; and, more particularly, popular education is benefited in most cases directly, by special work which these men are fitted to undertake, but always indirectly and largely by the education, taken as a whole, of which this is a partial result, and by the encouragement and respectability thus extended to the entire class of popular instructors.

Early in 1862 Derwent published *The Teachers of the People; A Tract for the Time.* This was originally going to be an Appendix to his Letter to Sir John Coleridge, but grew into a booklet of 110 pages, in which he expresses the ideals he had been pursuing at St Mark's for the past twenty-one years and his aspirations for the future. He begins by saying 'the value of education as such, – as the birthright and privilege of man, irrespective of class distinctions and particular occupations, – is in many quarters secretly slighted, if not openly decried. More especially is this true as regards the education of the humbler classes. To combat this feeling . . . is the ruling motive of the following Tract.' The particular subject he set out to discuss was: 'Is the elementary schoolmaster too highly trained?'

Bust of Derwent Coleridge.
(Courtesy College of St Mark and St John, Plymouth)

Bust of Derwent Coleridge.
(Courtesy College of St Mark and St John, Plymouth)

Derwent began by stating that by far the largest amount of time and labour in the Training Colleges was expended on the most ordinary rudiments of instruction: correct, fluent and intelligent reading; the spelling, pronunciation and meaning of words; English grammar and composition; history, geography and arithmetic. Much of this ought to have been learned before.

But I forget: it is the forwardness, not the backwardness of these young aspirants that is now deprecated. And doubtless there is a small percentage of their number who have enjoyed peculiar advantage, or who possess such powers of acquirement, accompanied by such patient and vigorous industry, that they cannot but rise above their fellows ... And is this to be regretted? The garden is tilled ... better by these men than by more ordinary labourers ... And what if, in the end, one here and one there should be called away to a finer and more extended husbandry? The loss of the individual, if loss it be, is far more than repaid by the encouragement thus extended to the class. So long indeed as the appropriate discipline of the schoolmaster and elementary teacher can only be had in the Training Colleges, there will be an urgent and increasing desire for the services of these men in the higher walks of the ... scholastic profession ... For my own part, I will never consent to educate down to any standard, to avoid an imaginary risk of inconvenient excellence ... Let the instruction offered be appropriate – Yes, but be it ever borne in mind that we are educating men, not forming machines.

Derwent argued that the art of elementary tuition demanded, on the part of the teacher, all the mental culture which could be bestowed on him.

Now of course I do not expect all our schoolmasters to be scholars and men of genius: all I maintain is, that their acquirements are not to be stinted, nor their intellects cramped. That our popular schools can safely or hopefully be entrusted to a set of laborious drudges, removed but one degree in knowledge from the children that they teach, may be an attractive, but is a delusive vision. As a rule, you will neither find the power nor the will for the work of a schoolmaster in men of low attainments; no, nor the moral fitness ... The education of the country ... will be advanced, both morally and intellectually, by the employment of a class of teachers more, not less thoroughly trained than at present; from which thorough training mental cultivation cannot be dissociated ... It was with these views ... that the system originally pursued at St Mark's College was constructed. It was to supply the requisite education.

Derwent went on to write about Kay-Shuttleworth's regulations: 'These provisions were scanned at first with a very jealous eye. By me they were accepted, with all their drawbacks, frankly and thankfully, as the best boon ever conferred by a government upon a free, a progressive and a religious people ... The training of schoolmasters, on an extended scale ... first became practicable when the College was supplied with suitably prepared students, when funds were provided for their maintenance and instruction, and when a career was held out to them in the line of their calling.'

To the objection 'But we do not wish to make a set of second-rate gentlemen and ladies!' Derwent replied:

Certainly not ... but it *is* our business to impart or to develop many of those qualities which are supposed to be associated with gentle birth, and which are certainly the best products of gentle breeding, – modesty, self-respect, manly courage and endurance, honour, courtesy, and simplicity ... For it is our business to train schoolmasters and schoolmistresses, men and women, whose occupation it will be to impart, ... not merely the rudiments of book knowledge, but all the essentials of religious and moral culture, and this not to little children only, but to young persons ... this in their official capacities, while simply as educated men and women they constitute a civilising and humanizing agency in the whole class of society to which they belong.

Derwent maintained that the substitution of religious principle for worldly motive taken alone would not work, and that it was necessary to appeal also to the desire of social advancement. He admitted freely that he had modelled St Mark's on a university.

The College must be an adapted copy, *mutatis mutandis*, of the elder educational institutions of the country, originally intended, even those of the higher class, with their noble courts, solemn chapels, and serious cloisters, for clerks to the full as humble as those whom I had to train – I looked, not in foreign lands, but at home for my exemplar, not of course to be followed blindly: it must be modified, lowered, yet remain the same in kind; the same theme transmodulated. It must awaken the same or similar associations. It must create the same *esprit du corps* among its alumni. As time went on it must be associated with the same *religio loci*. In a word it must be rendered attractive both to the student and to his friends. It must first attract, then elevate, refine, ennoble.

And he argued that there must be a career open to talent:

There must be at least a possibility of rising by a graduated ascent to posts of comparative eminence.

Derwent maintained that the mental culture and range of information given to the student in training were necessary 'to impart the barest elements of knowledge to the humblest class of pupils'. But he went on to argue the need for what was in effect secondary education. 'Let it be borne in mind that the labouring population, in whose interest these Schoolmasters are trained, is demanding ever more and more ... school-teaching of a higher character ... The rudiments of mathematical and physical science, with natural history and drawing, the first principles of social economy and constitutional history, together with that knowledge of common things (so called), which none but the best educated masters are qualified to impart...'

The State needed to co-operate in providing suitable instruction for 'the emergent as distinguished from the subsident class, for the intellectual upward-looking artisan'. There was a need for the State to aid in quickening their intelligence with a view to the industries in which they were engaged, and to prepare them for that political influence which they were increasingly called upon to exercise. Derwent was aware of the growing need in industry for skilled artisans and of the growing demand for extension of the vote to this class. He declared 'Our duty, fully stated, is to educate the people, our fellow-citizens and ourselves, the nation as a whole.' Finally he argued that the popular schoolmaster is the moral and intellectual guardian and tutor of the pupil-teacher: 'it is most necessary that he should be a man to whom his ward and pupil can look up with respect for guidance and example'.

Towards the close of his Tract Derwent put forward a scheme for the future whereby the training colleges should be collectively incorporated. 'They should be combined into one, or perhaps more than one aggregate, each with a central authority, and common organisation for corporate purposes, while the several colleges should be separately, and to a great extent independently administered'. Such a system was not established until the 1950s when Institutes of Education were set up by the universities.

With remarkable foresight Derwent went on to suggest that the training colleges should be thrown open for the purposes of general education – 'real education, of a liberal yet practical kind, dealing as at present with the lower rather than the upper branches of learning ... yet so as to provide not a school, but something analogous to a university training, for the sons of yeomen, tradesmen, artisans of the higher, and professional persons of the lower grade; while the training of the schoolmaster, no longer limited to a particular class of schools, though not the sole, continued to be the leading object, and characteristic feature of the system'. The diversification of the activities of training colleges to make them into general colleges of higher education in fact had to wait until the 1970s.

Derwent did not foresee the links which would take place in the second half of the twentieth century between the training colleges and the universities. He accepted the class structure of his time and thought his suggested system 'would fill up the space downward in the social scale which the elder universities and public schools have long left vacant, and which I do not think it desirable that they should attempt to resume, a space which no institutions not offering the advantages of collegiate residence can adequately fill'. But he did see the need for the training colleges to be places of real education with high standards of culture.

> Meanwhile, [said Derwent] I ask ... that we may be permitted and enabled to prosecute the great and useful work in which we are engaged, with the same helps and encouragements as heretofore. I ask more particularly that the young men, whom we have to train, may not come to us less fully prepared; that they may not remain with us for a shorter period; that we may not be compelled to educate them less thoroughly, and that they may not leave us with less encouraging expectations.

Derwent's plea was unsuccessful. The Revised Code was put into operation, with all the dire effects which he foresaw. Between 1862 and 1864 the Education Grant was reduced from £840,000 to £705,000. Both teachers and pupil-teachers suffered loss of salary. Good teachers deserted the profession. The number of pupil-teachers declined because their wages were reduced and their hours of instruction were cut; the quality of their instruction also declined as teachers no longer received payment for instructing the pupil-teachers. Schools taught the minimum necessary for getting the children through the Inspector's examination in the '3 Rs'. History, geography and grammar were generally neglected, and the standard of reading-books was lowered, so that it would be easier for pupils to pass the reading examination.

For the Training Colleges there was worse to come. The syllabus for the teacher's certificate was altered in 1863. As the Inspector, Rev. B. M. Cowie, explained in the Committee of Council Minutes 1862–3: 'The main features of the alterations are these: excision of the more ambitious parts of the original scheme, and the insertion of some particulars which will more specially require cultivation of the power of memory, facility in mental calculation, a close attention to English composition, and some knowledge of economy, political, social and sanitary.[1] In the first year Church History and algebra were dropped and the books of Euclid studied were reduced from four to two. Instead of studying these subjects each student was required to repeat from memory, and pass an examination in mental arithmetic, was exercised in writing English and more fully examined in English grammar, and was expected to show some knowledge of the elementary principles of social economy, sanitary precautions and the 'science of common things'. Religious instruction required a competent knowledge of Holy Scripture, the Catechism and the Book of Common Prayer. Dropped from the second year syllabus were physical science, including inorganic chemistry, mechanics, higher mathematics, English Literature and Latin. Instead the second year examinations required a higher standard in subjects studied in the first year. There was no encouragement to anybody to stay on for a third year.

By the Minutes of Committee of Council, 21 March 1863, the payment of grant to the Training Colleges was to be retrospective. It was not to depend on the results of the annual examinations but on the number of certificated teachers from the college who had been engaged for at least two years in elementary schools. The annual grant was not to exceed 75 per cent of the annual expenditure of the college. The number of students trained was not to exceed the number for which accommodation was provided in 1862. Queen's Scholarships were abolished and the Training Colleges were to settle their own scale of charges. Candidates for admission were to be examined by an inspector and no grant was to be made for students who did not stay for two years.

In his report on the Church Training Colleges in 1863, the Rev. B. M. Cowie stated that the maintenance of a supply of candidates for admission was very uncertain: 'The Lachrymose and peevish tone of the teachers in charge of elementary schools has discouraged many of their young pupil teachers, from seeking the office of schoolmaster,'[2] The future supply of pupil teachers was affected by the same cause.

[1]p. 203.
[2]Committee of Council Minutes. 1863–64. p. 310.

267

Kay-Shuttleworth summarised the effects of the Revised Code on the supply and training of teachers:

The whole system of public aid has been shaken to its very centre – the Managers of Schools have been discouraged – the emoluments of the teacher have been lessened, and his hopes disappointed. Pupil teachers are therefore scarce, and are easily attracted to other employment. Their education is not well cared for, because it has ceased to be the interest of the principal teacher; their qualifications at the end of their five years' engagement are much lower than formerly. The Training Colleges have an insufficient supply of inferior students, who pass a lower examination for their certificates...[1]

The Revised Code contributed to a century's delay in the working out of Derwent Coleridge's aspirations for St Mark's. He sought to give higher education to the teachers of the people, to raise their status and to enable them to climb the social and professional ladder, even into the Church. In these aims he achieved a high degree of success. He had printed in December 1864 *The National Society's Training Institution for Schoolmasters, St Mark's College, Stanley Grove, Chelsea. Occasional Report*, which included a list of students trained in St Mark's, showing their present employment. The number of men who had left St Mark's after training up to the end of December 1863 was 659. Of these, 391 were engaged in the education of the poor at the end of 1864.

In the eyes of Robert Lowe, Lingen and the Whig Government, bent on economy, these results were deplorable. Their point of view was expressed by the Rev. B. M. Cowie, Inspector, in his report for 1864.

Mr Coleridge has always maintained that his object was to raise the education of the middle grade as well as the lower grade; and hence he endeavoured to leaven the body of teachers of

[1] J. P. Kay-Shuttleworth, *Memorandum on Popular Education*. 1868. (Republished Woburn Books Ltd. 1969) p. 29.

TABLE SHOWING LATER CAREERS OF FORMER STUDENTS OF ST MARK'S COLLEGE (1864)

Employed in National Schools	329
Employed in schools for the poor other than National Schools	48
Employed in Training Schools or other work connected with normal training and school organisation	14
	391

The remainder were distributed thus:

Employed in grammar schools, middle class schools, private tuition	99
In holy orders and in clerical work not directly connected with education	13
Laymen not engaged in education	35
Unemployed (chiefly through ill-health)	9
Present employment unknown	29
In the colonies engaged in educational or missionary work	43
In the colonies not known to be engaged in educational work	8
	236
Deceased	32
	268

middle-class schools with the better article which he manufactured at St Mark's. He has done this with considerable success; and the friends of education may well be pleased with that success. But this work should be done, and paid for by those *who wish to do it.* And there cannot be a more evident proof of the necessity of recent measures in order to secure the application of Parliamentary funds to their intended object than is shown by the tabulated results of the 25 years [sic] work at St Mark's.

As Government aid to training schools is now directly proportional to the number of teachers who work in inspected schools for the poor, this system of training young men for the higher branch of the teacher's profession must either be abandoned or the funds must be provided by the National Society or from some other source. If neither of these conclusions is accepted, I do not believe that St Mark's College can stand.[1]

At St Mark's Derwent had sought to put his father's ideas into effect by educating the clerisy with the highest standard of mental cultivation. But the Government in 1864 was quite clear that it only intended to assist the education of the labouring poor, and their education was to be confined to the barest minimum. The '3 R's' were quite sufficient for children who would go to work at the age of 11. The teachers of the labouring poor should also be given the minimum education to enable them to instil the '3 R's'. Derwent's ideas of higher education for the teachers of the people, of holding out to them prospects of social advancement and of promoting also middle-class education were not going to be assisted by government grants. The Revised Code prevailed in 1862 and ended Derwent's attempt to apply Coleridgean wholeness, vision and culture to the task of educating the teachers of the people.

The narrow scope of the certificate examination and the poor standard of entrants to the training colleges led to much rote learning. The Revised Code, by making 'payment by results' the supreme principle in national education, lowered the standard of education of the teacher, restricted the curricula of the training colleges and encouraged a mechanical approach to teaching and learning.

The Church rewarded Derwent's years of struggle at St Mark's, not with a Bishopric, Canonry or good country living but with the offer by the Bishop of London in December 1863 of the poorly paid living of Hanwell, Middlesex, plus a pension of £200 p.a. from the National Society. At the age of 63, with his aspirations for St Mark's in ruins, Derwent had little choice but to accept.

---

[1]Commitee of Council Minutes 1864–65.

PART VI
Hanwell 1864–80

Derwent took up his appointment as Rector of Hanwell in the spring of 1864. Mary told Arabella Brooke[1] that he read himself in and preached on Palm Sunday and Easter Sunday and that he had presided at his first vestry and chosen his churchwarden. But the Coleridge family did not move to Hanwell until August, as the previous Rector, Sir Charles Clark, did not leave the Rectory until then. He also continued to collect £80 worth of tithes to which he was entitled until six months after his resignation. Meanwhile Derwent had to sell some securities to cover the expense of the move and of getting Derwent Moultrie off to Australia again. Derwent's successor at St Mark's, Rev. J. G. Cromwell, was not appointed until June. Derwent had a temporary curate at Hanwell but he suffered from overwork: 'Hanwell and St Mark's falling out sometimes very heavily'.[2]

Hanwell lay on the Great Western Railway, about seven miles from Paddington. The parish church of St Mary, rebuilt in 1841 to the design of Sir Giles Gilbert Scott, stood on a hill above the River Brent. The Rectory[3] stood beside the church and the glebeland sloped steeply down in front of the Rectory to the muddy waters of the Brent curving through the wooded valley below. The river valley was spanned by the great Wharncliffe viaduct, built in 1838, across which thundered the trains to the west. To the south-west of the church was Brent Lodge, a large house in its own grounds, and all the older and wealthier residences were in the vicinity of the church. Beyond the railway lay the Uxbridge road, around which

[1]29 March 1864. Coleridge papers. HRC, Texas.
[2]Ibid.
[3]Demolished in 1920.

271

was rapidly growing the new Hanwell, with its rows of yellow brick villas and a large population of labouring and lower middle-class people, many of whom had moved from inner London.

As Derwent wrote to Moultrie, his new parish was 'no haven of rest'. His flock was deeply divided by social class and by urban and rural origins. Many of the people were dissenters or atheists and the church was far from the real centre of population. At the age of sixty-four, Derwent set to work to meet this new challenge, with the help of Mary and the other members of his family, which included Christabel (known as Cissy) who remained unmarried, Sara's orphan daughter Edith, and after her husband died in December 1865, Mary's sister, Sarah Dusautoy, who remained at Hanwell Rectory until she died in December 1875.

A picture of the Coleridge family's early days at Hanwell comes from Mary's letters to Arabella Brooke, her old friend of Helston days, who now lived at Waddington, a few miles south of Lincoln. On 22 August 1864 the Coleridge family were staying at Brent Lodge but

> we hope to sleep in the Rectory tonight. Yesterday was our first Sunday – a doleful, irresponsive service, with melancholy hymns and a very thin congregation. There is plenty of work to do here.' Cissy had taught in the Sunday School and liked it. 'Derwent comes home quite ill of sick and miserable babies and the details of bad legs etc. etc. – he is so tender-hearted – but he will get hardened by and bye – the dismal children are his great trial for though it is on the whole a well employed parish there are specimens of great suburban misery and neglect ... The charities are muddled and complicated – all wants organisation. We are pining for a good working curate – nearly 2000 of rich and poor is no sinecure.[1]

On 21 September Mary remarked on the number of 'smart retired small tradespeople who all pay us the compliment of calling – and expect us to do ample duty in return. Cissy and I do the needful as far as we can.' In the parish were '3 gentry, 3 or 4 pleasant fellows –

---

[1]Coleridge papers. HRC, Texas.

artists, lawyers, etc. – who live here for cheapness', dozens of
suburban, retired or otherwise, tradespeople – 'vulgar and narrow',
shopkeepers who were civil and obliging – 'the best of them
dissenters', and hundreds of labouring people. The neighbouring
clergy consisted of the chaplain of the great industrial workhouse
school, the chaplain of the great Lunatic Asylum, and the chaplain of
St George's Cemetery. The church was far from the village, and
Derwent could not hold an evening service on that account, but the
Coleridges had already decided to have a weekly evening service in
the school.

On 14 November 1864 Mary wrote:

Alas! for leisure – I have less than ever – parish – parish all
day long ... dearest E. T. if she could look down upon us
all. She would put her dear head on one side, prick up her
mouth, and consider parish work good discipline for us, be
glad that we had it to do – and shed tears out of her human
eyes for that her beloved old pastor had not a little more
rest in his old age. We are getting into harness. Cissy and
Edith have their districts – and their Sunday School-clubs
etc. I have the care of funds, the buying of wine and meat,
the distribution of blankets – and alas! a Bible class on
Sundays wh. frightens me out of my very small wits, I
having no skill to teach – the big stupid ones – and the
small sharp ones – are exceedingly alarming but I begin to
see a little improvement, wh. is encouraging. I was grand and
solemn upon the subject of respect to superiors and especially
what I required myself so the Hanwellian free and easy tone is
subsiding – and I am beginning to impress upon their minds
that I am not the obliged party. Our congregations are
improving – and I hope in time we shall do a little by God's
help.
 ... I think his [Derwent's] greatest trial of a small sort is
mixing with his clerical brethren – they do talk such sad stuff
... His own club discuss the great stirring questions of the day
with great learning and great piety – Dr Wordsworth, the Dean
of Canterbury, Maurice Kempe of Piccadilly etc. etc. – men of
various views but undoubted earnestness. So you will forgive

273

him if he feels sleepy at our excellent neighbour's talk of the 'dear missionary who has just addressed us' – and who is just escaping from some Red Indian costume (Query paint and feathers?) which he has tried on for the edification of his audience. Said neighbour is a very loveable man . . . but thinks it right to talk stuff – he sent us loads of Tracts for distribution – but so unsound in doctrine – and as we think morally that they live in the cupboard.[1]

On 11 February 1865 the Bishop of London, A. C. Tait, wrote to Derwent: '. . . you seem to have done a great deal during the past year, especially considering that your connection with St Mark's lasted during a great part of the time and that you have been without a curate'. Mr Snow was now to be licensed as Derwent's curate.

On St Mark's Day 1865 (25 April) Derwent was invited to preach the anniversary sermon at the College. Mary wrote to Arabella that the service was perfection, and after dinner a testimonial was presented to Derwent by Archdeacon Sinclair in the name of the students 'in a most gratifying manner' – a splendid and rare book, *Walton's Polyglot*, and a purse with £140.

The Hanwell Rectory was a large rambling house, rebuilt by Sir Charles Clark 16 years previously with funds from Queen Anne's Bounty to which Derwent had to repay £50 p.a. for a further 15 years. It was beautifully situated with a fine view. Mary told Arabella that she liked the house very much – it was commodious, the garden was lovely and there were delightful walks round about. Derwent, also, derived a good deal of quiet satisfaction from his immediate surroundings, despite financial and parish anxieties and his disappointed hopes of preferment. In May 1865 he had been staying in town for a night or two, where he had been to his clerical club and to a concert. He had left Mary and Christabel there and returned to Hanwell for a vestry meeting. He wrote to Moultrie: 'I am now alone in my glory, such as it is . . . well, in spite of much anxiety, a good deal of fatigue and a little spring biliousness – in a calmish – qualmish – warmish-senile or senescent sort of way I do rejoice. Out

[1]Ibid.

of doors I have my pretty view – with the cuckoo all the morning – and the nightingale all the evening – and indoors I have my fire – this wet day – and my books about me – among the latter, my *Walton's Polyglot* – who is half an inch too high for my shelves.'[1] The congregation of St Mark's Chapel subscribed £60 in July 1865 as a testimonial to the late Principal, and Derwent used it to make good his boundary towards the Brent.

Pleasant as the Rectory was, Derwent was not the man to settle there with his books in comfortable semi-retirement. He told Moultrie in July 1865 that the congregation was increasing and he was writing sermons again: '. . . now I do not preach an old sermon with comfort; but as I take great pains with what I now write my time and strength are somewhat taxed'. Mary wrote to Arabella in December 1865: 'Derwent is wanted to write his Father's life and has been offered well to do it – the only proper person to do it – but it is simply impossible as he is situated – no <u>time</u> and no strength wherewith to <u>make time</u> as he did when he wrote his book in Cornwall.'

The Sunday evening service in the schoolroom was a great success with the poorer part of the parish. On the evening of 11 January 1866 Derwent gave a public reading of Southey's narrative poem *Thalaba* to raise money to pay for 'making the schoolroom snug for his evening services against the piercing wind'.[2]

As might be expected, the Coleridge family took great interest in the National Schools in Hanwell. Cissy taught History in the girls' school. Derwent exercised constant oversight. In 1871 he succeeded in getting the school enlarged, and wrote to Moultrie that he hoped to open the new schoolroom for divine service in the first Sunday of the new year, but there was much to do to collect the necessary £60.

The success of the Sunday evening services in the schoolroom convinced Derwent of the necessity for building a new church in this part of the parish, where the bulk of the population lived. He wrote to the Bishop of London, John Jackson, on 25 April 1872, requesting his advice about a second church or chapel in the village itself.[3] The increase in population sharpened the need. He foresaw

[1] 11 May 1865. Derwent Coleridge MSS. HRC, Texas.
[2] Mary Coleridge to Arabella Brooke. 11 January 1866. Coleridge papers. HRC, Texas.
[3] Derwent Coleridge MSS. HRC, Texas.

difficulty in raising funds, as the parish was poor in the number and size of contributors, and he had just lost the only wealthy contributor. The dissenting interest was strong, particularly among the tradespeople, and was recruited by the new residents. Although at present in good health, he could not run two churches without a second curate, which the parish could not afford. 'But I am most unwilling to yield to these impediments without a vigorous effort to remove them.'

He wanted a site and mentioned a small field 'belonging to your Lordship's estate, now in the hands of the Ecclesiastical Commissioners', close to the schools and very favourably placed. At the age of seventy-one, Derwent set out to raise the money for the new church – a large part of it from the contributions of himself, his family and his friends. The cornerstone of the new church was laid on St Mark's Day, 1879, and the church was consecrated on 31 December 1879, and dedicated to St Mark. It stood on the corner of Green Lane and Lower Boston Road, surrounded by contemporary yellow-brick small villas, but opposite the church was a triangular green, fringed with plane and poplar trees. The church was a modest yellow-brick building with Gothic windows; the apsidal end was an echo of St Mark's Chapel.

The move to Hanwell was 'disastrous in a money point of view', as Mary wrote to Arabella.[1] Derwent wrote to Sir John Taylor Coleridge in 1866: 'The net proceeds of the living are already about £40 p.a. less than represented to me when I accepted it. The expenses are far greater than I had reason to expect – until something can be done to increase my income, my small capital cannot be preserved intact.'[2] Derwent explained that for this reason he was unable to take a leading part in proposals for the removal of the Coleridge tomb and for putting a memorial to STC in the chapel at Highgate School and in Westminster Abbey. Besides himself and Mary, Derwent had to maintain Cissy, Edith and, at least partly, Mary's sister Sarah, and Ernest Hartley, who went up to Balliol in October 1866. He was also sending out money to Derwent Moultrie in Australia. He wrote to Moultrie on 1 February 1868

[1] 21 December 1865. Coleridge papers. HRC, Texas.
[2] 30 January 1866. Derwent Coleridge MSS. HRC, Texas.

that he was 'downhill in the way of money' and had just had to sell out another £200 worth of stock. So, as at Helston forty years earlier, Derwent decided to take in pupils.

In the autumn of 1868 the Rector of St Paul's School, Concord, New Hampshire, USA, who was then in England, arranged for Derwent to take as a pupil a boy from this school. Augustus Swift went to live at Hanwell Rectory, where he remained for the next three years and was virtually adopted into the Coleridge family, to whom he became 'Gus'. He was joined and succeeded by other young Americans, coming to Europe for a classical and literary education, and Derwent had a steady succession of American pupils until 1879.

Derwent and Mary watched the progress of Ernest Hartley with some anxiety, after the disastrous career of his elder brother. Ernest was born on 8 December 1846 at St Mark's. From 1857 to 1858 he was at C. A. Johns' first school at Watford. After another two years at school in Highgate and a period of private tuition at home, he tried twice, unsuccessfully, for a scholarship to Eton. Derwent probably felt he should have sent Dervy to Eton, as recommended by Sir J. T. Coleridge, but he could not afford the fees for Ernest without a scholarship. After four years at King's School, Sherborne, he went up to Balliol in October 1866.

Derwent described Ernest to Moultrie in 1868 as 'far from a severe student'. In December 1870 Ernest obtained a fourth class degree in *Litteræ Humaniores*. Derwent wrote to him:

> What is past is past. What cannot be cured must be endured, by you and by me. Let us now set about curing what is still curable, and this is much ... I have so long foreseen the result of your Oxford career and was so well prepared for its probable consequences that it has hardly occasioned me a momentary disappointment, or increase of anxiety. Do not impute this to a despondent temper; it has proceeded from nothing else but a clear judgement all the clearer that its eyes were unbandaged by affection.

He went on to say that there must be a change in his habits of indolence.

In January 1871 Ernest went as a temporary assistant master at

C. A. Johns' School at Winchester, where he 'earned golden opinions'.[1] As Derwent remarked to Moultrie, 'Perhaps he takes to teaching as pointers do to pointing from an inherited instinct.' In March 1871 Derwent went down to Winchester for the day to talk over Erny's prospects with C. A. Johns. Ernest wished to start his own private school for teenage boys, relying partly on Mr Johns' recommendation – a scheme which Derwent and Mary viewed with considerable anxiety, in view of Ernest's very limited means and their own shortage of money. In June Derwent, Mary and Ernest went to look at a house called Pickhurst, near Chiddingfold, Surrey, and in September 1871 Ernest started his school there, with his sister Christabel as housekeeper. Derwent had to subsidise this venture. He wrote to Erny in May 1872 that he had been to the bank to put £15 to his account – 'completely exhausting my own balance'. He went on: 'You now owe me £95 to say nothing of my railway fare and omni-buses – 2/9 – which I mention to remind you that I am obliged to attend to such items.'

He wrote to Moultrie in April 1873 that Erny would start with six pupils – '8 would make him independent – an unspeakable comfort to his mother and myself, for I have no prospects of more pupils and cannot nearly live on my income. However, the future, though not brilliant, is not altogether dark. The cloud might be thicker, and blacker, and I ought to know, or rather feel, that the sun is shining behind.'[2] By December 1873 Ernest had 12 pupils and was thinking of leaving Pickhurst, as the house was too small. In May 1874 he moved to Beomonds, Chertsey, Surrey, where he set up another private school and Derwent lent him money to enlarge the house.

The American pupils, taken on because of Derwent's financial difficulties, proved to be a source of much happiness on both sides. Augustus Swift was the first to come to Hanwell Rectory, in the autumn of 1868. By December 1871 Derwent had three American pupils. In September 1872 he wrote to Moultrie that he had just interviewed a new American pupil – Alexander Mackay Smith. 'I

---

[1]Derwent Coleridge to Moultrie. 24 March 1871. Ibid.
[2]30 April 1873. Ibid.

must make hay while the sun shines – and make the best of the aftermath.'

Augustus Swift wrote, after Derwent's death:

between his sixty-ninth and eightieth years, Mr Coleridge was never without a young American companion, to whom he stood *in loco parentis*, as well as undertaking the entire charge of his mental training. This contact with America became most interesting to him. Our friends and relatives from over the water were welcomed by the score at his house and table; and ... he soon acquired, by means of his familiar converse, a far more accurate and unprejudiced idea of American social, political, educational and religious institutions than even the best informed of his countrymen. The love of teaching, moreover, was so fixed in him, that it had grown into a habit that could scarcely be broken without regret. It was almost essential to his happiness to have near him one or two young men, whose minds and tastes he could form, and in whose youthful sports and gaiety he could sympathise. In this sense he never grew old. He was old in wisdom, it is true ... but in energy and animation and bodily vigour he was young even when past seventy. As a matter of simple like and dislike, apart from the love and respect we bore him, we preferred his society to any other. He was a great walker, for instance, and would put any one of us on our mettle. In 1870 I took three walks with him within a week, and each walk was over twenty miles long ... We were received, almost as sons, into one of the most intellectual and delightful homes in England. We formed the acquaintance of many social and literary celebrities, and were made welcome by his friends in any part of England or Europe.[1]

Derwent's letters to Mary when he was touring with 'Gus' reflect his keen enjoyment of this shared exploration. From 23 May to 30 May 1870 they went to Canterbury, Hastings, Brighton, Chichester,

[1]Derwent Coleridge, Scholar, Pastor, Educator – An Address delivered 19 June 1883 at the Public Meeting of the Library Association of St Paul's School, Concord, N. H. by Augustus M. Swift. Charles F. Roper & Co. New York, 1883.

Winchester, Romsey, Salisbury, Stonehenge and Bristol. 'In my strongest days I could not have done so much with less fatigue', wrote Derwent. After his death Augustus Swift wrote: 'It was my privilege to visit in his company every cathedral of note (with one exception) in Great Britain, and to hear him descant upon their various beauties or relative merits, was almost an architectural education ... And he delighted also in the great abbeys and parish churches...'[1] In July and August 1871 both Derwent and Mary took Gus to Exeter and Ottery St Mary, to Torquay and Plymouth, and then to Penzance, where they stayed for a fortnight with Derwent's old pupil, William Bolitho. Both there and at Helston, Derwent was much touched by the grateful remembrance of his old pupils. From Helston they explored the Lizard peninsula and at Falmouth they had a day with the Fox family. Mary left them at Bristol and returned to Hanwell while Derwent and Gus went on to spend 12 days touring in Wales.

As Derwent grew older his love of the Lake District and of natural beauty was as deep as ever. He had in his study a panoramic view of the Lake District and used to trace with his finger the route he and Hartley walked to school.[2] The work and money worries at Hanwell did not permit Derwent and Mary to return to the Lakes until July 1867, but then they were able to stay with Mrs Joshuah Stanger at Field Side, Keswick. 'Here I am in the valley of Beulah – with the Delectable Mountains all around and in the House that is, or ought to be called Pleasant, with the widow Friendly for my hostess', wrote Derwent to Moultrie.[3] 'When we came hither I hardly hoped that the old scenes would bring back the old feelings – but when I looked out of the window on Tuesday morning I found that I had changed apparently as little as they have ... there is no better kind of beauty and nothing better in its kind ... but I fear I shall hardly get far up, or among the hills – which is a loss to me of the highest enjoyment of which I am susceptible.'

In fact Derwent went on climbing the hills in the Lake District with his young American friends until well into his 70s. Augustus Swift recalls:

[1]Ibid.
[2]William Benham. 18 April 1883. Obituary of Derwent Coleridge in *The Guardian*.
[3]26 July 1867. Derwent Coleridge MSS. HRC, Texas.

'Ah,' he exclaimed one day in 1868, as we were walking through the level haze of Middlesex, 'if only I could run down to the North and see the hills. I want to hear the Greta, and look at Blencathra against the sky, and walk over the Nathdale fells to Watendlath!' And a week later we set forth, he and I and one other, and went to the Lakes, where, for six weeks we regaled ourselves with 'the things of earth, water and skies'. This was the first of several such trips. The dew of Skiddaw was his elixir of life; and no one would have thought, to see him tramping over moor and fell, leaping over a beck or scaling Raven's Crag, that he had fulfilled the allotted time of mortal man. Every mountain was voiceful to him, and every vale and stream; Causey Pike and Scawfell, and 'the mighty Helvellyn', and Loughrigg, and Airey Force, and Troutbeck, and Borrowdale, had each their message from the past – were each peopled, to him, with visionary forms.

From Kendal to Cockermouth he was welcome, especially in the cottages of the poor, whom he would delight by talking in broadest Cumbrian. No child failed to get a sixpence who would 'oppen t'yat'. He would order, periodically, from pure sentiment, shoes from Robinson, his old cobbler friend in Keswick, oblivious of the fact that these shoes had been accumulating in his dressing-room for at least one generation. And the stores of poetry he would pour forth! Wordsworth he knew largely by heart, and did more, possibly, than any individual to engraft in others that deep and subtle charm; and when he would pause at the Yew Trees, or look down on Grasmere from Silver How, or scamper through Paterdale, what stores of lyric music he would roll out, in tones sonorous or tender at will!

In August 1874 Derwent and Mary were again at Field Side, Keswick. Derwent told Moultrie that he had done two walks of some eight miles – 'one a mountain scramble with good effect, as regards spirits, and I think my general health, but I have of course less endurance and less recuperative power than I had two years ago'.

In the summer of 1871 Derwent and Mary did not go to the Lakes, owing to the tours in the west country and Wales, and Derwent wrote a long letter to his friend Dr David Leitch in Keswick.

Well, I am old now, and know not the day of my death – when my 'umbra' – to indulge in a pagan fancy – half-baptised – shall quit this resting place of my body, to hover over and about, the wide and beautiful God's acre of my heart. Wordsworth, in perhaps the choicest of his water pieces (July 30th, 1802, be it well noted) thus expresses himself –

> 'Brook! Whose society the Poet seeks
> Methinks the Eternal Soul is clothed in thee
> In purer robes than those of flesh and blood
> And hath bestowed on thee a safer good,
> Unwearied joy, and life without its cares...'

– What if the separate streamlet assigned me in the great departition, were hereafter to be so clothed, so individualised? What if I were to flow on, from beneath some white-mossy coverlet, in some upland moor, over rocky steeps and at the bottom of rocky clefts – down the side of one of my native fells – amid ferns, and star flowers, shaded by alder-trees, decked with the ruddy glow of rowan-berries – music in my voiceful flow, sweeter silence in my still, pure depths...

Yes, the brook would be well – but then, tho' a traveller, it is always confined to one route – and with this I could be content, but then, it is subject to fits of passion, of which one has had enough – perhaps one would rather be

> 'The Spirit of the breeze
> That singeth in the trees
> Making low music when the young leaves dance'

– the mountain breeze, carrying down upon its wings the perfume of the heath blossom, winding through the valley-

tracking Glenderterra − following the course of Greta − floating over Derwent, up into Borrowdale − with a soft murmur of enjoyment − or 'histing' along, 'like the mute silence' − with quiet lulls and dreamy sleeps?

Love of nature and a fine taste in scenery were among Derwent's most prominent traits. His sermons were full of analogies from nature. Augustus Swift recorded his love of Wordsworth's lines:

> Thanks to the human heart by which we live;
> Thanks to its tenderness, its joys and fears;
> To me the meanest flower that blows can give
> Thoughts that do often lie too deep for tears.

In 1877 Derwent wrote to his old friend Thomas Dyke Acland, at Killerton: 'Spare as many of the old Devonshire hedges as high farming will permit − with their primroses and violets below, their blackberry bushes and honeysuckle above − and nurse them all, the elmtrees and oaks that spread over them their kindly shade, and look up, as if on their behalf, to the sky.'[1]

Derwent was a voracious reader, but his great mental recreation was the comparative study of language. He told Moultrie in 1873: 'I am looking up my Syriac − it occupies my head without troubling my heart − and requires no effort of the will.' STC had trained him in grammar from his infancy. In the 1830s H. N. Coleridge wrote to Sara from Helston: 'Derwent is at the height of the Lingomania.' By 1870 Augustus Swift tells us: 'Mr Coleridge had complete mastery of about fourteen languages, and was sufficiently well versed in eight or nine more for all practical purposes.' He recalls Derwent writing a letter in Hungarian one day, without premeditation, to one of the Budapest newspapers. 'He began Icelandic at seventy, and in six weeks could translate the Reykjavik news to us, without a halt. When Bishop Staley (one of his former Vice-Principals at St Mark's) brought him from Honolulu one or two volumes in Hawaiian, he worked at them for weeks till he had mastered the curious

[1] 5 November 1877. Ibid.

grammatical forms of the language, composing a little grammar of his own.' Swift recalls; 'The late Dean Stanley once said, at a garden party at Fulham Palace: "You young Yankees may not realise that you are reading with the greatest master of language in England."' For Derwent languages were a real relaxation. For instance, in May 1866, he told Moultrie he was not at all well; he goes on to comment on Renan's new book *Les Apôtres*, and J. R. Seeley's *Ecce Homo*, but says he is 'very idle' and accordingly has been reading Shakespeare in Hungarian.

Although, when Derwent went to Hanwell, he retired from the centre of the educational stage, he continued to be consulted on educational matters. The Schools Inquiry Commission set up by the Government in 1864 under the chairmanship of Lord Taunton to enquire into the endowed schools and proprietary schools asked Derwent for his opinions. In his reply Derwent said good schoolmasters needed a fixed income and the opportunity to add to it by boarders, when the day school was not very large. He thought there should be no free admission but small quarterly payments of 16s to £2. Retirement pensions for schoolmasters were very desirable. He recommended regulated supervision by a central authority and Government aid as 'by far the quickest and most effectual remedy for the existing want'. Masters should be trained and certificated and he thought the existing Training Colleges' courses should be extended to three years to supply teachers in middle-class schools, as had been the case at St Mark's. Public inspection and examination of the endowed schools was most desirable.

On 28 February 1867 Derwent delivered a speech at a meeting of the London Diocesan Board at London House, which was subsequently published by Moxon as a pamphlet entitled *Compulsory Education and Rate Payment*. The gist of his argument was that compulsory education must be free education. He might agree to this if it were paid for out of taxation but this, he thought, was not proposed, and it was intended to saddle the cost upon the rates. He maintained that rates were an unfair tax quite unrelated to income, whereas funded and floating capit'al was comparatively exempt from 'the relief of that poverty which it so largely contributes to create'.

In general Derwent believed 'the one thing needful is to improve and multiply such schools as we now have, that they may spread over the length and breadth of our land; schools I mean maintained by school fees, by local subscriptions and by Government grants, freely regulated by their local supporters in harmony with their religious convictions, and freely recruited with scholars through the attraction of their own excellence'.

In 1870 he was advising in detail on the organisation of the Welsh school in Ashford, Middlesex, and he also examined there. In December 1874 he replied to an enquiry from the Rev. J. Duncan about education.

> What is wanted is <u>better</u> – much <u>better</u> – education – not merely or mainly more general instruction ... We want much more and much better <u>teaching power</u> ... We must seek to teach the teachable to the extent of their capabilities – we must aim at a <u>high maximum</u> rather than a low minimum, however widely spread ... I see no reason why, with a conscience clause, denominational schools should not have the power of enforcing attendance ... An army of teachers would detract far less from the national wealth than the armaments which we now maintain – even in a financial point of view: in fact it would eventually effect a saving – it would pay for itself, and more.[1]

In 1876 Derwent wrote to E. C. Tufnell (who with Kay-Shuttleworth had founded the Battersea Training College) on the subject of a training college for teachers in middle-class girls' schools. He thought boarding institutions indispensable and the choice of the Lady Principal crucial – 'she must possess mental culture, and teaching power – that faculty of self-transference, which is the secret of all education worthy of the name...' The teaching must be mainly individual. He spoke of the need for a preparatory Boarding School '... such as I proposed at St Mark's before the pupil teacher system supplied the need'. He believed the best pupils from Whitelands and Salisbury would make the best

[1]20 December 1874. Ibid.

285

teachers in the very highest class of Ladies' Schools 'supposing them to possess suitable manners and deportment'. With regard to pupils in the new college he thought 'gentle birth and breeding an advantage, but vigorous natures are so often found in a lower sphere of life and so much may be done to polish them that I do not think the door should be shut against their admission'.

He was 'always an advocate of the highest attainable culture of the female mind' and he had 'admiration for female talents and genius, in whatever department it may have been displayed. I believe that . . . the intellect of women may run parallel to that of men, to a great height, but never in the same line, for the most part not strictly parallel . . . This difference – this distinctness – cannot and ought not to be disguised. A woman is never so obtrusively female as when she puts on man's attire.'[1] Derwent had good reason to admire 'female talents and genius' in view of all he owed to Mary in his personal and professional life, and after working so closely with his sister Sara in editing their father's works. He had helped to educate both of them in their youth.

In his political and social ideas Derwent was very much an individualist. Augustus Swift says: 'It was a tendency of the man's mind, which his instinctive honesty caused to operate against his own interest, to see both the good and the bad side in all party organizations.' It was for this reason that he never gained preferment in the Church, which was determined by political patronage. Alexander Mackay Smith, another of his American old pupils, wrote after his death that it was the good and bad fortune of Derwent Coleridge that he could see so clearly the evils as well as the merits of both political parties and could never attach himself openly to either.[2] 'The English Church was still too much governed by party spirit for such a man to succeed.' He had no patience with violent extremes, with bigotry in any shape, whether Tory or Radical, sectarian or freethinker. 'Thus he was considered by the Liberal leaders a Conservative, and by the Conservatives a Liberal. Between these two stools he fell, but not without perfect apprehension, and not with discontent'.

[1]14 August 1876. Ibid.
[2]New York Evening Post. 30 March 1883.

Derwent's cousin, John Duke Coleridge, son of Sir John Taylor Coleridge, later Lord Chief Justice and the first Baron, was Solicitor General under Gladstone's ministry of 1868–74. In 1869 Derwent wrote to him, on account of a piece of preferment which he wanted: 'I am certainly not a "party man", and if I have any claims for preferment, personal or inherited, I never have, and never will, put them forward on this score: but as certainly I am not a clerical obstructive.' Alone among the clergy of his Deanery, he had refused to sign a petition against Gladstone's disestablishment of the Irish Church.

As little can I be called a Tory, whether in the historical or the popular acceptation of the term. In my preface to the additional volume of Coleridge's notes (1853) I wrote as follows: '... Warmly attached to the institutions of his country and especially anxious for the permanency and well-being of the National Church, he sought to enlighten ... the Conservative Party in the State, but the whole bearing of his mind was towards liberty – that freedom alike of thought and action which he believed to be essential to the dearest interests of man,' – [this] conveys the real sentiments of his younger son.

My friends may call me a liberal-conservative, or a con-servative-liberal, but liberal – I do not say A Liberal' – I assuredly am and ever have been ... As an Educationist I have actively supported ... the cause of progress, and have not scrupled to associate myself with the party of progress whenever I thought, which I did often think, that they were on the right track. Thus ... I entered heartily into the movements set on foot by Sir James Kay-Shuttleworth. .... I believe that I was instrumental in reconciling the Church to the provisions of the Privy Council, the organ of a Liberal government, and in so doing exposed myself to some misconstruction. I have always been favourable to a conscience clause.[1]

A conscience clause was a clause in the trust deeds of new schools

[1] 13 November 1869. Derwent Coleridge MSS. HRC, Texas.

giving dissenting parents the right to withdraw their children from religious instruction. This statement of Derwent's reveals the extent to which he differed from the National Society, which refused grants to school managers who accepted a conscience clause. In 1874 we find Derwent writing to an author who had sent him his book: 'As to schools, I should be content to have morality taught on any sound religious principle however general – and to this I suppose we must come, or to something worse: but I don't see my way to getting religious morality taught except by religious men and women, who will be apt to be very 'denominational' for some time to come.'[1] This liberal statement, which appears to sympathise with the Cowper-Temple clause in the 1870 Education Act, which provided for non-denominational teaching in Board Schools, is also in marked contrast to the attitude of the National Society, which was anxious to perpetuate denominational teaching in Church schools.

A letter from Derwent to the same correspondent, Rev. G. D'Oyley Snow, written on 25 January 1875, reveals much of his social outlook. 'I honour you for the part which you are taking in the labour question, but I cannot follow you.' He thought strikes 'as at present conducted' were iniquitous in the process and disastrous in the result. Christian Socialism must come by spontaneous growth. Wages could not be permanently increased beyond certain narrow limits, clearly defined by economic considerations. 'This much from an old Tory-radical (not D'Israeli) who while he respects and values the social order – or orders – of his course, has yet done all he could to soften its insidious distinctions, and remove its injurious barriers...'

In his 60s and 70s Derwent continued to read widely in old and new philosophy, scientific theory and historical criticism of the Bible, and he corresponded vigorously about what he read. These were years in which fundamentalist acceptance of the Bible was undermined by biblical criticism, and, after the publication of *The Origin of Species* in 1859, the theory of evolution led to scientific agnosticism. Derwent was critically interested in the new findings, but his concept of the essence of Christian belief was on a plane

[1]Derwent Coleridge to Rev. G. D'Oyley Snow. 15 October 1874. Ibid.

which was secure from what many of his fellow churchmen saw as a threat to their faith. His religious and philosophical thinking shows a tolerant and assured conviction about man's duty to God and to his fellow men, which rested partly on his father's teaching on Christianity and partly on classical philosophy. The essence of STC's religious teaching was that religious truth is evolved from within a man. Fundamentalist teachings about the Bible he called 'bibliolatry'. He says in *Aids to Reflection*: '*Evidences* of Christianity! I am weary of the word. Make a man feel the *want* of it; raise him, if you can, to the self-knowledge of his need of it; and you may safely trust it to its own Evidence.'[1]

One of Derwent's letters in 1866 has a strangely modern ring, at a time when electricity was only just beginning to be used for carbon-fibre lamps in lighthouses and the incandescent filament lamp was yet to be invented. Derwent foresees a time when coal will be exhausted and 'we shall have to burn the force of wind or gravitating water ... I have often thought of this; but do not see my way to a comfortable study fire ... Alas, for the time when pokers shall be discovered, and kept in museums, shewn at conversaziones, in evidence of the poker age ... Shall we grind up electricity by windmill, with a service for each house? – turn it on into our grates to set asbestos aglow – or light our rooms with it through ground glass ceilings as with a diffused daylight?' He goes on to say:

I have no quarrel with science, and am proud of its acquaintance, though I be but on shaking hands terms with it. I have always believed in continuity and always, from a boy, seen the one in the many, the many in the one – always from a boy looked through the multi-fold and diverse, to a primordial unity ... I have no quarrel with science or with scientific men, so long as they stick to their text ... 'Heaven is my Throne, and Earth is my Footstool' is as true as astronomy and without disparagement to that glorious revelation – far more important.[2]

[1] Samuel Taylor Coleridge. *Aids to Reflection*. Bohn. p. 272
[2] Derwent Coleridge to 'My dear Glover'. 11 September 1866. Coleridge MSS, Victoria University Library, Toronto.

In 1874 Derwent commented on a lecture against the Darwinian hypothesis: 'Mr Rowe's assault upon the Darwinian hypothesis is very powerful ... But the question is not vital ... Whatever the process may be, the result is not less admirable, nor the original less divine. Such enquiries into the course of nature may be examined with entire equanimity. The mystery of creation is not thereby solved, nor the divine truth in any way compromised.'[1]

Writing to Dr Maudesley in 1869, Derwent praised his 'great work' on psychology. He accepted that all mental phenomena were in some sense the results of physical organisation – 'but I do not hold that this is an ultimate explanation. There is an Infinite behind and before and all through, which cannot be and will not be ignored.'[2]

In the summer of 1873 Derwent wrote a series of letters to John Moultrie, who appears to have been deeply depressed and concerned about the state of his soul. These letters were a remarkable contrast to that earlier exchange, when both were young and Derwent was assailed by religious doubt. They show how, despite all the blows of Fate, Derwent had arrived at a tolerant but deep religious faith, through which he sought to comfort and sustain Moultrie.

'As for your past life, let bygones be bygones,' wrote Derwent on 4 June. 'Few men will be able to show a cleaner bill of health than you: nor many leave behind a record of more usefulness, in a quiet way, very few a richer legacy to those that come after. You will say this is but a poor balm for a Christian conscience – no better than a placebo – Well, let us appeal to the Christian conscience. It replies with a call to repentance. But what is Christian repentance? Not regret for the past, but a change of mind; not mere sulk ... We should forget things behind and press forward.'

On 31 July Derwent wrote:

You speak of my cheerful acquiescence in the approach of death. I do not find that death is set forth in the New Testament as the King of Terrors, showing in this, as in all

---

[1]Derwent Coleridge to J. Petrie, Esq. Philosophical Society of Great Britain, 10 Adelphi Terrace, Strand. 11 April 1874. Derwent Coleridge MSS. HRC, Texas.
[2]14 January 1869. Derwent Coleridge MSS. HRC, Texas.

other ways, its divinely-human character. To the natural man death is very much a matter of course. He gets out of its way as long as he can, but takes it very quietly when it comes: and such I think should be the attitude consciously maintained of the educated man who would live *convenienter naturae.*[1] I am not ashamed to confess, or avow, that I gain much from (so called) Heathen philosophy, and I should be very sorry to see the study of it slighted in schools and colleges.

'If I try to number my days it is that I may apply my heart unto wisdom; – that I may take account of my remaining opportunities – and set my house in order, in a worldly, which I do not take to be an irreligious sense. I look forward to death with calm, but serious earnestness, with dim but not dark awe. I have no triumphant anticipation – no clear previsions. I resign myself to a faithful creator. Certainly I derive no confidence from my past life – and no comfort, except as an evidence of, and pledge of the divine goodness, wisdom and mercy. Not what I have done, but what I do: – not what I do, but what I am; not what I am, but what I will be and am becoming: not I at all, but Christ that dwelleth in me, the Light and Life of the Eternal.

'... Dear Moultrie, in God's treasury of good deeds, the two mites of the old and feeble may outweight all the rich offerings of the young and vigorous. Remember too Milton's noble lines – 'They also serve who only stand and wait'.

On 19 August Derwent was confined to bed at Pickhurst, 'laid up by a swelling which occasions extreme pain on standing upright – in itself distressing, disquieting, and disabling in a high degree ... The truth is we're wearing awa', John – in one way or another – let us hope to the land of the leal, and bearing this in mind, we may properly adopt a less solemn strain and Never say Die.' Since he arrived he had read Herbert Spencer's *Social Statistics* and a volume and a half of Zeller's Greek philosophy. On 25 August he wrote that his trouble was enlarged prostate and a swollen testicle, and his usual

[1]Conformably to nature. Cicero.

291

skin complaint. But by this time he could walk 'or rather crawl about' and was 'by no means out of heart'. He went on to ask Moultrie: 'Why, in matters of general interest or again of personal concernment to a friend, think first and foremost, if not solely, of <u>yourself</u> – and of your own spiritual improvement? My dear, dear Moultrie, I wish you would let your soul alone: <u>it is in far better keeping than yours</u> ... I have no patience with men and women who are always troubling themselves about their souls, and not much with many who busy them-selves about other people's – <u>not trusting</u> – <u>not trusting fully</u> – <u>in God.</u>'

This series of letters ends in a screed of 16 pages, dated 10 September 1873, and marked 'Private' which Derwent called his *confessio fide*. He began by saying he was

> once more at home, very much better – convalescent I hope and believe, though still weak with much remaining infirmity, some of which will doubtless be permanent, as it is of long standing. I am surrounded with every comfort, and with all means and appliances at hand, that my case requires – for which I cannot be sufficiently grateful. Still more fervently do I give thanks for my remaining powers of mind, and indeed of body, much as the latter may be impaired; for my love of reading, and meditation, for my unimpaired – I may even say for my quickened, and strengthened sense and enjoyment of beauty, whether in art, or in nature, – but especially in nature; most of all for my increasing fruition of God's truth, which is all truth, whether developed from within, or supplied from without; – such as it is, partial, and imperfect, – ever yearning, never satisfied, – waiting for the unvailed light ... Much of what I have written and all that now follows you may regard in that light, – simply as my confessions.

He read the Bible as the book of Life, divine but also human, '...and in the latter aspect, partial, progressive, limited, liable to error, changeful – transient'. The Old Testament had been subject to searching criticism 'with results widely different, I believe, from the traditional belief', but he read it as a devotional exercise, 'to lean upon the faith of Abraham and of Moses – of Job, of David, and of Isiah – to believe without sight, and against it: to pray on in glimmer, or in darkness; to hope on in trouble, and in gloom; to dwell with my heavenly Father – amid the promises of Israel, and to join the sacred quire'.

In the New Testament, I find the same God, brought very nigh to every one of us ... Power from on high, enabling me to wrestle with sin and death ... Love, Goodness, Power, brought very near to us in Christ, the Divine Man, and even now dwelling in us as the Paraclete. And here, as confessing my own thought, I might be tempted to speak of God as the eternal I, dividuated in man and separated by the alienated will, with the prospect of ultimate and complete coalescence ... But I am treading on shadowy ground; the cloudland in which the vista terminates.

With regard to the New Testament he wrote: 'we have this excellency in earthen vessels'. The New and Old Testament 'must, in my opinion, be subjected to human criticism ... No tenable theory of divine inspiration can in my judgement withdraw them from this ordeal ... For myself I watch the process with extreme interest, yet not as a matter of life and death. For me the word shines by its own light. My faith, whatever struggles it may have to pass through, is not in the least troubled by biblical difficulties...'

With regard to the Church he said: 'In plain terms a worship, intended to be a service of the spirit and truth, became transformed by the introduction of alien rites, spurious practices, essentially idolatrous ... unspiritual and untrue ... I would express my grateful attachment to my own branch of the Church, in which I can minister with much comfort and edification upon the whole. Not that I look upon it as perfect...' He thought the Lord's Prayer contained indeterminate meanings. Did 'daily bread' mean 'bread of tomorrow' or 'the bread of spiritual life'? Did 'deliver us from evil' mean 'particular ills' or 'the evil of this world'? '... So little may we trust in the mere letter'.

This is a remarkably broad-minded statement. He is critically interested in the new findings of science and history on Christian documents, but his concept of the essence of Christian belief, in Love, Goodness, Power, is secure from Biblical criticism.

The last part of Derwent's life was increasingly a struggle, with financial difficulties which made retirement impossible, hard work in a difficult parish, and increasing ill-health. He met all these difficulties with stoical acceptance which owed much to classical philosophy. In 1877 he wrote to Sir Thomas Acland (who had sent him a donation for his new church) – 'of the "old books", the Greek and Latin authors gain more and more upon my liking. Whether I look to form or substance I feel an ever recurring admiration for the legacy which they have left behind them.'[1]

Derwent retained his sense of humour in his later years. On 30 November 1872, when he was recovering from an illness, he wrote a charming verse letter to Christabel, who was at Pickhurst, helping Ernest with his school, and who had had a novel published. The letter begs her to come to town for her Christmas shopping:

To eat Christmas pudding and ditto mincepies
And to gladden the sight of your old Father's eyes
And let Ernest for once turn his back on his club
And come home for his bed (if we've room) and his grub.
For myself, I am better and mean to be well:
Your presence, dear Daughter, will act like a spell.
And now, be it known, I have read through your book,
All alone by myself in my own quiet nook.
For as to those nasty proof sheets
Reading backwards and forwards, with strictest directions
To look out for fumbles, and to notice objections,
'Twas like eating a packet of dirty mixed sweets
With an earnest injunction to spit out the grits.
But now that I've pleasurably read it right through
With much joy in my heart and some tears in my eyes

[1] 5 November 1877. Derwent Coleridge MSS. HRC, Texas.

Let me tell you at once, without more ado,
That I find it – I own with some little surprise,
That I find it – no matter
I don't wish to flatter –
You would think it absurd
So I wont add a word –
Except that I like it and love it
No novel, no tale set above it.
These chords have I struck from an old broken lyre,
Hang it up! hang it up! cease from clanging the wire,
Even so, says D. C. your affectionate sire.

Derwent's oldest friend, John Moultrie, died on 26 December 1874 – 'he leaves a blank behind which in my case cannot be filled up'.[1] Derwent wrote on 25 January: 'Death has been busy in thinning the band of my nearest friends and most valued intimates.'[2] Within the last few months he had lost Moultrie; Sir Alexander Spearman, his most influential parishioner; James Back, chaplain of the cemetery, the most companionable of his brother clergy within reach; Charles Kingsley, whom Derwent and Mary had recently visited at Westminster, and who had sent his son to be educated by Ernest Hartley; and Charles Johns, Derwent's old second master at Helston.

Derwent set to work to produce a new edition of John Moultrie's poems, with an introductory Memoir by himself, which was published in 1876.

But by 1879 Derwent was becoming incapacitated by neuralgia in his right arm. Mary wrote to Arabella Brooke on 8 April: 'we are mending slowly, Derwent can take the services and enjoys them but still has acute neuralgia pains in his arm rendering his right arm too feeble for writing – he can just sign his name.' They were going to Beomonds (Ernest's School) to be out of the way of Easter business. The cornerstone of the new church was to be laid on 25 April, St Mark's Day. 'Derwent will be present at this if he can stand . . . he had set his heart on meeting this great need in his parish.' Derwent in

[1]Derwent Coleridge to 'My dear John' (presumably Sir J. T. Coleridge). 28 December 1874. Ibid.
[2]Derwent Coleridge to Rev. G. D'Oyley Snow. Ibid.

fact delivered an address at the laying of the cornerstone of St Mark's Church, Hanwell:

> Fellow parishioners, and you kind and liberal friends who have joined in promoting the work assigned to us by our Divine Master, brothers and sisters in Christ! In accordance with the hope which I have never ceased to cherish, but contrary to the expectations of my friends and medical advisors, I appear before you personally on this solemn and joyful occasion... You will now have a church of your own at a convenient distance from your homes, with its attendant pastoral ministrations. As this church will be raised for the people of Hanwell, so I desire that it should be raised, as far as possible by the people of Hanwell, with whatever aid from without...'

In his Pastoral Address of May 1879, Derwent stated that the chancel, transepts and vestry and three bays of the nave of the new church were partially roofed in. The estimated expense for this portion was £3,600, leaving a deficit of £550. The new church was consecrated on the last day of 1879.

On 1 April 1880, owing to the state of his health, Derwent resigned the living of Hanwell. The Vestry passed a unanimous resolution:

> It desires to place on record its appreciation of the faithful service rendered to the parish by the Rev. Derwent Coleridge during his incumbency of 16 years, of the manner in which he has devoted himself to the interests of the Church, especially by sanctioning and promoting the building of a second church in this rapidly increasing neighbourhood. It also desires to acknowledge the attention he has given by himself, his family and his curates to the National Schools, and to the spiritual and temporal wants of the poor, and it recognizes the courtesy, dignity and impartiality he has uniformly shewn when presiding over the deliberations of this vestry.

At an age when many would have sought an easy life, Derwent

Mary Coleridge, 1880, aged 72, pastel by Lowes Dickinson. Presented to Derwent Coleridge by 102 friends and inhabitants of the Parish of Hanwell 'in the belief that you will value it as a proof of our affectionate remembrance of Mrs Coleridge as well as of yourself, more than any other gift of a costlier character that we could have offered.'

(By permission of Capt. Gerard Peter Derwent Coleridge)

had exerted himself to the utmost to meet the needs of his difficult and growing parish. He had maintained a lively interest in the affairs of the wider world, had endeared himself to his young students, and, in spite of growing infirmity, he had continued to enjoy life.

EPILOGUE
Torquay 1880–83

When Derwent and Mary at last retired they moved with Christabel and Edith Coleridge to Eldon Lodge, a small villa at Torquay, where it was hoped the climate would be beneficial to Derwent's health. But his last years were a time of almost constant pain. Mary wrote to Arabella in January 1881 that Derwent was a sad sufferer – 'the neuralgia pains are terrible – nothing seems to relieve them – it prevents him from reading, almost from thinking'. In December 1881 she wrote to Canon Cromwell, who had asked for information about the history of St Mark's College: 'Mr Coleridge is suffering too acutely even to dictate a note – but he will help me with his reminiscences.'[1]

Derwent's last years were further saddened by the news of the death of Derwent Moultrie in Australia which arrived in January 1881, and in the same month the sudden death of Ernest's baby boy, 'choked by a spasm in the throat', while staying with his mother at Eldon Lodge.

Derwent died on 28 March 1883 and was buried at Torquay.

A deeply affectionate memoir of Derwent Coleridge was written three months after his death by his American pupil, Augustus Swift.

In personal appearance, Mr Coleridge, like his father, was 'a noticeable man'. He was not above the middle height, but his great breadth of shoulder, and the noble poise of his head fully compensated for any lack of inches. When he came down in the evening, scrupulously dressed for dinner – for he disliked to see anyone sit down to dinner in morning dress — his

---

[1] Archive: College of St Mark and St John. 30 December 1881.

appearance was very striking. The head was large – 'oppressive with its mind' – and his hair clustered in curls of silvery white ... As one thinks of such things, the very memory of the years spent so near him seems like a benediction. For he was a man to love as well as to admire ... No one would ever have dreamt of taking a liberty with him; he was a man of great personal dignity and self-respect; but all heart flowed forth to him; every child would run to his arms; every dog would lick his hand. And yet, with all his gentleness, whenever he found aught to despise, whether of cant, effeminacy, or oppression, he could express infinite scorn in the stern lines of his mouth, and the contemptuous tumult of his brow ...

But beyond all that has been said of his work and character, the very crown and flower of it all was his supreme goodness. This was his own first consideration, and the only point of view from which any character had value to him. Too modest to set himself up in judgement, always with the kindest possible word to say of every one, even of those who might ill deserve his toleration – never by any chance sanctioning gossip or backbiting, he was ever intolerant of the slightest misuse of natural gifts ... He consecrated his life to the good of others; and this he would have considered his highest title to praise.

Swift tells us: 'While at St Mark's (as indeed during the greater part of his life) he rose at six, and heard a class before breakfast. He never spared himself. He undertook, in spite of all his administrative cares, the formation of special private classes of the more promising students; and in many instances he won over those who seemed most to respond to his influence to take orders, preparing them himself for the sacred office, and gaining their hearty affection. Many such used to visit him in his old age.' Derwent's power to inspire affection in his students is shown by the fact that his nickname at St Mark's for twenty-three years was 'Old Dad'.

Fate was unkind to Derwent Coleridge from birth till death. He was born of an incompatible marriage; his father had no money nor the kind of influence which was essential to preferment at the time; he went to the wrong university for him to achieve academic distinction; his successful school at Helston failed because of the belated coming of the railway to Cornwall; his considerable achievement at St Mark's was ruined by the Revised Code; his lack of political influence and refusal to placate the National Society meant that his efforts were not rewarded by the preferment which he merited; he spent his old age struggling with financial problems, a difficult parish and increasing ill-health; his eldest son was an alcoholic failure and two of his much loved children died in infancy; his last years were racked with physical pain and saddened by the untimely death of his son and grandson.

St Mark's College became the College of St Mark and St John in 1926 and moved from Chelsea to Plymouth in 1973. It seems somehow inevitable that, when the Chelsea building was empty, the memorial which Derwent's friends and admirers had placed in the floor of St Mark's chapel below the altar steps, a very fine full-length brass engraving of him in full canonicals, was ripped up by vandals and has disappeared, presumably into the melting-pot.

Why should Derwent Coleridge be rescued from oblivion?

In the first place, he overcame the blows of fate without bitterness, keeping to the last his idealism, his sweetness and light and his sense of humour. The turning-point of his life was his meeting with Mary Pridham, who inspired his new-found religious faith. Throughout the 56 years of their remarkable marriage partnership, she gave him emotional and intellectual support and practical help in all his undertakings.

A remarkable amount of evidence survives about his life. His personal history, and family history, is profoundly interesting, as part of the history of Victorian society and ideas, and as a voyage of self-discovery which still speaks to our condition today.

Derwent applied his father's religious philosophy to the scientific findings of the later nineteenth century and retained a liberal but secure religious faith, as well as a poetic vision of the natural world. He was the only member of his immediate family who coped with the arduous business of earning his living. He combined this with a serious attempt to put into practice the educational ideals of STC.

At St Mark's Derwent converted a college founded by the National Society as a political move by the Church to outwit the State's bid to take over education into a college working in partnership with the government scheme of Kay-Shuttleworth, and very largely state-financed. The National Society wanted a college to promote 'the education of the poor in the principles of the Established Church'. They saw the purpose of the college as training teachers of the '3 R's' and religious dogma to the children of the poor. Derwent believed that every child or student is an individual and worthy of education to the top of his or her bent. He tried to provide all his students with a liberal education to the highest level of which they were capable. He sought to bridge the gap between teachers in elementary schools and teachers in secondary schools, between training colleges and universities. Other Victorian training colleges established a rigid distinction between the training of the elementary school teacher and the education at public school and university of the sons of gentlemen, who would go into the Church or teach in grammar schools. A large proportion of Derwent's students bridged the class gap and achieved successful careers in the Church and in grammar schools.

The Revised Code delayed the realisation of Derwent's ideals until the second half of the twentieth century, but many individuals owed Derwent Coleridge a deep debt of gratitude for their liberal education and their careers. Among many others, Charles Kingsley and Cowley Powles at Helston, William Benham and Storer Lakin at St Mark's, Augustus Swift and Alexander Mackay Smith at Hanwell bore witness to that debt.

Derwent's principal claim to be remembered lies in his conviction, ahead of his time, that the teachers of the people should be educated men.

Derwent, by his editorial work and memoirs, preserved the work of his brother Hartley and of his friends Praed and Moultrie. He contributed substantially to the editing of his father's works. He never achieved his ambition to write an extensive memoir of his father's life and ideas, but he made a valiant and largely successful attempt to apply his father's philosophy, both to his own religious and personal life and to the education of teachers.

Select Bibliography

Acland, A. H. D. *Memoir and Letters of Sir Thomas Dyke Acland, edited by his son*, privately printed, London, 1902

Coburn, K. *In Pursuit of Coleridge*, Bodley Head, Oxford, 1977

Coleridge, Derwent. *The Scriptural Character of the English Church*, Parker, London, 1839

The Christian Minister's Account with Time: a farewell sermon preached at Helleston in Cornwall, 10th January, 1841, Parker, London, 1841

An Account of the Training College for Schoolmasters at Stanley Grove, Chelsea (Appendix V National Society Annual Report 1844)

Second Letter on the National Society's Training Institution for Schoolmasters (Appendix III, National Society Annual Report 1844)

The Education of the People. A Letter to the Rt. Hon. Sir John Coleridge, Rivingtons, London, 1861

The Teachers of the People; A Tract for the Time: with an introductory address to the Rt. Hon. Sir John Taylor Coleridge, Rivingtons, London, 1862

Lecture by the Rev. Derwent Coleridge, M.A., to Chelsea Literary and Scientific Institution (Poetry as a Teacher) 1862

A report cut from a newspaper and mounted in a notebook. Presented by the author to Sir John Taylor Coleridge. (British Library).

Coleridge, Hartley. *Letters of Hartley Coleridge*, ed. G. E. Griggs and E. L. Griggs, London, 1936

Poems with a Memoir of his Life by his brother, Moxon, 2 vols., London, 1851

Coleridge, Lord. *The Story of a Devonshire House*, T. Fisher Unwin, London, 1905

Coleridge, S. T. *Biographia Literaria*, Rest Fenner, London, 1817
    Aids to Reflection, Taylor and Hessey, London, 1825
    On the Constitution of Church and State, 3rd edition, ed. H. N. Coleridge, Moxon, London, 1839
    Collected Letters, ed. E. L. Griggs, 6 vols., O.U.P., Oxford, 1956–1972
Coleridge, Sara (Mrs S.T.C.). *Minnow among Tritons: Letters of Mrs Sara Coleridge to Thomas Poole*, ed. S. Potter, London, 1934
Coleridge, Sara. *Memoir and Letters of Sara Coleridge*, edited by Edith Coleridge, Henry S. King & Co., London, 1875
Cottle, J. *Early Recollections, Chiefly Relating to the Late Samuel Taylor Coleridge during his Long Residence in Bristol*, London, 1837
Fox, Caroline. *Memories of Old Friends, being extracts from the journals and letters of Caroline Fox from 1835 to 1871*, ed. H. N. Pym, Smith, Elder & Co., London, 1882
Griggs, E. L. *Coleridge Fille*, Oxford, 1940
Holmes, Richard. *Coleridge*, Oxford University Press, Oxford, 1982
    Coleridge: Early Visions, Hodder & Stoughton, London, 1989
Hutchinson, Sara. *Collected Letters*, ed. K. Coburn, Oxford, 1954
Kay-Shuttleworth, J. P. *Four Periods of Public Education as reviewed in 1832, 1839, 1846, 1862, in papers by Sir J. Kay-Shuttleworth*, London, 1862
    Memorandum on Popular Education, London, 1868 (republished by Woburn Books Ltd., 1969)
Kingsley, Frances, E. *Charles Kingsley: His Letters and Memories of his Life*, 2 vols., H. S. King & Co., London, 1877
Lefebure, Molly. *Samuel Taylor Coleridge, A Bondage of Opium*, Gollancz, London, 1974
    The Bondage of Love. A Life of Mrs Samuel Taylor Coleridge, Gollancz, London, 1986
Moultrie, John. *The Dream of Life, Lays of the English Church and other poems*, London, 1843
    Poems edited with an Introductory Memoir by Derwent Coleridge, 2 vols., Moxon, London, 1876
Mudge, Bradford Keyes. *Sara Coleridge, a Victorian Daughter*, Yale, 1989
Praed, W. M. *Poems of W. Mm. Praed edited with a Memoir by Derwent Coleridge*, Moxon, London, 1864
Rainbow, Bernarr. *The Choral Revival in the Anglican Church, 1839–1872*, Barrie & Jenkins, London, O.U.P. New York, 1970
Southey Robert. *New Letters of Robert Southey*, ed. Kenneth Curry, 2 vols., New York and London, 1965
Swift, Augustus M. *Derwent Coleridge, Scholar, Pastor, Educator*. An Address

delivered June 19th, 1883, at the Public Meeting of the Library Association of St Paul's School, Concord, N. H. Charles F. Roper & Co., New York, 1883

Toy H. Spencer. *The History of Helston*, Oxford University Press, Oxford, 1936

Trevenen Emily. *Little Derwent's Breakfast* by a Lady, Elder & Co., London, 1839

Wordsworth, Dorothy. *Journals of Dorothy Wordsworth*, ed. M. Moorman, Oxford, 1971

Wordsworth, William and Dorothy. *Letters of William and Dorothy Wordsworth*, ed. de Selincourt, *The Early Years 1787–1805*, rev. Chester Shaver; *The Middle Years 1806–1811* rev. M. Moorman, Oxford, 1937–1970

The Letters of William and Dorothy Wordsworth, the Later Years, revised, arr. and ed. by Alan G. Hill from the first edition ed. by de Selincourt. Part I 1821–1828, Part II 1829–1834, Oxford, 1979

OTHER PRINTED SOURCES

NATIONAL SOCIETY FOR THE EDUCATION OF THE POOR IN THE PRINCIPLES OF THE ESTABLISHED CHURCH

(Now: National Society (Church of England) for Promoting Religious Education, Church House, Great Smith Street, London SW1P 3NZ)

Annual reports
Minutes of the Committee of Enquiry and Correspondence
Minutes of the General Committee
Minutes of the School Committee
Minutes of St Mark's Sub-Committee of the School Committee
Minutes of the Council of St Mark's College

THE COMMITTEE OF THE COUNCIL ON EDUCATION IN ENGLAND AND WALES

Minutes

These are available in the Library of the Department of Education, Sanctuary Buildings, Great Smith Street, Westminster, SW1P 3BT

ARCHIVES OF THE COLLEGE OF ST MARK AND ST JOHN,
  Derriford Road, Plymouth
First College Register 1841–1849
Address by Rev. Derwent Coleridge, August, 1847
Old Days at St Mark's. By One of the First Students. (Reprinted from the Year
  Book of 1914)
Derwent Coleridge. *The National Society's Training Institution for School-
  masters, St Mark's College, Stanley Grove, Chelsea. Occasional report. 1864*
ed. Gent, G. W. *Memorials of S. Mark's College, 1891*

KEY TO REFERENCES
HRC, Texas: Humanities Research Center, The University of Texas at
  Austin, Texas.

Index

Regular correspondents and diarists have not been indexed, nor have single mentions of any except well-known people and DC's relations. DC's relationships and interests have been indexed under the other name, not his. Page numbers in italic refer to illustrations; an asterisk indicates a reference in a note. References to Derwent Coleridge (DC) are mainly grouped according to chapter, and alphabetically within the chapter group.

311